The Ceramic Narrative

D1607153

The Ceramic Narrative

Matthias Ostermann

WITH AN ESSAY BY

David Whiting

A & C BLACK • LONDON

UNIVERSITY OF PENNSYLVANIA PRESS • PHILADELPHIA

10-17-2006
WW
$49.95

This book is dedicated to my mother,

Lila Ostermann,

raconteuse extraordinaire,

who has supported me

in all my endeavours.

First published in Great Britain 2006
A& C Black (Publishers) Limited
38 Soho Square
London WID 3HB
www.acblack.com

ISBN-10 0-7136-6851-2
ISBN-13 978-0-7136-6851-3

Published simultaneously in the USA by
University of Pennsylvania Press,
3905 Spruce Street
Philadelphia, Pennsylvania 19104-4112
www.upenn.edu/pennpress

ISBN-10: 0-8122-3970-9
ISBN-13: 978-0-8122-3970-6

Copyright © Matthias Ostermann 2006

CIP catalogue records for this book are available from the British
Library and the U.S. Library of Congress.

All rights reserved. No part of this publication may be reproduced in
any form or by any means – graphic, electronic, or mechanical, including photocopying, recording, taping or information storage and retrieval
systems – without the prior permission in writing of the publishers.

Matthias Ostermann has asserted his right under the Copyright,
Design and Patents Act, 1988, to be identified as the author of
this work.

Book design: Penny & Tony Mills
Cover design by Peter Bailey.

COVER (BACK): Dish depicting 'Adam and Eve'. England,
Brislington, c.1680. Tin-glazed earthenware, ht: 6.3cm (2⅜in.), dia:
33.5cm (13¼in.). *Gift of George and Helen Gardiner, Courtesy of The Gardiner
Museum of Ceramic Art, Toronto*
COVER (FRONT): *Metamorphosis I*, 2004, by Matthias Ostermann.
Earthenware with vitreous engobes and copper sgraffito. *Photograph
by Jan Thijs.*

FRONTISPIECE: Vessel: *Staircase*, 2004, by Matthias Ostermann.
Earthenware with vitreous engobes and copper sgraffito. *Photograph
by Jan Thijs.*

HALF TITLE: Plate: *Metamorphosis I*, 2004, by Matthias Ostermann.
Earthenware with vitreous engobes and copper sgraffito. *Photograph
by Jan Thijs.*

Printed and bound by Tien Wah Press

A & C Black uses paper produced with elemental chlorine-free
pulp, harvested from managed sustainable forests.

Contents

Introduction

The *Concise Oxford Dictionary* defines the word 'narrative' as follows: 'A tale, a story, a recital of facts, especially told in the first person; a kind of composition or talk that confines itself to these.'

In the context of the ceramic narrative, we are dealing with a pictorial format, one involving an image associated intimately with an identifiable object. I have chosen to expand the above definition somewhat, to include not just the concept of a story, but any image that portrays a specific message or visual sequence and association of ideas, one that touches upon some kind of human activity or drama beyond the merely ornamental and decorative, and that has the intention of perhaps provoking some kind of thought response in the viewer.

Thus an image of an anonymous Greek nymph disporting herself on a Sèvres porcelain vase, I would consider as a fashionable and decorative image of the times. If however that image referred to a **real** mythological person in the context of a retold **particular** story, then I do see a narrative. A ceramic sculpture of a cherub or of the Madonna by one of the della Robbias, I might consider more iconic than narrative. However, a full Crucifixion scene by the same artist depicting this story from the Bible clearly constitutes a narrative in my view (see Figure 23 on page 71).

As can be seen by those chapter divisions in this book relating to contemporary ceramic narratives, I am including within the narrative concept those visual images that deal with mythology and re-explored archetypes; cultural icons reshaped into new idioms; personal visions, private stories and memory; and the exploration of the human figure as it embodies our aspirations, our relationships and our identity. I am further exploring social commentary touching upon pertinent political issues such as gender politics, as expressed through humour or irony. Finally, I examine the object itself as a metaphor for the presentation of a more allusive kind of narrative, through an association of ideas. Certainly these categories are loose ones at best, given that often a particular artist's work may freely explore more than one theme. I have thus tried as much as possible to let the artists speak for themselves, and perhaps the narrative categories I have proposed can be left open to debate.

Narratives of all kinds, whether they be oral, text or image, have the tendency to reflect the point of view and attitudes of the narrator. Sometimes an ancient story from a living oral tradition may very well lose its heart and impetus

OPPOSITE PAGE

FIGURE **1**
Plate with image of Crucifixion scene. Northern Italy, 16th century. Earthenware with carved slip and transparent lead glaze, dia: 37cm (14½in.).
Gift of George and Helen Gardiner
Courtesy of The Gardiner Museum of Ceramic Art, Toronto

through over-pedantic translation. For example, in his 1902 preface to Lady Gregory's magnificent Irish hero epic *Cuchulain of Muirthemne*, Y.B. Yeats states the following:

> [...] Generations of copyists who had often but little sympathy with the stories they copied, have mixed versions together in a clumsy fashion, often repeating one incident several times, and every century has ornamented what once was a simple story with its own often extravagant ornament. We do not perhaps exaggerate when we say that no story has come down to us in the form it had when the storyteller told it in the winter evenings.

In praise of Lady Gregory's particular work, Yeats continues:

> Lady Gregory has done her work of compression and selection so firmly and so reverently that I cannot believe that any body, except now and then for a scientific purpose, will need another text than this. [...] When she has added her translation [of *Cuchulain*] from other cycles, she will have given Ireland its *Mabinogion*, its *Morte d'Arthur*, its *Nibelungenlied*.

When the heart of a story remains intact, then the qualities of fluidity and change of viewpoint can actually sustain a given narrative and allow it to transform across time and cultural borders in each successive retelling. In her introduction to *The Virago Book of Fairy Tales*, English writer Angela Carter comments on the mutability of the story (in this case the fairy tale):

> The chances are the story was put together in the form we have it, more or less, out of all sorts of bits of other stories long ago and far away, and has been tinkered with, had bits added to it, lost other bits, got mixed up with other stories, until our informant has tailored the story personally to suit an audience of, say, children, or drunks at a wedding, or bawdy old ladies, or mourners at a wake ...

In discussing the impetus and resilience of the narrative, Carter continues:

> The narrative drive is powered by the question: 'What happened then?' The fairy tale is user-friendly; it always comes up with an answer to that question. It survives today because it has transformed itself into a medium for gossip, anecdote, rumour; it remains hand-crafted, even in a period when television disseminates the mythologies of advanced industrialised countries throughout the world, wherever there are T.V. sets and the juice to make them flicker [...] Now we have machines to do our dreaming for us. But within that 'video gadgetry' might be the source of a continuation, even a transformation, of storytelling and story performance.

In other words, the narrative from ancient times until today, and in whatever art form it chooses to emerge, continues to be a pervasive and adaptable vehicle for the expression of human concerns.

The ceramic narrative object, in particular, is a fascinating study in itself. Throughout history, it has incorporated material and technical advances where fabrication procedures and craftsmanship are concerned, and has shown evidence of stylistic changes in iconography that reflect the visual language and concerns of each particular culture and era. These shifts and changes are also reflected in the content of the actual depicted narrative. As in oral and written traditions, the same narrative themes, often the same specific stories, have been retold at different times in a variety of ceramic contexts. The oral (and later literary) narrative, which probably goes back as far as any other human creative endeavour, brings home to the listener the ever-relevant themes of struggle and of the human condition, exemplified by every culture's creation myths, heroic legends, parables and fairy tales.

These same themes, often taken directly from those oral and literary sources (and from painting and print-making sources as can be seen in some Chinese, maiolica and porcelain traditions), prevail throughout centuries of image making in ceramics. The ancient Greek myths that first appeared as imagery on the great Attic wares of the 6th and 5th centuries BC reappear later on many Renaissance *istoriato* maiolica pieces, on later 18th- and 19th-century European porcelains, and on the even later works of 20th- and 21st-century ceramic artists. Chinese literary themes, such as the classic story of the *Romance of the Western Chamber* from the drama *Xixiang ji*, appear on Qing dynasty porcelains (see Figures 11 and 12 on page 43), and on a later Du Paquier porcelain jar from Vienna (see Figure 31 on page 88).

There is a staying power, and an on-going profundity inherent in many narratives, exemplifying the need to re-explore those universal and often unresolved themes that have preoccupied mankind since time immemorial: the endless existential issues concerning our mortality, our identity as individuals and members of a community, our need for survival, for love, for acceptance and so on. The narrative, in all its forms, has been and remains a potent vehicle for the expression of such issues.

As I have said, my definition of what constitutes the ceramic narrative is a fairly broad one. The ceramic object, through its inherent diversity, be it as a container or drinking vessel, as a ritual or commemorative object, or as an architectural component, can provide a number of venues for exploring the narrative by its very function and association. I believe that this function and association can lead to a further level of contemplation and involvement on the part of the viewer/user — the object itself is often linked to the image it supports. Indeed, in some instances (as will be seen in the last chapter of this book) the object **is** the image, and becomes the metaphor for a more subtle, or indirect message or narrative.

The great 20th-century narrative painter Marc Chagall (1887–1985) was well aware of the potency of the ceramic object in his own ceramic work, especially that of a domestic scale, with its propensity for touch and handling, thus entering into the immediate body and home space of the viewer (as opposed to a physically more distant and perhaps less touchable work on canvas). His biographer Sylvie Forestier (*Les Céramiques de Chagall*) mentions this accessibility and intimacy of his ceramic narrative objects, notably in his cycle of portrayed Bible stories from the early 1950s.

There has always been a long-standing tradition for painters and sculptors to engage in ceramic work, either because of the above-mentioned object intimacy, or perhaps out of a simple fascination for the inherent possibilities of expression provided by ceramic materials and processes. Chagall himself states:

> I have wanted to use this earth like the old artisans, and to avoid accidental decoration by staying within the limits of ceramics, breathing into it the echo of an art which is near, and at the same time distant.

Artists such as Paul Gauguin and Raoul Dufy, as well as Henri Matissse, André Derain, Maurice de Vlaminck, Georges Rouault, and later Pablo Picasso, A.R. Penck and Mimmo Paladino among others (see Figure 36 on page 97 and Figure 37 on page 99) have all created narrative ceramic works in the 20th century, in collaboration with established ceramic studio artists. Such works, introduced into the fine art market, were highly valued and found equal footing with the painted and sculpted works of their time. The ceramic works of some of these artists are reviewed in-depth in Chapter Six.

Throughout many ceramic-making cultures, objects have been ornamented, and used as vehicles for the narrator. Tempting as it may be to dip into all of them, the purpose of this book is not to present an all-encompassing history of the ceramic narrative. Rather, it is to offer a brief synopsis of **some** of the more pertinent narrative traditions that precede and perhaps inform the main content of this book — contemporary ceramic narratives. In order not to drown in an overwhelming (and tantalising) sea of historical information capable of filling volumes, I have tried to focus on a few images that I have found personally exciting, and to place them in some kind of logical historical context.

For example, in my exploration of historical pre-20th-century ceramic narratives, I have given more page space and emphasis to three particular ceramic traditions: those of Ancient Greece, Italian *istoriato* maiolica, and some of the later European porcelains. There are two reasons for this. First of all, each of these seems to have embraced the narrative with great verve, possibly due to the above-mentioned variety of ceramic painting techniques that encouraged ceramic painters of the time to express their chosen themes to the maximum of their ability in this medium. The desire and willingness of their respective cultures (as regards the marketplace) to embrace and promote that particular type of work, has led to a large quantity of work being produced and hence a great number of ceramic objects have survived for documentation and study. Another reason for concentrating on these three ceramic traditions is that they are essentially European, and chronologically predate, and no doubt influence, our own Western culture and the largest portion of contemporary ceramic work reviewed here in this book.

To my regret, I have been obliged to omit a great deal, simply because the mandate of this book and page restrictions preclude an in-depth study of each and every ceramic narrative tradition preceding the 20th century. In touching lightly upon a few of them, I can only hope to encourage further study of this most fascinating and important subject. Historical experts in their specific fields, from whom I have gratefully gleaned so much information, have written extensively on their respective subjects, from ancient Mesoamerican ceramics to 18th-century European porcelains. Works by some of these specialists can be found in the 'Sources and Recommended Reading' section of this book. I am not proposing an encyclopaedic work of scholarship here, but rather a book which I hope will be appreciated from the point of view of a ceramicist writing about a subject close to his own heart.

My own particular love of the narrative, whether in oral, literature, painted, or ceramic form, comes no doubt from my mother, who in her early days was a professional *raconteuse* in Germany. I grew up with stories, legends and poetry and a constant sense of both the beauty and the power of the spoken word in the context of narration. The vivid imagery engendered in my mind by those narratives has surely remained and has been an ever-present and important catalyst in my own work.

It is my hope that this book will not only pave the way for further study but will also provide an insight into the great diversity of narrative ceramics of all types (be they vessels, sculpture, installations or architectural works) being produced by ceramic artists today. Even though I have been unable to include so many artists at this time, I do hope that this book will be a celebration of the work of all artists who have made a commitment to the ceramic narrative, both within these pages and elsewhere.

Matthias Ostermann

Montreal, 2005

Ancient Greece

1

Background, Vessel Types and Functions

If one is looking to the beginnings of any major ceramic narrative tradition in Europe, it is most likely the black- and red-figure painted vases of Classical Greece that first spring to mind. It is believed that the approximately 50,000 vessels excavated to date represent only 1% of the total output of this type of work, produced from the late 7th century to the 4th century BC. These two types of ceramic figure painting, best known to us through museum collections world wide, are the principal focus of this chapter.

Since most Attic vessels have been recovered from tombs (largely in Etruria in the Italian peninsula), their survival has been ensured. The lack of other surviving domestic objects, such as wall and panel paintings, fabrics and metalwork, makes it difficult to make price and personal-value comparisons with objects of ceramic manufacture. For the same reason, it is not clear to what degree ceramic shape styles and surface embellishment may have been influenced by other art forms. Judging by the large number of surviving works, their great sophistication and their extraordinary expertise (by any historical ceramic standards as regards both potting and painting skills) it can be assumed that the ancient Greeks, as a society, highly valued and promoted fine objects for use, especially ceramics. The narrative imagery painted on these vessels provides one of the major sources of insight into ancient Greek daily life, attitudes and beliefs.

Although the largest number of pottery finds come from Etruria, it is believed that these were popular imports. Corinth was certainly an influential production centre in the 7th century BC, and a likely progenitor for some of the earliest pictorial ceramic narratives (as will be discussed further on). Later some of the western Greek colonies based in Apulia and Sicily produced some fine

OPPOSITE PAGE

FIGURE **2**
Attic amphora with image of 'Herakles Wrestling the Nemean Lion'.
Greece, Vulci, c.520–10 BC.
Black-figure painted earthenware, ht: 36.7cm (14½in.).
Courtesy of Staatliche Antikensammlung und Glyptothek, Munich

13

figurative work, but Athens in the Attic peninsula remained the primary centre of production and the major arbiter of style and taste, certainly throughout most of the Classical Period of the 6th and 5th centuries, and well into the advent of Hellenistic times around the beginning of the 3rd century BC.

Apart from the more simple and mundane pottery designated for kitchen use, the more spectacular painted vessels under discussion here were produced for three basic purposes, and presumably for a wealthier upper middle class. Since many images on pottery depict the rituals of worship, such as sacrifice and libations to the gods, that particular function becomes self-evident. Another major vessel use takes place within the context of the male symposium, or drinking party, which usually excluded women, except those of the *hetairai* or courtesan class. (It is generally believed that in ancient Greek society, the woman's role was one usually relegated to household duties, worship and child-rearing, with limited access to public and political life outside of the home.) Some of the vessels associated with the symposium include: the large *krater*, for mixing the potent Greek wine with water, the *amphora* for storing of wine or oil (see Figure 2), the *hydria* for carrying and pouring water, the shallow handled *kylix* used as a drinking bowl and the *lekythos* or cosmetic flask (more associated with the woman's boudoir), used for the storage of precious oils and unguents. Many more vessel types than these exist, and all reflect their specific uses in terms of size, shape, number and placement of handles, and so on.

The final use for most Greek pottery was funerary, not particularly as ossuary containers, but simply as personal treasures placed in tombs to provide continuing earthly comforts in the afterlife. Although some may have been ordered expressly as commemorative offerings, it is clear from the number of finds lovingly repaired that the deceaseds' favourite and much-used objects were often interred with them. Another type of ceramic narrative may have occurred on painted or low-relief panels used as architectural ornamentation or furniture coverings (see Figure 5 on page 23).

Black- and Red-figure Wares

The techniques involved in the manufacture of Attic wares are fairly apparent. The analysis and examination of found vessels and shards indicate that the basic ceramic manufacturing processes in use at that time have in some instances remained unchanged since ancient Greek times. Greek pots were wheel-thrown using terracotta clay, and predate the use of glazes in a two-firing process. Lead glazes did not come into use until later Roman times. The standard black and red (and at times white) colouring associated with most Attic wares came from the use of finely deflocculated, highly burnished slips (terra sigillata), once-fired with brushwood to around 950°C/1742°F. Judicious control of oxidation and reduction atmospheres during the firing cycle helped to promote the strongly contrasting black and red colours.

Black-figure wares were predominant in the 6th century. As their name implies black figures appear as silhouettes on a basic red background, with fine incised lines through the black to the red for delineating details (see Figure 3). Occasionally a white slip was also painted in for added details or highlights, or to denote female figure skin tones. A stylistic innovation in the next century was the development of red-figure wares where the figure and background colours were simply reversed (see Figure 4). Fine-line black contour brush drawings, sometimes raised, outline the red figure, which is now seen against a black burnished background. Some white background wares, from the mid 5th century onwards became popular, especially in the form of flasks (*lekythoi*) designed largely for funeral use.

The artist known as the Andokides-painter is credited with being the inventor of red-figure painting. His remarkable 'bilingual' *amphora* pictured here (*c.*520–10 BC) exploits both black- and red-figure painting techniques on opposing sides of the same vessel. The repeated image of Herakles at his ease, his reward on Olympus after his trials, also shows us some interesting iconographic detail variations. In Figure 3 (black-figure painting, on the left), he is greeted by the god Hermes (far left) and the goddess Athena (left), while a servant on the right is preoccupied with mixing his wine. The presence of Hermes, messenger of the gods, indicates that some distance has been travelled, and the hero's quiver, bow and sword hang on the wall behind him.

Figure 4 (red-figure painting, on the right) shows a similar scene, but without the presence of Hermes and the servant. Herakles is larger, more upright in his posture, supporting his weight on his knee. Athena appears smaller, almost

FIGURE **3** (below left)
Detail of Andokides amphora with image of 'Herakles Reclining'.
Greece, Vulci, c.520–10 BC.
Black-figure painted earthenware, ht: 54cm (21¼in.).
Courtesy of Staatliche Antikensammlung und Glyptothek, Munich

FIGURE **4** (below right)
Detail of other side of Andokides amphora with image of 'Herakles Reclining'.
Red-figure painted earthenware.
Courtesy of Staatliche Antikensammlung und Glyptothek, Munich

15

secondary in stature, as she hands him a small blossom. As in Figure 3, Herakles clasps a drinking cup, and a side table displays another cup, some cakes and pieces of meat. There is more tension and drama in this depiction — Herakles' head encroaches into the border pattern above, and his body tension is mirrored in the vigorous-curving grape vine. His weapons are absent, perhaps indicating that he is now truly in repose on Olympus, and no longer requires them. His identity must be surmised by his association with Athena alone, in the absence of the standard symbols associated with him (his club, weapons and lion pelt).

Narratives: Beginnings and Themes

To best examine narrative Greek vase painting of the 6th and 5th centuries, one should perhaps briefly look further back in time at some of the Attic Geometric-Period vessels of the 8th century BC. Some of the first figurative imagery occurred on these around 750 BC, where for the first time banded geometric patterns enclosed panels with drawings of highly stylised battle scenes, horses with chariots, and funeral processions. Some of these vessels, often over a metre in height, served as funerary monuments for the dead. Eastern Mediterranean influences in terms of drawing styles and pictorial themes can be assumed in the earliest figurative works of potters from the islands of Euboea and Crete, with their outward-looking maritime trade cultures. The Cretan potters in particular favoured imagery often found on votive metal shields of hunting scenes, flying birds, goddesses, sphynxes and other fabulous monsters. Imagery here displays ancient Minoan and Oriental influences, somewhat distinct from the leading Attic school of painting on the Greek mainland.

One of the first vase painters in Attica, called the Dipylon master (named after the cemetery where most of his works were found), portrays what may be the first known true ceramic narrative. The image on a large *krater*, from *c.*750 BC, conveys a sequential storyline of a battle scene where in one instance, the depiction of Siamese-twin warriors (possibly Aktonione-Molione) can be directly linked to their participation in the Trojan wars. The Trojan war saga would of course have been widely known from popular oral culture. Another image occurring on a pitcher around 690 BC shows what may be the thanksgiving crane dance of the hero Theseus and Ariadne on Delos, after the vanquishing of the Minotaur. These works by Attic Late Geometric painters can perhaps be seen as the precursors to the later black- and red-figure ceramic narratives.

The first completely unambiguous mythological imagery is found on vessels from the Proto-Corinthian Period early in the 7th century (as mentioned earlier, Corinth was at the time a rival production centre to Athens as regards figure painting, until the mid-6th century). Scenes such as the Death of Ajax, the

Judgement of Paris, the Rape of Helen, etc., probably inspired by the circulating epic works of Homer (namely the *Iliad* and *Odyssey*), show an increased interest in the depiction of mythological themes. Some historians believe that this interest stems from popular awareness of the Mycenaean past (again evidenced in the works of Homer, among others). Another factor could be an orientalising influence — where Near-Eastern mythologies, their heroes and monsters as seen on imported artefacts caught the Greek imagination and were adapted to a more specifically Greek story-based iconography.

The real flowering of figurative narrative vase painting occurred around Athens in the 6th and 5th centuries. Much later, in Post-Hellenistic times, after the conquests and death of Alexander the Great early in the 3rd century BC, there was a decline in the great figure painting tradition. With power centres shifting away from Athens to such cities as Antioch, Alexandria and later Rome, ceramic work had a more regional focus, and surface embellishment of vessels was more in the hands of decorators, rather than highly-skilled narrative painters.

Interpreting the Image

Many historians consider the Greek vase painters to be true painters, rather than mere vessel decorators. Some have described their imagery as 'paintings on vases' (as opposed to 'painted vases'), especially since the images on a given vessel so often have no direct relationship to its actual function. To me this is irrelevant — a pot can function as a serviceable object and on another level can elicit added pleasure by showing a story to be viewed from different angles as the piece is turned about and handled. (You may remember that in this book's Introduction, the 20th-century painter Marc Chagall revealed a similar attitude.) The imagery on the shallow *kylix* drinking bowls proves this point. The symposium drinker enjoys the central interior image as the cup is brought up to the lips and his drinking partners at the same time can view the imagery encircling the bottom (often of an erotic and titillating nature).

From an art history point of view, there appear to be a number of approaches to evaluating and understanding Greek vessel imagery. Provenance, manufacturing techniques and painting styles certainly need to be established, but the real challenge might be in actually interpreting the meaning of any given image. Since Greek potters were mostly anonymous, and their works predate the kinds of biographical and contextual documentation associated with later artists, virtually all extrapolation and analysis, the Hows and Whys, must be deduced from the works themselves. For example, from the early Renaissance onwards, painters always signed their work and there was plenty of archival information (letters, contracts and sometimes written biographies) available to help put these artists' work into an historical and cultural perspective. In the case of Greek black- and red-figure painting, the interesting questions to ask might be how did the ancient Greeks interpret this imagery and how might their interpretation differ (or not) from our own, many centuries later?

There are basically two types of narrative that most commonly occur on Greek vases. The one deals with human figures engaged in such mundane activities as household duties, worship, the symposium, and so on. The other popular image type deals with mythological characters and their participation in epic dramas. Landscape depiction appears to be almost entirely absent, but it should be noted here that the recited epic poem played a leading role in the development of thematic imagery on pots. These performed songs (and later dramas) were popular throughout ancient Greece, not just as courtly or symposium entertainment, but assuming a didactic function as well. For example, Hesiod's *Theogonia* (The Genealogy of the Gods) created around 700 BC, with its chronology from Chaos to the Reign of Zeus, amplifies the heroic aspects of such characters as Herakles, reinforcing the hero cult and serving as a mirror for aristocratic societal values.

On particular ceramic works, especially those made in the western Greek colonies in Italy later on in the 4th century, images of satiric plays and dramas specifically allude to theatre settings. Performances are literally translated into vase imagery. Theatrical presentations by visiting troupes to the colonies may have been an important means of maintaining contact with the Greek homeland, cut off by the Peloponnesian wars at that time. Epic poetry and drama remained highly popular in the 4th century, through the great works of such authors as Sophocles and Euripides, and they continued on well into Roman times with the works of Ovid, among others.

In looking at Greek vase imagery from a more literal-minded 20th- and 21st-century perspective, we should be aware that we have a history of viewing painting, photography and film that explore realism (i.e. 'real' events, 'real' characters, 'real' perspective, etc.). We might be tempted to interpret a Greek seemingly realistic and meticulously rendered image as being an actual or documentary depiction of ancient Greek life.

I think such an interpretation might be overly reductive. Although certainly partially true, one should note that on vessel imagery 'mundane' figures are often seen interacting with 'divine' figures. Greek mythology itself certainly has its gods endlessly interacting with mortals, not to mention displaying such mortal attributes as lust, jealousy, envy, compassion, and so on. It seems very likely that the ancient Greeks identified very strongly with their divinities, and so their imagery may not be so much a reflection of their own social history, but rather a representation of personal ideals and cultural values.

Like most cultures, the Greeks used myths as parables for contemporary events. Frequently retold pictorial narratives (such as the heroic deeds of Herakles and Theseus) reinforced the ancient Greeks' world vision and even mainstream political thought. For example, a period of warfare might engender more depictions of epic battle scenes. Theseus, an Athenian prince, is found as a central figure on much vase imagery in the 5th century. He is then associated in the public mind with a certain number of Athens' leaders, especially in the light of that city's achievements against the Persians at that time. Herakles, the greatest of Greek heroes, later is often seen in the company of the goddess Athena, the city's patron deity, and so Athens can be associated with him. He becomes in fact a hero serving as a symbol of the state.

I think historian Mary Beard in the book *Looking at Greek Vases* best sums up the way in which the ancient Greeks may well have expressed their world vision in their painted vase imagery:

> Gods and the characters of myth did not inhabit a separate world, a set of vague, rather remote symbols. They were part of human experience; they intervened directly in human life; they were a necessary means of re-presenting and of making sense of the world. Like Athenian drama, Athenian pots celebrate the interrelationship in many different ways. Sometimes a named mythological figure is balanced on the other side of a pot by an anonymous figure of 'real life'. Sometimes an individual or group of figures is understandable in mythological and 'everyday' terms: a scene of a warrior saying farewell to his wife, for example, may represent the Homeric Hector taking his leave of Andromache, but it could also be the tender farewell of any Athenian fighter leaving home; the Maenads in the entourage of Dionysius [Bacchus], mythical women of the wild, may not be easy to distinguish from the 'real' women of Athens. It would be a crude oversimplification to try to determine in each case what precisely is represented, to try to invent a single, unproblematic title for each scene. The meanings of these images depend on the subtle interplay of both registers: myth and 'real life'. We are not just dealing with a figure who is **either** Hector **or** an Athenian hoplite; we are dealing with a figure who can be and is **both**.

Herakles: The Divine Hero

Orpheus with his lute made trees,
And the mountain tops that freeze,
    Bow themselves when he did sing:
To his music plants and flowers
Ever sprung, as sun and showers
    There had made a lasting spring.

Every thing that heard him play,
Even the billows of the sea,
   Hung their heads, and then lay by.
In sweet music is such art,
Killing care and grief of heart
   Fall asleep, or hearing die.

Act III, King Henry VIII

William Shakespeare's haunting ode to Orpheus, Auguste Renoir's voluptuous bronze *Standing Venus*, Michael Cacoyannis' powerful film *The Trojan Women* — these are but a few examples of the ongoing fascination and preoccupation of artists throughout the ages with ancient Greek mythology. That mythology, with its archetypal themes of heroic questing, achievement, romance and ideals of a physical and moral beauty, still seems to have relevance as source material for present-day creators. This applies of course to ceramic narrative imagery as well. One has only to look at the wealth of mythological references on Renaissance *istoriato* maiolica images, and those appearing on later porcelains and the works of 20th-century artists such as Matisse, Picasso, Jean Puy and William Newland, among many others. The heroic myth still remains one of the most popular and enduring of all narratives.

My focus here will be on the great Greek hero Herakles, and to a slightly lesser degree on the Athenian hero Theseus. Herakles was (and perhaps still remains) the most popular and renowned of all Greek heroes. Certainly his is the heroic image most often portrayed on 6th- and 5th-century Greek vases. He is always recognisable by his overly large and fiery-seeming eye, his short curling hair (the mark of the athlete) and, after the conquest of the Nemean lion, by his wearing of the lion pelt. Although seen at times carrying such weapons as bows and spears, he is most usually portrayed carrying his club.

Interestingly enough, at the time his exploits were recorded on Greek vases, there was no written epic dealing with his chronology, and most particularly, that of the famous 'Twelve Labours'. Oral culture was of course strong and ever-present in ancient Greece: some of the first allusions to Herakles (although not as a central thematic hero) occur in the 9th century BC in Homer's *Iliad* and *Odyssey*. In the *Iliad*, the great warrior Achilles in lamenting his own heroic departure from life, likens his death to that of the hero Herakles, and the poem also touches on the eleventh Labour of Herakles, the bringing forth from Hades of the three-headed watchdog Cerberus. Around 700 BC, Hesiod's *Theogonia* (The Genealogy of the Gods) briefly mentions our hero at times, but even Peisander's later *Herakleia* in the early 6th century BC does not yet give the chronology or details of the renowned Twelve Labours. It is the historian Diodorus who first chronicles the Labours of Herakles in 30 BC — any previously existing text sources may simply not have survived, and those images seen so frequently on vase paintings were no doubt completely familiar to the ancient Greeks from popular oral sources.

Herakles can be seen as the archetypal 'divine' hero, exhibiting some of the frailties of his human heritage but more remarkably his inherited half-god attributes. His chosen path of hardship and travails, although seemingly imposed upon him by circumstance (fuelled by the antipathy of the goddess Hera), nonetheless reflects his own choice and desire to overcome his human weaknesses to attain greatness. The fairy tale hero's story is usually one of surmounting hardships in a prolonged quest, and of finally being rewarded by the hand of the princess, with perhaps a kingdom thrown in as well. Not so for Herakles; as a demi-god his struggles are more monumental and elemental. Their roots go back to the father and mother of all gods and men, Zeus and Hera. Herakles' suffering and achievements are a reflection of the power struggle and resolution of Zeus' and Hera's marital conflicts at both an Olympian and cosmic level, reflecting the fundamental order of all things. Herakles' reward is not on earth, but finally in heaven. After many long hardships, humiliation and expiation, his mortal half is burned away (quite literally) and he is finally brought to Olympus to be fully reconciled to Hera, the god-mother, and given an assured place among the gods.

His entire story is of course much too long to recount here, but makes wonderful reading in its many available translations. In summary, it goes as follows: Herakles is born to mortal Alcmene, fathered by the philandering Zeus in the guise of Alcmene's husband Amphitryon, king of Thebes. Zeus' consort and equal on Olympus, Hera, vents her legitimate jealousy and spleen on the child, symbol of the demi-god she was not allowed to create. As a first act of malice she sends two serpents to destroy the new-born child, who promptly strangles them in his cradle, thus revealing his hero and demi-god stature. To add insult to injury, Hera is later tricked into briefly suckling the infant, and so his claim to later immortality is assured through a few ingested drops of her divine breast milk.

In later life (always pursued by the vengeful Hera), Herakles performs many great deeds in the course of his difficult destiny. Driven to madness at one point by Hera, he mistakenly slays his own children, and the laws of punishment and penitence require that he demean himself in the service of the weak king Eurystheus, the usurper of his own birthright (again by Hera's connivance). In the expiation of his crime, Herakles must perform the Twelve Great Labours, the first of which is the destruction of the Nemean lion. This first task is the one most often depicted on Greek vases, and perhaps was one that most stirred public imagination, for the lion was a heroic beast in itself and invulnerable to all weaponry, and had to be destroyed bare-handed. In this Herakles is successful and the first of his labours is accomplished. Most imagery depicting later labours shows him wearing the vanquished lion's skin, symbol of his victory.

Figure 2 on page 12 shows a magnificent Attic *amphora* (c. 520–10 BC) depicting this popular Herakles narrative. Because no weapon can penetrate the lion's hide, Herakles is obliged to divest himself of everything and conquer the beast naked, with nothing but his bare hands and strength. His useless weapons and clothing can be seen hanging up behind him, and his raised head above the lion indicates his inevitable victory. Primeval strength is pitted against primeval strength, and this, the first of his Twelve Labours, sets the pattern for those to follow. His *protégé* Iolaos stands to the left, holding Herakles' club and urging him to victory. Athena (on the right) also spurs him on, and a thin black line at the most crucial point in the *amphora*'s shape, forms the flat ground against which Herakles and the lion are so forcefully braced in their momentous struggle.

It should be mentioned here that in Greek mythology the theme of vengeance by the gods visited upon particular mortals was as common as was their partisanship and support of others. Odysseus, for example, was vengefully pursued and continually shipwrecked for ten years by the sea god Poseidon for the slaying of his son the cyclops, Polyphemus, after the ten-year siege of Troy. Herakles found staunch supporters in the gods Hermes, and most notably in Athena, both of whom frequently appear with him on vase imagery.

Perhaps Herakles' story was (and remains) so popular as a reflection of one of the great themes of Greek mythology, and indeed of most cultures' heroic narratives, because it establishes the concept of destiny and the inevitable consequence of assuming (or not) the responsibility for one's actions. Good is usually rewarded, and crime is followed by punishment, expiation and sometimes redemption. To be a demi-god, Herakles **must** be fathered by Zeus; to be a hero, he **must** be subject to Hera's legitimate vengeance and overcome all obstacles. And finally, to become immortal, he must first have endured the loss of family, kingdom and his mortal life. Only then is destiny fulfilled, and all things brought into final balance.

Theseus: The Mortal Hero

After Herakles, it is Theseus who most often appears on Greek vases as a hero. This is not surprising, considering that Theseus was thought to have been a ruler of Athens, and Attica was of course the focus of both political power and mainstream culture during the 6th and 5th centuries BC, and the place in which most black- and red-figure vases were being produced. Theseus is a somewhat different hero from Herakles, for he is entirely human, and his human frailties, in the long run, bring him to an unhappy end, as is the case with so many Greek heroes. Meleager dies at the hands of his own vengeful mother, Jason commits suicide after the murder of his children by his wife Medea, Agamemnon is murdered in his bath by his wife, the perfidious Clytemnestra, and so on.

Certainly in his prime, Theseus follows a very 'Heraklean' hero pattern, in ridding the world of criminals and monsters, and performing great deeds before his ascension to the Athenian throne. Like Herakles, with whom he occasionally interacts, and who serves as a heroic role model for him, he also carries a club, and even performs similar tasks. He defeats the Minotaur, the same in fact that Herakles had once captured and released (according to Diodorus) in the seventh Great Labour, and his killing of the Krommyonic boar mirrors Herakles' capture of the Erymanthean boar in the fourth Great Labour. Figure 5 shows us a low-relief clay plaque (c. 460–50 BC) from the island of Melos, most probably a covering for a small coffer. It is meant to depict either the boar hunt of the hero Meleager, or more probably to represent Theseus in the process of slaying the Krommyonic boar.

The deed for which Theseus is best remembered is the killing of the Minotaur, half bull, half man. This creature was housed in the labyrinth beneath the palace of King Minos of Crete. For the unwarranted murder of one of Minos' sons in Attica, the gods plague the region with drought and pestilence. As expiation to Minos, the Athenians are obliged to send fourteen youths and maidens as tribute to be sacrificed to the Minotaur every nine years. The young prince Theseus insists upon his own inclusion as tribute and leaves Athens with the firm intention of destroying the monster for good. A propitious sacrifice to Aphrodite, goddess of love, ensures that Minos' daughter Ariadne falls in love

FIGURE **5**
Coffer covering with image of 'Theseus and the Krommyonic Boar'. Greece, Melos, c.460– 50 BC. Low-relief carved earthenware, ht: 15.2cm (6in.).
Courtesy of Staatliche Antikensammlung und Glyptothek, Munich

with Theseus and provides him with a sword and a ball of twine to find his way out of the labyrinth. The Minotaur is successfully slain, and Theseus escapes unharmed with the Athenian youths and maidens in the company of Ariadne.

A visitation by the god Bacchus forbids his love to Ariadne, and with a heavy heart he abandons the girl on the island of Naxos, to fulfil her destiny as bride of the god. In his sorrow at her loss, Theseus forgets to take down the black sail that announces his apparent defeat. His aged father, King Aegeus, waiting anxiously on a cliff top for the outcome of the voyage, sees the black sail and hurls himself in despair to his death. Thus Theseus' triumphant homecoming is full of grief, and his ascension to the throne a sad one. He nevertheless shows himself to be an able ruler, and is credited with the creation of Athens as a truly centralised city state under benign rule.

It is in his old age that folly and sorrow dog his footsteps. With his bosom companion Peirithoos he embarks upon questionable adventures, beginning with the theft of the lovely Helen of Sparta (who later of course is again abducted by Paris from her husband Menelaos, thus provoking the great Trojan War). Peirithoos sets his sights on Persephone, the wife of Pluto, ruler of the underworld, and here the two heroes are cursed to immobility for their rashness. Eventually Herakles in his travels through Hades does manage to free Theseus, but is unable to do the same for Peirithoos, who must be left to his fate.

Figure 6 shows a small painted detail from an elaborate Apulian *krater* from Canosa (*c.*340–30 BC). Stylistically there are obvious differences between the earlier Attic red-figure paintings and later Apulian work; the drawing is less precise and stylised and there is a fresh sketch-like quality to figure depiction. There are more white-slip details (the hats, clubs, jewellery, etc.) and garments are rendered in a much more naturalistic manner. This scene detail, one of many occurring in the densely stacked registers over one another on the *krater*, shows an 'allegorical' meeting of Dike, goddess of justice (left), with the seated Theseus (centre) and the standing Peirithoos (on the right). Dike has pulled her sword from its sheath and addresses the sitting Theseus, who looks back at her over his shoulder, still wearing his sun hat (*petasos*) and comfortably braced on his club. The standing Peirithoos, also with his club and his hat slipped off, is gesturing with his left hand, and all three appear engrossed in their conversation.

In late life, the lonely Theseus courts and marries Phaedra, Ariadne's younger sister, in the hope of regaining some of his lost love. Phaedra, very much younger and not in love with Theseus, has lustful leanings towards his young and innocent son Hippolytus, who appears to her like a youthful and desirable version of his father. Hippolytus spurns her advances and flees, and a chagrined Phaedra hangs herself, but not before leaving a spiteful letter to Theseus, denouncing the youth as despoiler of her honour. Theseus curses his own son and brings about the latter's destruction through the help of Poseidon. In the

FIGURE 6
Detail of Apulian krater with image of 'Theseus, Dike and Peirithoos'.
Italy, Canosa, c.340–30 BC.
Red-figure painted earthenware,
ht: 124cm (48⅞in.).
Courtesy of Staatliche Antikensammlung und Glyptothek, Munich

end, the truth of the matter regarding Hippolytus' innocence comes to light, and Theseus succumbs to remorse. The unjust death of his son is the turning point in Theseus' compromised destiny. His rulership crumbles, and Theseus ends up in exile on the island of Skyros, where a traitorous hand sends him to his death over a cliff's edge, much like his father. According to legend, it is many centuries later that the hero's bones are found on Skyros, and brought back in triumph and honour to Athens, his final resting place.

Here the elements of tragedy, so beloved of Greek mythology and theatre, are played out to the full, and of course as a narrative, there is rich food for the telling of the story or the painting of the image. Unlike Herakles, Theseus' fate did not bring him any rewards of an everlasting kind — he was but a human hero, and as such (by ancient Greek beliefs) ends as a shade in the underworld kingdom of Hades. Yet as a mortal, he did fulfil his destiny in the order of things, and perhaps, like his compatriot Herakles, it is no mean reward to be remembered and celebrated in painting and literature some two thousand years later.

CHAPTER

2

The Maya

Background: Classic Elite Maya Pottery

In the early 16th century, Europe first made contact with those peoples inhabiting Mexico and Central America. Before the incursion of the Spanish into this region, various civilisations had been building great cities for many centuries, developing intricate systems of calendrics and writing, and achieving high levels of proficiency in the arts of poetry, music, dance, sculpture and painting. These Mesoamerican cultures flourished in the area now comprising southern and eastern Mexico, Guatemala, Belize, El Salvador, parts of Honduras, and the Pacific coast as far south as Costa Rica.

The Protoclassic Period (from 100 BC to AD 200) marks the beginning of Maya civilisation in two particular regions; the lowlands of the Yucatan peninsula and the Chiapas Pacific coastal highlands. Its great achievements in writing, architecture, painting, calendrics and ceramic manufacture are usually associated with the Classic Period, from AD 250 to 850, particularly at such important sites as Palenque, Yaxchilán, Tikal and Copán. It should be understood that the Maya were by no means a unified empire or confederation. They spoke diverse languages and maintained separate competing city states, where ascendencies changed according to the social and political upheavals of the times. When the Spanish arrived in the 16th century, Maya Postclassic culture (AD 1250 to 1521) was in decline. By this time the fragmented Maya civilisation had abandoned its great established sites, and had ceded cultural dominance to such peoples as the Aztecs and the Mixtecs.

It is the elite narrative ceramics of the Classic Maya that I wish to examine briefly and that certainly deserves to be ranked among the greatest ceramic achievements of any ancient culture. To understand the complexity of painted figurative imagery and calligraphy that characterises these works, they should be studied in the light of the political and social framework in which they were

OPPOSITE PAGE

FIGURE 7

Maya cylinder vase with 'Ball Game' theme. Guatemala or Mexico, late Classic Period, AD 600–850. Earthenware with red, black and white pigment on orange slip, ht: 24cm (9½in.).
Gift of George and Helen Gardiner
Courtesy of The Gardiner Museum of
Ceramic Art, Toronto

27

conceived. By AD 500, Maya society had expanded to a level of prosperity, dynamism and cultural complexity rivalling that of China and Renaissance Europe. The Maya culture was based on a city state system both highly organised and hierarchical, with political dominance exercised by a ruling lineal aristocracy controlling the surrounding regions. Public and private rituals sponsored by the ruling elite were a means of promoting power and ideology, as well as maintaining authority. Monumental architecture served as the stage for impressive displays, and elaborate costumes and ceremonial vessels were among the important appurtenances of such rituals.

At this time the art of painting was very highly developed and valued by the Maya. Unfortunately, few of the great painted frescoes and screenfold books (or codices) have survived the ravages of time and the Spanish invasion. It is primarily the imagery from polychrome vessels (see Figure 7), usually preserved in elite tombs, that provides insight into the artistry of Classic Maya painting, and that helps us to decode the habits, beliefs and functioning of this complex and sophisticated society. Elite pottery served not only as high-status ritual serving vessels, but also as a currency of gift exchange, denoting the favour of the giver and status conferred upon the receiver. Scenes of various events and important individuals found on stone carvings also appear on elite painted vessels, with more specific allusions to particular ritual details and named people. Cosmological religious themes and post-death beliefs were also an important source of vessel imagery, such as narrative episodes from the epic Maya creation myth, the *Popul Vuh*, with the central theme of the Hero Twins and their various activities. Changing ceramic painting styles, especially those of the Late Classic Period (AD 550 to 850) reflect the ferment of change in Maya culture and social history at this time. The shifting of power bases along with their affiliated royal ceramic workshop sites no doubt had an important effect on techniques and painting styles, as did the style and vision of individual artists.

The Role of the Artist

Particularly worth mentioning in the context of elite Maya painted pottery is the status and role of the artists themselves. In ceramic-making cultures preceding the 20th century, potters tended to remain fairly anonymous and were perceived as coming from a more humble artisan class. As we have seen in Chapter One, some of the ancient Greek vase painters were among the first known artists to sign their works. It is likely that these artists were greatly valued and appreciated, and they may well have been publicly acclaimed. This is certainly true for the maiolica painters of the Italian Renaissance and for later European porcelain painters. In Japan, leading craftsmen and artists, including ceramicists, have always been highly acknowledged; some, such as Shoji Hamada, have even been accorded the title of 'National Living Treasure', an honour accompanied by stipends and an elevated social standing.

In Maya times there was certainly an artisan class of potters who along with other types of craftsmen produced the mundane necessary objects for daily use by the non-elite. The elite painters, however, were drawn more from the aristocracy and even from royal lineage. They were perceived as high-ranking artist-savants, with an education that encompassed history, religion, cosmology, mathematics, calendrics and philosophy. That their social standing was closely linked to the ruling elite is clearly apparent on some Maya vessels, where the artist's signature is given a visible associational prominence immediately behind the image of an important ruling figure. Above and beyond his skills, the elite Maya painter, by the creation of important ritual objects, supported and maintained the existing hierarchical social order, and was thus an integral and necessary adjunct to it.

Since no Maya workshop sites have actually been excavated, much of the information regarding ceramic manufacture and techniques comes from the pots themselves, along with some explicit imagery of the painters at work. The fact that certain signatures on vessels recur over time suggests a family continuity in the passing on of skills. As is the case in most traditional ceramic workshop settings, there may have been a division of skills and labour in the Maya pottery workshop. Vessel painters were also very likely engaged in fresco and codice painting (suggested by similar pigments and tools excavated in non-ceramic workshop finds). It is likely that the actual potters were not the painters but they may have worked through the universal apprenticeship system, advancing from the mixing of clays and pigments to vessel forming and the mastering of firing skills. The fact that vessel paintings often seem to surpass the quality of the pot itself, both in verve and delicacy, suggests that makers were indeed separate from painters, but still working as a team in the same locale. This apprentice and teamwork system was probably the same for all artistic disciplines, such as architecture, sculpture, and mural and codice painting.

Calligraphy and Image Meaning

One of the most striking visual attributes of the painted Maya vessel is the prominence given to calligraphic symbols, framing and freely interspersed with depictions of important human figure activities. The prominence and visual fluidity of these symbols lets us surmise that the artist, using the brush as primary tool, did not value his role as scribe any less than his role as painter. Calligraphic design on elite Maya pottery was as integral to the overall visual harmony of the piece as the image itself, as is the case in the Islamic ceramic tradition. It was at times used to frame or stabilise the overall composition, and its placement could enhance or emphasise a particular narrative. For example, horizontal calligraphy below the rim of a vessel joined to upright calligraphic panels might represent a palace structure within which an important activity such as a state visit is seen taking place.

From the point of view of semantic content, translation analyses indicate that the actual text meaning of the Primary Standard Sequence (the designation given to important Maya calligraphic texts) was not so much in support of the depicted narrative. It had a more dedicatory purpose and tended to elaborate the actual ritual or gift-giving function of the vessel, listing its proposed use, the patron giver's and recipient's names, and at times the artist's signature. In other words, the vessel as an important ritual object was sanctified and elevated to extreme importance by a clear calligraphic code, which did help to support the image function, but in an autonomous way.

Elite Classic Maya imagery usually dealt with a number of themes that had at their centre the human figure. As in the visual iconography of the ancient Greeks, it is assumed that depicted human figure activity moved freely between the 'real' and the 'supernatural' worlds. Narratives were not only charged with different levels of meaning, but as mentioned earlier, confirmed existing religious ideology, cosmology and the Maya world view. For example, animals (such as the bat and jaguar) were imbued with sentience and the ability to transform themselves and assume human characteristics. Animal imagery could be associated with the bridging of both worlds, the real and the supernatural, and could be used to consolidate totemic and emblematic power.

Popular human imagery dealt with historical scenes such as palace rituals, state visits, hunting scenes, vision-quest rituals and the journey after death. A frequently-portrayed subject was the 'Ball Game', seen as both sport and highly charged ritual (see Figures 7 and 8). It was the allegoric re-enactment of the gods' creation of the cosmos, with the ball court seen as the symbolic place of origin, connecting both worlds. Such imagery of the underworld, often depicting narratives from the great Maya epic, the *Popul Vuh*, was probably considered most suitable for burial vessels. Images of state functions and historical events may have been more associated with ritual serving or patronage and gift-giving.

Figure 8 shows a roll-out image taken from the reverse side of the chocolate beaker shown in Figure 7. Depicted here is the popular Mesoamerican Ball Game mentioned above, either shown as a ceremonial ritual or as an actual illustration of the Hero Twins' defeat of the underworld gods from the *Popul Vuh*. Three ball players are seen in front of steps such as on a temple or dance platform. All three wear chest yokes which are made of wood covered with stucco and painted. Under the yokes a heavy fabric belt holds a decorated deerskin rear apron. Each player wears a knee guard and the kneeling player is wearing a deer headdress while the opposite team wears feather headdresses. The ball in motion is made of dense rubber. As in modern soccer, the ball was not touched with the hands, but was deflected off the protective padding on the waist and knees. The

rim text, a Primary Standard Sequence, dedicates the vessel and makes it a sacred object. The vertical glyph blocks on the body of the vessel are not filled in, only indicating where the names and titles of the participants would have been.

FIGURE **8**
Detail of Maya cylinder vase with 'Ball Game' theme.
Courtesy of The Gardiner Museum of Ceramic Art, Toronto. Photograph courtesy of Barbara and Justin Kerr

The Maya ball game has mythological overtones: the Hero Twins play against the Lords of the Underworld and defeat them. This defeat allows the Hero Twins and their father, the Maize God, to keep the Lords of the Underworld in check. This mythological game is played by the Maya elite over and over again in commemoration, in a sense, of the triumph of good over evil.

Maya Mythology and the Popul Vuh

The *Popul Vuh* is the highland Maya Quiché chronicle that recounts the history of their origins, cosmological concepts and the chronology of their kings to the year AD 1550. It was first compiled in the 16th century and translated into colonial Quiché spelling from lost pre-Hispanic books and oral sources. Later the Quiché chronicle itself was lost, but had been translated into Spanish. In its epic portion, it deals with the story of gods and creation, notably the Hero Twins Xbalanque and Hunahpú who descend into the underworld of Xibalba to defeat the gods of death, and to pave the way for the creation of humankind.

In Mesoamerican cultures twins were viewed with misgivings, to the point where it was often common practice to kill one twin at birth. In Maya and Aztec mythology, twins appeared as monster slayers, cultural heroes and creators of order, preparing the world for human life, but also being seen as the disturbing harbingers of conflict and change. The Hero Twins appear to have been in evidence well before Postclassic Quiché times, and were a part of Protoclassic and Classic Maya mythology centuries earlier.

The *Popul Vuh* is far too comprehensive and lengthy to fully narrate here, but I will attempt a very brief synopsis. It is probably the first great epic of the Western hemisphere, and has all the drama and adventure of any other culture's heroic creation myth. It is well worth pursuing, simply as a wonderful story. The first part of the epic deals with the abortive attempts of the gods to create an inhabited world. The creatures of the earth, water and sky were fashioned first to praise the gods. Lacking sentience and voices, they failed and were not given dominion. A race of clay people, and another made of wood and rushes, were created and successively found wanting and destroyed. After this the world remained unpeopled.

The second part of the *Popul Vuh* recounts the many exploits of the Hero Twins Xbalanque and Hunahpú, their quest to trick and vanquish the death gods, to resurrect their vanquished father and uncle, Hun Hunahpú and Vucub Hunahpú (also twins), so that maize might be brought forth into the world for the creation of the first true humans from corn. In this of course, the Hero Twins succeed and after many adventures, vicissitudes, deaths and resurrections, they finally defeat the death gods in the underworld of Xibalba.

Among their adventures, and one frequently depicted in Maya art, is the episode of the Ball Game. Historian Karl Taube, in his *Aztec and Maya Myths*, presents the following version:

> The twins then play ball with the death gods, eventually allowing themselves to be beaten. That night they face another series of tests, but by their cunning they pass safely through the House of Knives, the House of Cold, the House of Jaguars, and the House of Fire. Finally they are sent to the House of Bats, a room filled with fierce knife-nosed bats. To protect themselves the twins hide inside their hollow blowguns, but Hunahpú peeks out to see if dawn is approaching, and at that moment the killer bat Camazotz snatches off his head. The head of Hunahpú is taken to the ball court and all of the death gods and demons rejoice, since their victory over the twins now seems all but certain.
>
> However, in the late pre-dawn hours, Xbalanque calls on all the animals to bring their various foods. Some creatures present rotten things, others offer leaves and grasses. Finally the coati [similar to a racoon] arrives with a large squash and Xbalanque places it against the severed neck of Hunahpú like a new head. Magically, the squash takes the form of Hunahpú's features, and he can see and speak. At dawn the twins appear together at the underworld ball court as if nothing had happened.

The death gods begin the game by throwing out the real head of Hunahpú to serve as the new ball. Xbalanque strikes the head so hard that it bounces out of the court and into the woods. A rabbit, previously told to wait in the trees, immediately bounds away, confusing the death gods who mistake it for the ball. While their attention is distracted, Xbalanque retrieves Hunahpú's real head and places it back on his body. When the death gods return, the twins throw the squash into the court:

'The squash was punted by Xbalanque, the squash was wearing out; it fell on the court, bringing to light its light-coloured seeds, as plain as day right in front of them.'

Thus the confused and astonished death gods are truly defeated in their underworld court of sacrifice.

Another version of this story has the tortoise, the last of the animals summoned by the twins to arrive, being transformed and used as the temporary false head.

After many more trials, the twins finally overcome the two principal death gods, Hun Camé and Vucub Camé, and vanquish the evil kingdom of Xibalba. They then recover and speak to the remains of their father and uncle, reassuring them of continued respect and worship. Xbalanque and Hunahpú then rise into the heavens to be transformed into the sun and the moon. Their quest to liberate their father Hun Hunahpú is doubly important since the Classic Maya identified him as the maize god, with his implicit role in bringing maize to the world, and the subsequent creation of humankind from corn.

The images on the beaker shown here may well be of a game played between human players, or recount the defeat of the death gods in the underworld ball court. In coming to terms with Maya imagery on elite painted vessels it is important that we do not limit our interpretation of an image as reflecting **either** history **or** mythology. In *Painting the Maya Universe: Royal Ceramics of the Classic Period*, the historian Dorie Reents-Budet states the following:

When the painted imagery moves into the realm of religion and its associated rituals, the visual and epigraphic distinction between historical and supernatural images — between history and myth — becomes much less clear. This blurring of the boundary between the two reflects the Maya belief that history and myth are not separate entities as they are in the Western world, but instead they are simply a part of the phenomenon of human-deity existence. Further, for the modern and pre-Columbian Maya, history re-enacts mythology. Many vessels that record vision-quest and religious rituals, then should not be categorised as representing either a historical event or a mythological belief; and the depicted events should not be identified as taking place in the human or numinous realm because of their overlapping and synchronous nature.

China, Persia and Japan

3

China

Background

Of the world's many ceramic-producing cultures, China must surely boast one of the most long-standing traditions of ceramic manufacture anywhere. Chinese ceramic history, from its Neolithic period (c. 6500–1700 BC) to the present day, reflects the country's geographic and ethnic diversity, as well as its many political, social and cultural upheavals. More than 20 dynastic changes over a 3000-year period have been accompanied by constant fluctuations of patronage and popular taste in ceramics.

The influence of Chinese ceramics in terms of techniques and aesthetics has also been globally pervasive, strongly marking Korean, Japanese and Western 20th-century high-fire ceramic traditions. The collaboration of the Japanese potter Hamada Shoji and the English potter Bernard Leach in the early 20th century went on to influence the prevalent stoneware and porcelain aesthetic in the English-speaking world. Certainly, one of China's great contributions to world ceramics was the early development of high-fire technology, in particular the use of porcelain, well before its advent anywhere else. The Tang dynasty (AD 618–907) saw the development of high-fired stonewares and some whitewares in northern regions, but the first true porcelains probably came into use in the mid-to-late Tang period in the province of Jiangxi, in south-central China. The pure kaolinitic clays and feldspars of the region led to the eventual development of well-vitrified (and much later, semi-translucent) wares associated with Chinese porcelains. The most important kiln site and centre of manufacture, and one enjoying frequent imperial patronage, was that at Jingdezhen, which has remained one of China's premier porcelain production sites.

OPPOSITE PAGE

FIGURE 9
Detail of beaker vase with image of 'Lotus Gatherers'. China, Jiangxi Province, Jingdezhen, late Ming dynasty, c.1650. Porcelain with underglaze cobalt blue, ht: 41 cm (16 in.).
Gift of Ann Walker Bell
The Robert Murray Bell and Ann Walker Bell Collection
Courtesy of The Gardiner Museum of Ceramic Art, Toronto

35

Narrative Precursors: Signs and Symbols

Perhaps one of the earliest Chinese ceramic narratives in evidence is a brick tomb wall from Hsi-chan Chiao in Nankin, dating back to the Northern and Southern dynasties in the late 4th or early 5th centuries AD. Here the image shows the Seven Sages of the Bamboo Grove seated on mats drinking tea and making music among carefully painted variegated trees. The wall is treated very much like a painting in its entirety and the image was most probably transferred directly onto the clay from an initial image painted onto brick-sized blocks. This type of work appears to be somewhat unusual in early Chinese ceramic history.

The first real venture into narratives, specifically on vessels, did not really occur until the early 1600s, during the final decades of the Ming dynasty (AD 1368–1644) and continuing on into the Qing dynasty (AD 1644–1911). Before discussing these later narratives in depth, I would like to mention the kind of 'allusive' narrative, or symbol decoration that has been pervasive on Chinese ceramics for thousands of years, and that forms the basis of a visual and thematic iconography that was clearly understood by viewers and users of ceramic vessels. The understanding and appreciation of such symbols becomes relevant to later more specifically narrative imagery.

The study of signs and symbols on Chinese ceramics becomes quite complex because image meaning can be specific to vessel function, as well as speaking to different social classes. From a Western perspective a particular image, a fish for example, could be seen as just that, having an association with movement, water or possibly food. For the Chinese viewer the interpretation is far more complex. An example of this might be an image of carp and water weeds on the inside of a bowl that served as a common household item. In her book *Designs as Signs: Decoration and Chinese Ceramics*, historian and curator Stacey Pierson gives us the following analysis:

> The carp is a particularly resonant image in Chinese mythology. It is significant on many levels including its name, which in Chinese is pronounced the same way as 'profit' and 'advantage.' Fish in general symbolise abundance, *yu*, but the carp is also a more precious golden fish with literary associations and a further symbol of endurance. Here the carp are shown amongst water weeds. As we know from the rediscovery of ancient culture and literature under the Song [dynasty, AD 960–1279] the fish among water weeds probably alludes to the famous Zhuangzi parable called *The Joy of the Fish*.

To the Chinese viewer the carp image would of course be evocative on a number of different levels, and to receive or own and use such a ceramic piece would be considered positive and auspicious. A bowl in the collection of the Percival David Foundation of Chinese Art in London shows four different fish images in a pattern. The Chinese names for these particular fish are homophones for good omens. The mandarin fish, *guiyu*, is a homophone for 'plenty of richness'; carp, as mentioned above, is *li*, like 'advantage, benefit'; and goldfish, *jinyu*, can mean 'abundance of gold'. A mysterious fourth fish remains unidentified, but nonetheless this would definitely be a good bowl to own.

The dragon is another very popular symbol-image occurring on Chinese ceramics. Some of the earliest literary allusions to dragons go back as far as the Eastern Zhou dynasty (770–256 BC). Other artistic dragon references predating writing appear as early as Neolithic times. Traditionally the dragon represents themes relating to power: the emperor, rain and water, and energy. The dragon is also seen as an emissary bearing deities through the skies, and as a guardian to the entrance of paradise. Later the dragon becomes a popular motif in the Tang dynasty and continues on imperial ceramics of the Yuan, Ming and Qing dynasties. The five-clawed dragon in particular is usually associated with the emperor, as is the phoenix with the empress (see Figure 10). In earlier times in art and literature, the dragon is seen as aerial, and in later times as aquatic.

FIGURE 10
Shallow bowl with 'Dragon and Phoenix' image. China, late Ming dynasty, *c.*1620–50. Stoneware with coil-relief modelling and celadon glaze, dia: 28 cm (11 in.).
Author's collection
Photograph: Jan Thijs

What is interesting in regarding any culture's specific symbols is that they are not necessarily universal. The bat is considered a symbol of good wishes in Chinese culture, but is associated with darkness and evil in ours (thanks perhaps to the European Gothic literary horror genre and such works as *Dracula* by Irish writer Bram Stoker). In China the dragon is a symbol of power, energy and royalty whereas in Western mythology it is associated with evil, the devouring of maidens and the hoarding of gold. Christian mythology has the good Saint George defeating the dragon, symbol of evil and sin.

Certainly in the case of Chinese ceramics, any decoration should not be viewed as random, but appreciated on a number of different levels. First, there is the most obvious painterly and decorative aspect of the motif to be considered, where a harmonious image is allied to a three-dimensional form. There is the image's symbolic connotation, where a distinct message (or homophonic pun) is being conveyed, or where a design can be seen as talismanic, conveying messages to the spiritual world. There is another descriptive aspect to be considered, where the specific function of the object (as ritual or serving vessel) is further defined by the image. All of these registers of image meaning can come together in a single ceramic object. As is very evident in previously discussed Maya and ancient Greek ceramics, design and pictorial traditions also support established ideologies, religious beliefs and the existing socio-political cultural framework.

17th-century Ceramic Narratives: Background

Most interesting from a narrative point of view is the period from about 1630 to the early 1700s. This is something of an anomaly in the history of decorated Chinese ceramics, where prevalent symbol and sign decoration was to some extent replaced, or at least heavily augmented, by more specific narrative imagery. There are a number of reasons for this change in my view, the first being the advancement of new painting techniques at Jingdezhen. The classic high-fire blue-and-white underglaze painting on porcelain most usually associated with Ming wares had its origins earlier in the mid-14th century. At this time, with the fall of the Mongol Yuan dynasty (1368), the new Ming dynasty saw an increase in both foreign and domestic trade markets for these immensely popular blue-and-white porcelains. The next two centuries witnessed ever-increasing refinements in cobalt underglaze painting techniques, due in part to this popular demand.

A further important technical development that favoured ceramic narrative painting was the reintroduction by the mid-15th century of third-firing overglaze enamel techniques. This was a carryover from much earlier 13th-century Cizhou wares, using lead-fixed glazes fired on-glaze at a much lower temperature. Overglaze enamels (used in conjunction with cobalt underglaze painting, but most often by themselves in later Ming and Qing wares) provided not only a full and brilliant colour palette, but could also be used to advantage with great precision and delicacy as a fine painting medium.

Perhaps the most important reasons for the development of ceramic narratives in the 17th century were socio-political. By the 1630s a new class of literati-gentry was taking over as arbiter of taste and aesthetics, while the prestige, influence and affluence of the imperial court was waning. Profound economic and social changes in a newly-inflationary economy led to the rise of this new bourgeois 'literary' class of merchants and scholars, all aspiring to high levels of culture. This new economic elite with extensive outward-looking mercantile connections began a trend of investing surplus wealth in large collections of art and artefacts, among these a whole range of ceramic objects made for the scholar's studio.

At the same time the late Ming dynasty was a period of great social instability, with internal fighting throughout the eastern coastal regions from Northern to Central China, until the Manchu took Beijing in 1644 and established the Qing dynasty. The potters at Jingdezhen were not immune to the vagaries of civil unrest — the kilns were burned down in 1674 and did not attain their former levels of production until the 1680s, when the Kangxi re-established imperial patronage.

Landscapes and Scholars' Motifs

With the decline of imperial influence and the rise of a new and prosperous scholar and merchant class in the early 17th century, such popular imperial imagery on ceramics as the dragon and the phoenix was being supplanted by images of landscape painting, scholars' motifs and scholars' narratives.

Although not specifically narrative, the emergence of landscape themes on porcelains should be briefly examined as an important new development. The kind of symbolism previously discussed was still significant in the depiction of landscapes, especially that of mountain scenery. For the Chinese, from the most ancient times until today, the mountain remains the symbol of the most conspicuous manifestation of *qi*, or the universal life force. Mountains were seen as the home of spirits and gods, and as a source of life-giving rain and vegetation. They were the 'cosmic pillars' connecting the emperor to the gods, and were worshipped from the Eastern Zhou dynasty (770–256 BC) and onwards. This reverence and belief in mountains as a cosmic manifestation of life force remained constant, and was absorbed into Confucian, Daoist and Buddhist thought. The imagery of mountains on 17th-century porcelains became a reflection of sorrow for the lost Ming dynasty, and an escapist symbol of sanctuary and seclusion, away from the dilemma of divided political loyalties, or even actual persecution.

Landscape scenes were often allied to poetic script, supporting and reflecting the visual themes of escapism, seclusion and nostalgia. A famous vase in the Shanghai Museum shows a poetic inscription above a landscape of water, pines, rocks and mountains. It is a reference to the *Peach Blossom Spring* by the famous Six Dynasties poet-recluse Tao Yunming, alluding to an idyllic mythological village far from the turmoil of 4th-century dynastic upheavals. Many centuries later such imagery and poetry had great significance for the Ming literati-gentry, attempting to come to terms with their own turbulent dynastic changes.

Another prominent feature of ceramic decoration of the mid-to-late 1600s was the scholar's motif. Jingdezhen potters and painters at the time produced objects and vessels with particular scholars' themes, and of course found a very ready market in the merchants and scholars identifying with such themes. Scholars' motifs often portray the individual scholar or scholar-official, as well as his various pursuits and activities. Other scenes allude to success in imperial examinations — most important, since by imperial mandate two levels of examination had to be passed in order to be admitted to the civil service.

Figure 9 on page 34 shows a detail from a Ming beaker vase imitating the shape of an archaic ceremonial bronze drinking vessel. It depicts the popular scholars' pastime of lotus gathering. At dawn, the literati gathered lotus buds from muddy ponds and returned to their studies to watch them gracefully unfold. The figure to the right with two attendants behind him might well be a representation of the philosopher Zhou Dunyi (AD 1017–1073). In Zhou's poem *On the Love of the Lotus* he observes that the lotus grows out of the mud but remains pure.

Finally, there was a range of iconography that dealt with symbols of the scholar, and the depiction of scholars' virtues and accomplishments. The scholar was painted in many guises: as lonely wanderer, as exiled simple fisherman, or as meditator. He was often painted with animal and floral symbols that enhanced his virtues: the carp and pine, symbolising endurance and constancy; the prunus or plum, standing for perseverance and rejuvenation; the orchid, representing inaccessibility and seclusion (also a subtle significant protest against autocratic Qing rule); and so on. Many of these scholars' motifs made use of literary and poetic allusions from the past, as well as using references to mythological parables, all supporting scholars' beliefs and their particular world view.

Scholars' Narratives: The Romance of the Western Chamber

Not surprisingly after an intense period of political unrest and turbulence in the mid-1600s, there was a tendency to look back to the past for thematic inspiration in ceramic painting. Scholars' narratives were often inspired by existing older literary subjects that had been illustrated in hand-scroll paintings and woodblock printed books created for the merchants and literati of the Wanli period from the mid-16th century onwards.

Many of the tales and moral parables seen in imagery on 17th-century porcelains were inspired by stories going back as far as the Shang and Zhou dynasties (c. 700–256 BC). Such ancient literary characters as the previously mentioned Seven Sages of the Bamboo Grove for example, served as models of exemplary behaviour to the Ming literati, who resented and passively resisted the new Manchu 'barbarian' Qing regime. These 'sages' lived in the late 6th century during the Six Dynasties period and openly flouted Confucian conventions of the time and refused to abandon loyalty to an existing ruling house. Their examples of resistance and loyalty inspired much imagery in later 17th-century painting and ceramics.

The drama *Xixiang ji*, generally known in English as the *Romance of the Western Chamber* was perhaps one of the best known and most popular dramas of pre-modern China. Its origins go back to a Tang dynasty prose tale, *Yingying Zhuan* (or the biography of Yingying) by Yuan Zhen (AD 779–831). This tale of frustrated and finally requited love so captured the Chinese popular imagination that it cropped up again in ballad form later in the 12th century, revised by the poet Dong Jieyuan. Later on in the 13th century, it was further embellished into *zaju* dramatic form by author Wang Shifu. In the form of this drama the story has maintained its popularity to the present day.

Although secular book illustration had come into vogue by the 13th century and some scenes from other dramas appeared painted on porcelain pillows, the drama *Xixiang ji* has not been specifically identified in either context from this period. The first illustration of the drama on porcelain may date from the 14th century from an isolated vase in the collection of the Victoria and Albert Museum in London. From then on, late 15th- or 16th-century ceramic depictions of the drama seem to be rare. This is surprising, since this period saw a great proliferation of woodblock prints for books created for the literati-gentry of the time. The *Romance of the Western Chamber*, as a very popular drama, was thus frequently illustrated in that particular art form.

To what degree woodblock printed images affected ceramic imagery is not entirely clear. Certainly by the mid-17th century woodblock prints had been in wide circulation, and although not necessarily being directly copied, they may well have found their way into Jingezhen painters' studios, to provide at least some thematic inspiration. A treatise from 1911 called the *Jingdezhen Tao Lu* discussing ceramic production techniques, states the following:

> Those who paint on paper and silk do not concern themselves with painting on porcelain; and those who are skilled at painting on porcelain are not usually skilled at painting on paper or silk.

This statement seems to hold true when comparisons are made between earlier painting styles of paper and silk artists with later ceramic painting styles of the Kangxi period (AD 1662–1772). It seems that the painters at Jingdezhen maintained their own stylistic integrity, even if well aware of circulating woodblock printed works.

The story of the drama is a relatively simple one, and goes as follows: the talented but impoverished scholar Zhang Sheng, while staying in a monastery, meets the beautiful girl Cui Yingying, accompanied by her maid and formidable mother Madam Zheng. Aided by the clever and scheming maid Hongniang, the lovers gradually form a clandestine liaison, which of course is strenuously opposed by mother Zheng as unsuitable. Our scholar is sent away to pass his imperial civil service examinations, and in this he succeeds, finally returning in inevitable triumph to claim his bride. The story is of course replete with many details of faltering love, anxiety, and love letters passed back and forth, always with the presence and help of the ubiquitous maid.

The examples I have chosen here to illustrate the story of the *Romance of the Western Chamber* are two stylistically different objects, both made during the Qing dynasty in the early 1700s. Both depict vignettes from this particular love story. Figure 11 (opposite) shows a porcelain overglaze enamel-painted *famille verte* tile (possibly meant for inclusion in a piece of furniture). Here we see the scholar Zhang Sheng on his knees, perhaps making his first declaration of love to Cui Yingying. The maid Hongniang can be seen behind the garden door keeping watch for the lovers. Figure 12 (opposite) shows the rounded lid of a porcelain box painted in underglaze blue and white. The lovers can be seen through a window on the right, perhaps embracing for the first time, while the maid (or the disapproving mother?) looks on from the garden outside. (A passage entitled 'Beauty's Enchantment' from Part I, Act 1 of the play that describes the lovers' first meeting, can be found in Chapter Five on page 88, accompanying Figure 31.)

Interestingly enough, the scenes of the drama portrayed on both prints and mid-17th- and early 18th-century ceramics are not those that would be perceived as the most 'dramatic' by Western viewers. It is the Chinese literary convention of exploiting the static climax, or a brief moment of heightened perception in the story, that is reflected in both woodblock and ceramic imagery. The *Romance of the Western Chamber* scene most often portrayed on 17th- and early 18th-century ceramics is that entitled 'Listening to the Qin' (the solo stringed instrument favoured by the Chinese gentleman). It is this particular scene in which the young scholar pours out his heart in music and finally moves Yingying to favour his suit, that is portrayed so often.

In any case, any 'climactic' scenes of love and embracing would have been seen as downright licentious in courtly or elite Chinese society. The entire drama as such was considered so undesirable and vulgar in the mid-1700s during the Qianlong period that its translation into Manchu was forbidden. Nonetheless,

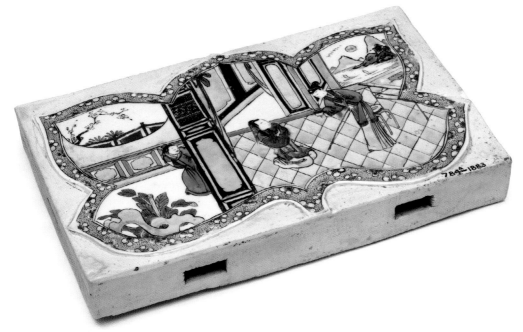

FIGURE **11**
Tile with illustration from the *Romance of the Western Chamber*. China, early Qing dynasty, Kangxi Period, c.1663–1722.
Famille verte porcelain with overglaze enamels,
w: 24cm (9½in.).
Courtesy of V&A Images, Victoria and Albert Museum, London

FIGURE **12**
Covered jar (lid) with illustration from the *Romance of the Western Chamber*. China, Qing dynasty, late Kangxi Period, early 1700s.
Porcelain with underglaze cobalt blue,
dia: 6.7cm (2¾in.).
Courtesy of the Percival David Foundation of Chinese Art, London

for the merchant class who even patronised *huabu* theatre (in which women were allowed to appear on stage with men) the *Romance of the Western Chamber* continued in popularity. No doubt the central character being a successful scholar added to the drama's appeal to a scholarly audience, although even here it was still considered somewhat *risqué*.

The narrative tradition in decorated ceramics continued into the 18th century to some degree. But by the end of the 17th century with the reassertion of imperial control of the kilns at Jingdezhen, there was a gradual resurgence of imperial motifs and auspicious rebuses at the expense of the more specific scholars' narratives. Yet that important anomalous period in Chinese ceramic history, from *c.* 1630–1720, saw a remarkable flowering of unsurpassed ceramic painting skills, which certainly formed the groundwork for much later decorative imagery.

This period also coincided with a heightened Western interest in Chinese art. The narrative imagery on the many ceramic objects that were making their way into European collections no doubt strongly influenced European appreciation of, and fascination with, all aspects of Chinese culture, even to the extent of imitation (particularly in the realm of European porcelain manufacture). The *Romance of the Western Chamber* theme can be seen yet again in Figure 31 in Chapter Five on a hard-paste porcelain tureen from the Austrian Du Paquier Factory, *c.* 1725. This particular narrative has been borrowed and renewed within another culture's ceramic imagery, as is the case with so many popular narratives.

Persia

Background

The Arab conquest of the Near and Middle East during the first quarter of the 7th century AD initiated the spread of Islamic culture over a vast territory that in time covered an area from the Spanish peninsula in the west to the borders of India in the east. It is the lustred and *minai* enamelled ceramics of the central Asian Turkish Seljuks (AD 1038–1194) that I wish to examine in a narrative context, but it first might be relevant to go back in time to look at some earlier Islamic styles and technical developments that led to these later Seljuk works under discussion. It will also be evident that the examination of later European slipware and tin-glaze traditions (Italian *istoriato* maiolica and Dutch and English delftware, as discussed in Chapter Four) are intimately linked to Islamic ceramic history.

In the early centuries of Islamic culture in and around the Near and Middle East, architectural building styles and basic decorative trends in crafts (such as ceramics) were initially adopted from conquered indigenous cultures, and later adapted and modified specifically to suit Islamic models. New and revived older techniques were introduced by migrating craftsmen seeking new patronage, or subject to the shifts and vagaries of political upheavals of the times. Before the 9th century, it appears there were two types of ceramic wares prevalent in this area. The first were more functionally-oriented vessels, such as ewers, serving

FIGURE 13
Seljuk lustre plate with
illustration of Sufic theme.
Iran, Kashan,
AD December 1210.
Stone-paste with
overglaze lustre,
ht: 3.7cm (1⁷⁄₁₆ in.),
dia: 35.2cm (13⅞ in.).
*Courtesy of Freer Gallery of Art, Smithsonian
Institution, Washington, D.C.,
(Purchase, F 1941–11)*

dishes and water containers. These were made of unglazed moulded earthenware and tended to be relief-patterned, with decoration based on stylised earlier Graeco-Roman or Sasanian models.

This 'adaptive' style change in early Islamic ceramics can be seen in 9th-century incised glazed wares known as 'splashed sgraffito' wares. Here purely Islamic incised palmetto motifs are allied to loosely splashed green, brown and honey-coloured glaze patterns. These are in direct imitation of Chinese Tang dynasty three-coloured splashed wares. This Chinese/Islamic influence travels even further. For example, Figure 1 on page 6 is an example of Islamic style and techniques seen on even later Italian slipware, most likely transmitted via Spain or Sicily. The splashed three-colour glaze theme and the stylised palmetto allied to the Christian Crucifixion theme are evidence of the adaptation of one culture's style and technique to another's. One constant design element that seems to have remained pervasive throughout most of early Islamic ceramics of all types was the use of vegetal motifs (arabesques), geometric patterns, calligraphy, and later on, of figural iconography. The above-mentioned types of ceramics maintained their popularity throughout the Near and Middle East due to a constant demand.

The 9th century, under Abbasid rule, saw the beginnings of major ceramic innovations in the first capital of Samarra in Mesopotamia (Iraq). The Abbasid dynasty (founded earlier in AD 750) is associated with the great caliph Haroun-al-Rashid (AD 766–809), whose magnificent court was famous for its wealth, its learning and its patronage of the arts. The splendours of his court are most associated with the famous stories of Scheherezade, in the *Tales of One Thousand and One Nights*.

The most important innovation in 9th-century Islamic ceramics was the rediscovery by Iraqi ceramicists of an earlier Egyptian invention of a white opaque alkaline or lead glaze combined with tin oxide. By this time, a number of earlier Chinese porcelains had been reaching the Near and Middle East through well-travelled trade routes. The new tin-glazed wares could emulate the whiteness and brilliance of Chinese porcelains, and form a more stable ground for elaborate in-glaze and lustre pictorial iconography. They became the foundation for the two most popular types of Islamic luxury ceramics of the late 12th and early 13th centuries: lustre wares and *minai* overglaze enamelled wares.

Islamic Lustre Wares

Ceramic lustre is the result of the application of such metal compounds as gold, silver and copper, to an already-fired glazed surface. The lustres fuse into the glaze at a much lower temperature in a third firing, and leave a residue pattern of shimmering iridescence. It is believed that early ceramic lustre techniques were carried over from Egyptian glass lustre painting going back to the 4th and 5th centuries AD.

Both earlier glass and ceramic lustre producers may well have been influenced by existing precious metalwork. The richness and associated status of valuable metals such as gold and silver, seen on these new metallic iridescent ceramic surfaces, no doubt made lustred luxury ceramics such a valued commodity. They may have been considered if not as a replacement, then at least as a noble addition to precious courtly metal and glass wares. Early Islamic lustre wares were first developed in the 9th century primarily inland around the cities of Baghdad, Basra and Kufa in Iraq. Another notable lustre-producing centre was established at Fustat in Egypt, near present-day Cairo, under Tulinid rule. These lustres rarely seemed to achieve quite the elegance of the Baghdad Abbasid lustres. After the Fatimid conquest of Egypt from the west in AD 969, Fustat still remained an important lustre production centre for the next 200 years.

The earliest lustres produced were polychrome, but these remained relatively short-lived, possibly due to the complexity of firing and low success rates. They were quickly replaced by monochrome golden lustred wares, and by the 10th century these had achieved a previously unattained refinement in technique and style, and might be seen as the precursors to the later dramatic narrative Seljuk lustres. Ceramic lustre techniques became pervasive in the Islamic world, eventually spreading to Syria, North Africa and into Spain, following the course of Islamic conquests and culture. By the middle of the 12th century lustre techniques had become well-established westward in Persia (Iran), with Kashan being the predominant production centre there. It is likely that lustre techniques had been introduced into this region by craftsmen from Fustat in Egypt during the decline of the Fatimid dynasty.

Thematically, lustre painters began to abandon the previous polychrome simple vegetal and geometric patterns in favour of more figurative work. Human and animal figures began to predominate on various types of vessels, from shallow bowls with turned-out rims, to cups, beakers, jars, ewers and bottles. These displayed elegant images of musicians, court attendants, mounted warriors and so on, all painted with an eye to drama and a conscious use of the vessel shape as a canvas. The focus was not only on decorative display, but also on the conveyance of messages to reinforce the values and ideals of the nobility. For example, imagery of the hare, the peacock, and the winged lion implied good fortune, and calligraphic inscriptions (occurring on most courtly ceramics of the time) might invoke blessing (*baraka*), trust in God (*tawakkul*) and the heavenly realm (*al falak*). Where figurative imagery was previously considered inappropriate in any Islamic religious context, it was viewed as acceptable in a more secular context on luxury ceramic wares. Certainly these images were new to ceramics, but were already familiar from other sources such as wall paintings, textiles and ornate metalwork. Direct image-links can be made between artefacts in these media to ceramic lustre wares.

Seljuk Narrative Ceramics: A Kashan Lustre Plate

There is a spectacular Kashan Seljuk lustre plate in the Freer Gallery of Art in Washington (see Figure 13 on page 45). This piece is dated, dedicated to a patron and signed by the artist. It shows a seated figure sleeping by a pool of water, accompanied by a horse and five attendant figures. In the pool there is a floating nude female figure surrounded by swimming fish. The Arabic inscription on the rim translates (loosely) as follows:

> Happiness and safety and generosity and favour and grace to the amir, the great, the learned, the just, the supporter, the conqueror, the victorious, the experienced, the champion of the faith, the one who brings victory to Islam and the Muslims, the leader of the kings and sultans, the leader of princes [...] the amir of the faithful, may his defenders be endeared to God and his power be doubled [...] work of Sayyad Shams al-Din al-Hasani in the month of Jumada II of the year 607 H. of the Hijra [AD December 1210].

It is likely that this plate was originally made for a prince of the Atabegs of Ardebil, Shiraz or Yazd. The fragmentary Persian inscriptions on both sides of the scalloped walls (seen as dark script against white) are a combination of various odes, a quatrain and an expression of good wishes. The iconography of the plate is somewhat enigmatic, and has been subject to various interpretations. One version attempts to identify a scene from the writings of the poet Nizami, entitled *Khosrow and Shirin* (AD 1175–76), where the king resting by a pool surprises the bathing maiden Shirin. This version seems to be somewhat disputed, since the king is a less significant and smaller-appearing figure than the five attendants, and also in all text sources the maiden Shirin is always modestly attired and not nude, as portrayed in this image.

A more likely interpretation of the narrative might be one proposed by Grace Guest and Richard Ettinghausen, in 'The Iconography of a Kashan Luster Plate' (*Ars Orientalis*, Vol. 4, 1961). Their version first of all presents a standard Islamic 'horse and groom' motif, for which there are many other precedents in Islamic metalwork and ceramics (it in fact occurs on the Freer *minai* beaker, in the following section, as seen in Figures 14 and 15). The dream-like and languorous quality of the image and its composite elements might lead a viewer to favour a Sufic, more mystical and allegorical interpretation, where all the visual elements combine into a coherent whole. Thus the fish is the symbol of the gnostic, the mystic or prophet, and the water in which he lives and for which his thirst can never be quenched, stands for infinite Divine grace. Water is the element from which Allah made all life and (in Sufi terms) can also stand for the saintly spirit, which soiled by contact with human sin, renews its purity by union with God. The woman in the water, to whom the fish are drawn, and who perhaps forms part of the sleeping youth's dream or vision, might be seen as the reflection of Divine beauty. In the *Mathavi* of Jalalu' ddin Rūmī, although compiled half a century later than the Freer plate, the poet draws on pre-existing themes and states that of all earthly beauty, 'Woman is the highest type, but it is nothing except insofar as it is a manifestation and reflection of Divine attributes'.

The central and most prominent figure of the horse is usually the symbol of the body or carnal soul, which goes astray as a horse does without a rider. The seated youth on the left might be seen as dreaming, and perhaps enjoying the vision of 'absolute beauty' denied to him in a waking state. His juxtaposition and proximity to the woman conjures up the context of 'lover and beloved', and with it the theme of mystic union, providing a possible catalyst of thought that might provoke the posing of essential metaphysical questions.

Seljuk Narrative Ceramics: The Freer Beaker

After the arrival of the Seljuk Turks from Central Asia, Iran's ceramic production accelerated dramatically, and a large number of new ceramic techniques and styles were initiated. Although Seljuk rule (from AD 1038–1194) was relatively brief, Turkish influence still predominated until the onslaught of the Mongols during the first quarter of the 13th century, which brought wholesale destruction to most urban centres. Under Mongol rule, Chinese artistic influences asserted themselves strongly in all fields, including ceramics. A second truly Islamic renaissance in ceramic development only occurred much later after the late 1400s, when the Turkish Ottoman empire established its ascendancy.

From the point of view of Seljuk ceramics, however, one other important technical advancement should be discussed, and that is the development of *minai* enamelled wares by Iraqi potters in the 12th century. These enamels, in the form of soft, fusible glazes, were fired onto an already glaze-fired surface, and provided a new and rich panoply of colours for painting, hitherto unknown in the Islamic ceramic repertoire. Vessels were made from a hard frit-paste, and were often fairly thinly thrown and finely finished. Most surviving examples are smaller bowls, cups and containers (see Figure 14). Larger pieces may have been more susceptible to cracking in a third firing. *Minai* enamels were initially painted on a white ground, but fashionable variations of turquoise and cobalt blue backgrounds were soon added. The most spectacular examples of Seljuk pottery (both lustre and *minai* wares) were executed during the last quarter of the 12th century and the early decades of the 13th century. Although some production centred around the city of Rayy, the best works seem to be attributed to Iran's then premier production centre of Kashan.

One of the most famous and unusual of Islamic narrative ceramic works is an early 13th-century *minai* beaker, also in the Freer collection (see Figures 14 and 15). It illustrates the love story of Bizhan and Manizha from the *Shahnameh* (The Book of Kings), the great Iranian epic set down by the poet Firdausi between AD 975 and 1010. In the prelude to this 1300-verse cycle, the poet Firdausi visits his beloved, and tells her the story of Bizhan and Manizha.

The story goes as follows: Kai Khusrau, the Iranian king, is feasting with

Bizhan before the latter's departure to fight the terrible boars. Bizhan successfully overcomes the boars, and meets Manizha, the daughter of the Turanian king Afrasiyab. The young couple fall in love, but Afrasiyab, furious at the affair, has Bizhan imprisoned in a well. The great Iranian hero Rustam comes to the rescue at Manizha's bidding, lifts the colossal stone blocking the well, and frees Bizhan from captivity. (In the 12th and last scene on the beaker showing his release, Manizha is shown looking on, so we can only hope and assume that the couple made their escape together, and lived happily ever after.)

The story on the vessel is painted in three horizontal registers divided into 12 narrative panels. It is meant to be read much like a cartoon strip, but from right to left and from top to bottom. Thus the piece as it is rotated in the hand allows the narrative to unfold in a spiral fashion. In Figure 14 the top register shows the beginning and conflict of our story. The central panel is 'The Prelude to Love', with Manizha and her nurse seated in a pavilion; Bizhan rests beneath a tree on the left; and on the far left, we see the nurse (again) bringing him a message from the princess. Other panels in the upper register show Bizhan feasting with the king; the boar hunt; and the lovers' 'Tryst and Discovery'. Figure 15 on page 52 shows a further detail of this particular panel: Bizhan and Manizha (far right) are seated in her pavilion; Manizha fêtes Bizhan (centre); and Garsiwaz, an ally of Manizha's father Afrasiyab, approaches her palace (left).

The middle register's central panel, 'Imprisonment', shows Bizhan in the pit, its top sealed with a large boulder. The pit is flanked by a blue elephant on the right, with Manizha touching the boulder on the left. Other panels show Bizhan taken prisoner; Bizhan brought to judgement before the king; and being led away to captivity. In the bottom register, the small central panel is simply called 'The Wait', showing Rustam's horse Rakhsh with a crouching groom to the left gesturing outwards with his right hand, as if to point us to the rest of the story. (The theme of the 'horse and groom', as a standard popular Islamic image type that we have seen on the Kashan lustre plate, can be identified again here.) The other panels show Rustam travelling to Turan disguised as a merchant; Manizha approaching Rustam for help; and the aforementioned last panel of Bizhan's release from the well.

The sequential narrative of the beaker's imagery presupposes a deliberate desire on the part of the painter to illustrate the Bizhan and Manizha narrative along a story-timeline, rather than to impose a prefabricated visual system on a known tale. This is certainly reinforced by details of the presented characters who not only appear to change costumes (much as they would in a stage play), but also appear more than once in a panel, to suggest distinct before-and-after sequences. There is in fact a real sense of 'dramatic' progression in this imagery. It is not certain whether the story can be attributed directly to Firdausi's epic poem, or whether it simply constitutes a visual translation of previously known and widespread oral sources. Arab culture has a rich history of storytelling, and

OPPOSITE PAGE

FIGURE **14**
Seljuk *minai* beaker with illustrations from the *Shahnameh*.
Iran, Kashan,
c. late 12th century.
Stone-paste with painted underglaze colours,
ht: 12 cm (4¾ in.),
dia: 11.2 cm (4⁷⁄₁₆ in.).
Courtesy of Freer Gallery of Art, Smithsonian Institution, Washington, D.C,
(Purchase, F 1928–2)

FIGURE **15**
Detail of Seljuk *minai* beaker
with illustrations from the
Shahnameh, passage of
'Tryst and Discovery'.

OPPOSITE PAGE

FIGURE **16**
Square dish (*kakazura*) with
image of Mandarin Duck and
Plum Blossoms. Ogata
Kenzan (1663–1743), Japan,
Kyoto, Narutaki Workshop,
Edo period, early 18th century.
Buff clay with white slip, iron
pigments, transparent glaze
and overglaze enamels,
2.1 x 16.8 x 16.8cm
(1 x 6¾ x 6¾ in.).
*Courtesy of Freer Gallery of Art, Smithsonian
Institution, Washington, D.C.,
(Purchase, F 1905–58)*

indeed this was considered one of the more important social pastimes in all walks of life. Firdausi himself states: 'I have now told this adventure in its entirety, as I heard it recited according to the ancient tradition'.

One last and interesting aspect of the beaker's painting is the seemingly casual interspersal of non-related images apart from the main narrative theme. Among the 12 neatly laid-out tableaux are several ambiguous scenes, not easily read as part of the ongoing narrative. One of these is an image of enthronement. Other images of attendants and horsemen clearly refer to standard mediaeval Islamic image types such as the 'horse and groom' motif. These would be familiar to viewers of the time, and were perhaps meant to provide a sort of 'visual relief' and familiarity, and even to slow down the viewer in his viewing (and handling) of the object, to better savour the story and lively painting.

I would like to quote Alan Caiger-Smith, from his book *Tin-Glaze Pottery in Europe and the Islamic World*. His point of view in describing the character of *minai* enamelled wares reflects his great commitment to and affection for Islamic ceramics, as both researcher and maker. He states:

> *Minai* vessels were an extreme; aristocratic, romantic, exclusive, in which the treasures of the rugged world were gathered into the small compass of an enchanted space. Like all miniatures, *minai* pieces have their own inner space. But one cannot see it until, like *Alice in Wonderland*, one has eaten of the right side of the mushroom and quietened oneself down to the right scale. Perhaps this was always part of their appeal – that they make this pleasing demand on all who care for them?

Japan

Background

Much like China, Japan's ceramic history extends far back in time to the middle of the 5th millennium BC, if not earlier. The Jomon period in Japan (commencing *c.* 6000 BC) saw the production over several thousand years of unique earthenware vessels notable for their complexity and individuality of form, and very unlike any work being produced on the Asian mainland or anywhere else.

In time a growing Chinese influence reaching Japan's westernmost island of Kyushu led to the introduction of innovative bronze and iron technology. By 200 BC a fairly sophisticated unglazed type of earthenware known as *yayoi* was in popular use in Japan. Later by the 4th century AD the potter's wheel, as well as a

new type of sloping updraught kiln (*anagama*) based on a Chinese kiln prototype, had also become well established in the west of Japan. Higher firing temperatures favoured a new type of more durable earthenware known as *sueki*, which although Korean in style, paved the way for the even higher-fired unglazed later Bizen and Tamba wares which maintained their popularity for many centuries.

In other ways early Japanese culture tended to model itself along Chinese lines and Tang dynasty artists and scholars were welcomed at the imperial court at Nara during the Heian Period (AD 800–897). A new type of glazed pottery in yellow, green and white-mottled lead glaze (modelled on existing Tang wares) became popular at the Japanese court, even after the latter's relocation to Kyoto in AD 794. These lead-glazed wares remained popular until well into the 12th century.

By the end of the Kamakura Period (1185–1336) the next major important ceramic development occurred around Seto in the province of Owari (near modern Nagoya) on the main island of Honshu. High-fired Old Seto wares emulated Chinese celadon-type glazes, and by the late Muromachi period (1336–1568) kiln sites had spread further east well into Mino province, where the later popular Shino and Oribe wares were produced. By the late 15th and early 16th centuries the 'split bamboo' kiln had been introduced from northern Korea by *sue* potters in the Karatsu area in the west of Kyushu Island. These new kilns, much like a horizontally split and segmented bamboo section (hence the name), were also built against an upward slope, but had the advantage over the larger-chambered *anagama* kilns in terms of greater heat control, fuel-saving, and increased production capacity. From Karatsu this new kiln type spread rapidly to the rest of Kyushu and other parts of Japan.

There were two very important incidents in Japan's history that radically influenced both technical advancements and aesthetic change in Japanese ceramics. This was the invasion of Korea in both 1592 and 1597 by the Japanese *shogun* Hideyoshi. Korean potters were brought back as prisoners of war and settled into various fiefs, to produce their wares under the protection and patronage of local *daimyo*. Although these wares were initially modelled on Korean Yi dynasty prototypes, in time many kilns started producing work that was distinctly Japanese in flavour. By the end of the Momoyama Period (1568–1603) glazed ceramics of various types were produced in three main areas: Mino in Owari province, the Kyoto area in central Japan, and the westernmost island of Kyushu.

Porcelains came into being in Japan for the first time in the early 17th century. The Korean master potter, Ri Sampei, had begun to exploit porcelain clay deposits in the Arita district of Kyushu. Although the first and earliest Japanese porcelains were still modelled on Korean blue and white Yi dynasty wares, the demand to emulate the more colourful Chinese Ming dynasty enamelled porcelains led to the first truly Japanese overglaze enamel wares. These were developed by the Arita potter Kakiemon Saida in the middle of the 17th century. Some of these early enamelled Arita wares began to reach Western markets through the port city of Imari, and hence became generically known as Imari wares. Other porcelains of the time, created more for the domestic market, were Nabeshima and Hirado wares, also from the Arita district. A new and bolder-patterned, distinctively Japanese type of enamelled porcelain was being produced by the Kutani kilns — certainly Arita and Kutani remained the premier porcelain production sites in Japan over the next century. Overglaze enamel wares were also being made at Seto, and by the late 1700s during the Late Edo Period, porcelain production had spread to other sites. By the early 19th century, Seto was second in importance only to Arita in the manufacture of porcelains.

The Character of Japanese Ceramics

Japan's ceramic history is both unique and eclectic. To attempt to give an overview of its entire development is virtually impossible within the scope of a few pages. One might attempt, however, to examine some of the characteristics that help us to understand how Japan's unique ceramic heritage might be defined.

Two very distinctive attributes can be said to characterise Japanese ceramics. The first and foremost is the extraordinary variety of types of ceramics that coexist comfortably alongside one another in Japan. Earthenwares and stonewares (both glazed and unglazed) seem to fulfil their daily functions alongside the more 'sophisticated' decorated enamelled and gilt porcelains. Where for example in Korea the high-fired Koryo celadons tended to supplant the earlier earthenware models in popularity, in Japan it seems that diversity of expression is more the rule than the exception.

This Japanese appreciation for fine and diverse crafts was made very clear to me once during a visit to Japan some years ago. I was the guest of a museum curator in Kyoto, in a house that admirably combined extreme modernity with traditionality in the use of materials, and a very understated sense of decor and display. After being presented to my hostess as a visiting potter, she instantly took me past some magnificent Tang dynasty ceramic horses displayed in the entrance hall, and into her kitchen. The first pot she chose to show me was a simple unglazed Bizen-type jar for holding fat drippings, sitting on a corner of her super-modern kitchen counter. This pot had been in her family for many years, and was in fact still very much in use. It was undoubtedly as highly valued as the exquisite Tang horse sculptures that graced the entrance hall.

A second, and to me important defining characteristic of Japanese ceramics (and indeed of Japanese culture in general) is the ability and sensibility that allows Japanese makers to transform existing models borrowed from elsewhere, and to create innovative and distinctively Japanese models from them. For example, the Old Seto wares might well be modelled on Chinese tenmoku and celadon prototypes of the Northern Sung dynasty. Certainly the constant traffic and exchange over the centuries between the mainland and the Japanese islands becomes relevant in any comparison of works. Over time, however, different materials, firing techniques and perhaps a highly localised sense of individuality on the part of Japanese potters led to an entirely different ceramic model. Old Seto wares display a character that is quintessentially Japanese.

Ceramics and Tea

My main preoccupation with the Japanese ceramic narrative will focus on the works of Ogata Kenzan, as seen against the background of 17th-century Kyoto ceramics. I think that the influence of the tea ceremony and its associated rituals should be at least briefly touched upon in order to understand what became an all-pervasive aesthetic in Japanese culture, in its architecture and most certainly in its ceramics.

I think the philosophy of 'Teaism' in Japan is best summed up in the opening words of Okakura Kakuzo's wonderful treatise *The Book of Tea*, first published in the mid-1950s. He states:

> Tea began as a medicine and grew into a beverage. In China, in the 8th century, it entered the realm of poetry as one of the polite amusements. The 15th century saw Japan ennoble it into a religion of aestheticism — Teaism. Teaism is a cult founded on the adoration of the beautiful among the sordid facts of everyday existence. It inculcates purity and harmony, the mystery of mutual charity, the romanticism of the social order. It is essentially a worship of the imperfect, as it is a tender attempt to accomplish something possible in this impossible thing we know as life.
>
> The Philosophy of Tea is not mere aesthetics in the ordinary sense of the term, for it expresses conjointly with ethics and religion our whole point of view about man and nature. It is hygiene, for it enforces cleanliness; it is economics, for it shows comfort in simplicity rather than in the complex and costly; it is moral geometry, in as much as it defines our sense of proportion to the universe. It represents the true spirit of Eastern democracy by making all its votaries aristocrats in taste.

The drinking of tea as a pastime was adopted from China, and first enjoyed by the court nobles and clergy of the Kamakura Period (1185–1336). In the following centuries the practice spread among the more influential strata of society in the capital of Kyoto and its environs, and spread outward from there. The cult aspect of Tea as an aesthetic practice developed in the later half of the 15th century. The main precepts of the Tea cult stressed in both its rituals and its implements the absence of pretension, encouraging simplicity, humility and understatement (*wabi* or *sado* in Japanese), rather than costliness or lavishness. These precepts were first laid down by Tea master Murata Juko (1422–1502) and maintained by successive generations of Tea masters thereafter.

The fashion of tea drinking had gained popularity by the mid-1500s among landowners, and eventually had spread to the general farming population as well. With this popularisation of tea, the use of durable glazed ceramics in the form of tea bowls, caddies and other related utensils increased, and the hitherto imported Chinese vessels began to be replaced by distinctive Japanese ceramics in ever-increasing quantities. Advancements in firing techniques in the first half of the 16th century led to improved ceramic wares, and the increasing popularity of tea ensured a ready market for them.

Some of the established kilns at Seto, Bizen and Shigaraki were singled out as suitable producers of tea wares, especially by the great Tea master Sen no Rikyu (1521–1591). These uniquely Japanese wares known as *kuniyaki* (or native wares) became highly prized. Under Rikyu's tutelage and the later varying schools of Tea (largely Zen-inspired), the prevailing aesthetic of understated simplicity and avoidance of material pretension (*wabi*) touched upon all aspects of Japanese life. As mentioned earlier, Japanese architecture and ceramics were influenced as well. A typical example here might be the Iga wares made for Tea in the Kyoto area in the late 16th century. They embodied an aesthetic of 'deliberate asymmetry', in keeping with the precept of avoidance of 'perfection'.

Another example of ceramic innovation at this time in and around Kyoto during the early Momoyama Period (1568–1603) was the development of *raku*, a kind of light-bodied, quickly-fired ceramic ware invented expressly for the tea ceremony. New *raku* techniques incorporating the use of more colour and painted imagery gave new impetus to ceramic expression. *Raku* became a popular addition to the more subdued and traditional wares of Mino and Seto.

Kyoto Decorated Ceramics

The narrative ceramic works of Ogata Kenzan should be viewed against the background of both 17th-century Kyoto culture, and its particular ceramic history. In the early 1600s Japan entered an era of prosperity under Tokugawa rule that began the Edo Period (1603–1868). After 1600 Edo replaced Kyoto as the capital, but Kyoto nonetheless remained an important and prosperous centre of culture, with the arts and applied arts being fostered by an increasingly well-to-do merchant class. Consumer-oriented Kyoto began to attract a number of craftsmen, including potters (largely from the Mino area) who initiated new ceramic manufactories under generous Tokugawa patronage.

Sophisticated merchant and clergy tastes led to the production of distinctive new 'refined', and above all, decorated ceramics (*kyoyaki*). Elsewhere as market demand for decorated wares increased, other Japanese workshops producing Kutani, Kakiemon and Nabeshima-type porcelains were incorporating motifs from nature, as well as from Chinese woodblock-printed manuals. By the 1640s Kyoto potters were producing a large variety of different types of ceramics, from iron-glazed tea caddies and Korean-type tea bowls, to more complex under- and overglaze-painted decorated wares. Particularly distinctive for Kyoto ceramics was the increased use of overglaze enamel techniques. (We have seen in previously discussed Persian and Chinese Ming and Qing wares the versatility of enamels as a ceramic painting medium.) Again a sophisticated secular society encouraged a widening market and distribution venues for these new types of wares.

The master potter Rihei was notable as an innovator at this time, for his use of enamels applied in complex surface patterns. The other Japanese potter who perhaps received even greater renown was Nonomura Ninsei, active in the second half of the 17th century. Where previous Karatsu and Seto potters had earlier laid the foundations for painted decoration using simple iron and glaze brushwork, Ninsei took the art of overglaze painting to previously unachieved heights. He was the first potter to transpose motifs from other Japanese applied arts sources, such as folding fans, patterned stationery, musical instruments, Buddhist altar fixtures, and so on. His work is probably best known for its masterly marriage of pattern to ceramic form. Although his imagery cannot perhaps be seen as narrative, some of the more 'allusive' image references that characterise Chinese ceramics, were no doubt relevant in a Japanese context as well. This will become more apparent in my following discussion of Kenzan's work.

Ogata Kenzan: Ceramic Narratives

Ogata Shinsei Kenzan (1663–1743) came to ceramics rather later in life than is usual for most potters. He grew up in cultured and sophisticated surroundings and mingled with some of Kyoto's leading artists and craftsmen. His family had been related by marriage to Hon'ami Koetsu, one of the leading advocates of the revival of classical arts in Japan. The Ogata family was also related to Tawaraya Sotatsu, an associate of Koetsu, and one of Japan's most influential 17th-century painters. Kenzan's brother Korin, also a distinguished painter, founded the Rimpa school of painting which sought inspiration in earlier, purely Japanese art forms. Later the two brothers often collaborated in painting and ceramics, but Kenzan did not really begin his active career as a ceramicist until 1699, having been more inclined towards scholarly pursuits. His interest in ceramics was stimulated by a gift of the secret pottery notes of Koetsu, passed on to him by the latter's grandson Kano. His studies under the fourth-generation *raku* master Ichinyu finally led to his establishing a kiln at Narutaki near Omuro. It is believed that as a young man Kenzan had known the great potter Ninsei, and an additional present of the master's notes, given to him by Ninsei's younger son Seijiro, finally launched Kenzan's own ceramic career at the age of 37.

His amateur and fresh approach to the ceramic surface as a medium capable of expressing a range of pictorial iconography apart from vessel function made his work immediately endearing and popular. The popularity of his work did wane somewhat after he was obliged by financial difficulties to commercialise his establishment, and although very prolific, his work from this period was perhaps not his very best. By the early 1700s his supporters and patrons had fallen from influence, and he managed to lead at best a meagre existence. In 1731, under the new patronage of Prince Kimihiro, Kenzan finally relocated to the capital of Edo, and threw himself again into reading, painting and pottery making, until his death at 81 in 1743. His legacy was immense and his name passed on to other succeeding potters in titular descent until the 20th century.

The English potter Bernard Leach, who proved so influential in transmitting Japanese ceramic aesthetics to the West, was himself a pupil of the sixth Kenzan and received from him the *densho*, or secret pottery notes that in a way were considered the certificate of succession. With the tremendous interest in the mid-20th century in the revival of the works of Kenzan, with the formation of the Kenzan Society, and a subsequent fever of collecting Kenzan's work, there were of course many spurious works found attributed to him. Many works of Kyoto workshops from the 18th and 19th centuries are simply identified as 'in the Kenzan style'.

I am carefully avoiding this particular topic, because identification, classification and authentication of ceramic works do not fall into this purview, but indeed represent a complex subject on their own. For historians and curators, the Freer catalogue by Richard R. Wilson, *The Potter's Brush; the Kenzan Style in Ceramics*, ably and concisely outlines not only the history of Kenzan and his works, but also all the ramifications in later times of his succession and the collection and authentication of his works, and those in the Kenzan style.

Figure 16 on page 53 shows a square slabbed plate with an image of a mandarin duck and plum blossoms by Ogata Kenzan. It is from a series of 12 paintings of birds and flowers of the 12 months based on the paired poems of Fujiwara Teika from 1214, composed for the abbot prince Dojo. The poem itself reads as follows:

Plum blossoms:
It is that time when snow buries
The colours of the hedge,
Yet a branch of plum is blooming,
On 'this side' of the New Year.

Mandarin duck:
The snow falls on the ice of
The pond on which I gaze,
Piling up as does this passing year
On all years past,
And on the feathered coat of
The mandarin duck, the 'bird of regret'.

This allusive narrative harkens back to the Tang dynasty of China, where mandarin ducks were paired on marriage mirrors as symbols of human devotion; they were believed to mate for life, and following the death of one, the other pined away. The verse pair expresses sorrow for time irrevocably lost, supported by another symbolic image of separation, the plum blossom. Remarkable and unusual here is Kenzan's use of the flat surface as a painter's canvas. The back of the plate carries the poem itself in beautiful calligraphic script, painted over brush strokes that simulate traditional cloud-patterned paper (*kumogami*), and the overall poem composition suggests the format of the traditional Japanese poem card.

Figure 17 shows a lidded incense container with an image from the classical Japanese work *Tales of Ise*. The painted figures here refer to the ninth chapter of the work, in which the central figure, customarily identified as the courtier Ariwara no Narihira (AD 825–880) comes to a mountain pass called Utsutoge. This gloomy, ivy-overhung path plunges the travellers into profound melancholy, inspiring Narihira to write a poem (presumably to a lover):

Beside Mount Utsu
In Suruga
I can see you
Neither waking
Nor, alas, even in my dreams.

He hands this to a wandering ascetic of his acquaintance (the man in the white straw hat) to take back to the capital. This episode, known as *Tsuta no Hosomichi* (Narrow Ivy Road), came to express desolation and longing for home and for one's lover. It is perhaps also reminiscent of the scene of 'static climax' previously discussed in the Chinese *Romance of the Western Chamber* narrative, in 'Listening to the Qin', a poignant and contemplative, rather than climactic moment in the story.

The *Narrow Ivy Road* theme was already popular from the Kamakura Period, where it often appeared on lacquer ware and scroll paintings. Rimpa school artists (such as Tawarayu Sotatsu) further used this motif during Kenzan's time in painting, in lacquer ware, and in publishing. Kenzan's brother Korin made use of this theme as well, and was able to 'reduce' more complex imagery from other passages of the *Tales of Ise* to simple allusive elements, such as an iris theme, that would evoke in the viewer's mind a particular passage of the story. Thus this popular tale would involve the viewer in verse-guessing to 'complete' the image, or conversely require the visualisation of a familiar image, to evoke a particular text passage.

Stylistically and technically, the two works shown here (both from the Freer collection) exemplify Kenzan's narrative work and demonstrate his uniqueness as an innovative painter. His works are evidence of his love of traditional, reclusive scholarly themes, of history, of literature and poetry, and of his innate affinity with painting. His style and artistry remain unique and pervasive in Japanese ceramics, and indeed serve as an example against which contemporary painted ceramics can be still measured.

FIGURE **17**
Incense container with illustration from *Narrow Ivy Road*, taken from *Tales of Ise*. Ogata Kenzan (1663–1743), Japan, Kyoto, Narutaki workshop, Edo period, early 18th century. Buff clay with white slip, iron pigments, transparent glaze and overglaze enamels, ht: 2.5cm (1in.), w: 10cm (4in.).
Gift of Charles Lang Freer
Courtesy of Freer Gallery of Art, Smithsonian Institution, Washington, D.C.,
(Purchase, F 1907–84)

61

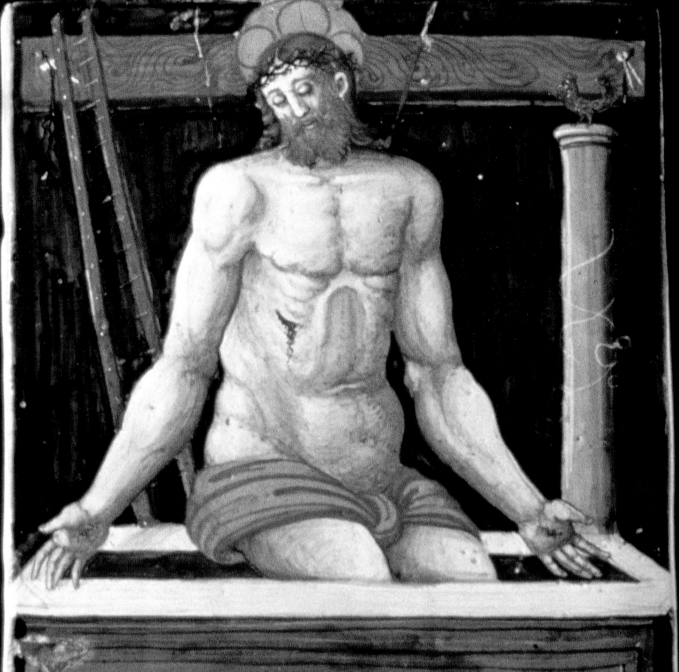

RESPICIE INFACIE CHRISSTI
TVI

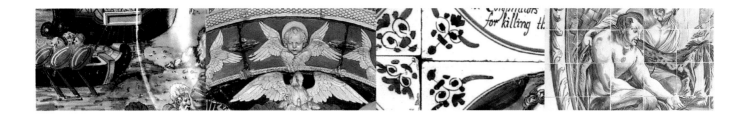

European Tin-glaze Traditions

4

Background

One of the richest ceramic traditions from the point of view of surface decoration and narrative expression is that of European tin glaze. As we have seen in chapter three the initial impetus for the use of tin glaze occurred in 9th-century Iraq, probably in imitation of early Chinese porcelains. The practice spread westward from the Near and Middle East into Europe through North Africa and the Iberian peninsula. Both inglaze painting techniques (on-surface pigments fusing into the glaze during the second firing) and lustre techniques, were established in Spain as early as the 11th century.

From there they spread to the Italian peninsula, and northwards into the rest of Europe. Throughout the 13th and 14th centuries, Spanish Hispano-Moresque wares produced at such important centres as Malaga and later Manises (Valencia), begin to exhibit a fusion of Near Eastern and European decorative motifs. These wares, along with migrant Spanish craftsmen, entered the Italian peninsula, where they found an active market during the 14th and 15th centuries. By the late 1400s, imported Hispano-Moresque wares with more Islamic-based motifs were being supplanted in Italy by the works of Italian potters, beginning to explore local themes and moving towards narrative depiction.

Before proceeding to a description of Italian *istoriato* maiolica, it might be worth clearing up some confusion regarding terminology. Until the mid-16th century 'maiolica' referred exclusively to lustre wares of Spanish and Islamic origin. The word itself may have its roots in the name of the Balearic island of Majorca, which was an important transit point of wares and techniques into Italy. The word might also be a corruption of the Spanish phrase *obra de málequa*

FIGURE **18**
Plaque with scene of the Resurrection. Italy, Urbino, mid-15th century.
Tin-glazed earthenware, ht: 28.2cm (11in.), w: 23 cm (9 in.).
Gift of George and Helen Gardiner
Courtesy of The Gardiner Museum of
Ceramic Art, Toronto

(work from Malaga). By the second half of the 16th century the term was being used in Italy to refer to tin-glazed wares of local manufacture. To confuse the issue further, the word 'majolica' is at times used interchangeably with 'maiolica', especially in the United States. (The term 'Majolica' also happens to be the general appellation of an entire range of decorative non-tin-glazed ceramics produced by the English Minton factories in the 1840s.)

Italian maiolica of the Renaissance was produced from the late 15th to the late 16th centuries, and we will look at these narrative works in depth. By the mid-1500s maiolica was spreading to France and Central Europe, there known as *faïence* or *Fayence*, a derivation of the name of the Italian city of Faenza, one of Italy's prominent centres of tin-glaze manufacture. As maiolica production spread, each part of Europe developed stylistic innovations. Antwerp in Flanders became an important centre, and by the late 1500s tin glaze had taken root in Holland and England from there. The passion for imported Chinese blue-and-white porcelains led to the immensely popular blue-and-white delftware, taking its name from the Dutch city of Delft. Later in 17th-century England, delftware became a general designation for tin-glazed work being produced there. The Chinese blue-and-white influence was also very marked in Portugal at this time, especially in the realm of architectural wall tiles. The Portuguese already had a long-standing affinity with tin glaze through their historical Spanish connections, and vice versa for the Spanish.

Figure 19 is perhaps an interesting example of the kind of cross-fertilisation of style and image types that were prevalent around the Western Mediterranean in the 1700s. This charming tile plaque from Alcora in Spain, north of Valencia, dates from the 18th century. It depicts the classic Hebrew story of Susannah bathing, while secretly being watched by the licentious two elders. The colour palette in predominately manganese and blue tones may well have been influenced by popular Portuguese or Dutch tile imagery. A certain naivety in drawing style might support this premise, and the treatment of plant shapes may even presuppose an Oriental painting influence. At this time a number of French artisans from the Provençal town of Moustiers-Ste-Marie were active in the Alcora region, and they may well have been sufficiently well-travelled to have absorbed and introduced varying stylistic influences into Spain.

By 1800, the traditional *faïence* producers in Europe were largely supplanted by new and more industrialised porcelain factories, such as Meissen in Germany, Sèvres in France and Chelsea in England. The newly discovered porcelain clays in Europe, previously the exclusive domain of China and Japan, were now exploited and moulded using more sophisticated casting techniques. This led to a marked decline in maiolica popularity as fashions, attitudes and tastes changed the face of European ceramics. (Some of these new porcelains and their narrative imagery will be discussed in the next chapter.) In the mid-18th century, notably in southern Europe, traditional tin-glazed wares were still in demand, but at

FIGURE **19**
Decorative plaque with illustration of 'Susannah and the Elders'. Painter: Vicente Pastor, after an engraving from the French Bible by J.B. Santerre.
Spain, Alcora, c.1728–43.
Tin-glazed earthenware, 17.5 x 25cm (6¾ x 10in.).
Courtesy of Museu di Ceràmica, Barcelona

perhaps a slightly lower level in the market. In such towns as Moustiers-Ste-Marie in France, and Gubbio and Deruta in Italy, traditional and contemporary types of maiolica are still being produced, as they have been for centuries.

Italian Renaissance Istoriato Maiolica

Perhaps the best-known tin-glazed ceramics of the Italian Renaissance are the narrative *istoriato* (story) wares, which came into being during the early 1500s. In earlier maiolica wares there had been a union of shape and decoration secondary to the actual function of the piece (serving dishes, jars, ewers, drug pots, and so on). *Istoriato* wares were a departure from this — they were conceived primarily as vehicles for painted stories, and hence shallow and open-surfaced dishes were favoured as shapes to best present narratives.

The brilliant, colourful surfaces associated with *istoriato* wares were the result of a more elaborate glazing and firing process. Bisque wares were covered with a white opacified glaze (*bianco*) of lead and tin oxides and silicate of potash from wine lees mixed with sand. This created an extremely stable ground for the controlled application of colour pigments, which remained sharp and well defined after firing. The skill of maiolica painters becomes apparent when an elaborate *istoriato* painted scene is examined. Very few colours were actually used: cobalt for blue, copper for green, antimony for orange and manganese for purple/black; yet the illusion of a full-coloured scene, with shading, volume, perspective and distance is complete. The precision of fine brushwork was enhanced by the sometime application of a *coperta*, or thin transparent fired glaze over the surface much like a canvas varnish effect, which lent additional brilliance to the colours.

Spanish lustre techniques were also incorporated into the maiolica decorative repertoire, and the mystique and intrinsic worth of gold enhanced the value of these ceramic showpieces. In the various workshops of such towns as Florence, Gubbio, Deruta, Urbino, Casteldurante and Faenza, distinctive works were painted by recognised maiolica artists. As is still usual in Italy, the basic shapes were made by potters and the painting was executed by master painters.

Before discussing the actual iconography of these works, it might be worth briefly looking at the type of thinking that characterised Renaissance attitudes, and made this work so very popular. In the 16th century artists and craftsmen were not perceived as inhabiting different spheres of work. For example, Duke Guidobaldo II of Urbino commissioned the great painter Michelangelo (*c.*1475–1564) to design a silver inkwell for him. He likewise ordered a painted harpsichord cover from Agnolo Bronzino (1503–1572) — in other words, unlike today artists/craftsmen were not only multi-skilled, but very much involved in the process of wealthy patronage.

Whereas during the Middle Ages the emphasis in the creation of works was on the spiritual, the metaphysical and the afterlife, the Renaissance promulgated a very different 'mental climate'. There was a new appreciation of material luxury and consumer goods that allowed objects of gold, silver and ceramic manufacture to be valued for their intrinsic worth and artistry. Wealthy patronage encouraged their production, in both a secular and ecclesiastic context. The eminent humanist Leonardo Bruni (1370–1440) had already spoken out against 'unwarranted frugality' and the saving of riches for an elaborate tomb — it was better to be known for one's virtuous spending in this life.

The actual imagery of the times, particularly that found in *istoriato* maiolica painting, also reflected Renaissance attitudes and new humanistic values. The influence of contemporary fresco and oil painting of the humanist tradition was especially evident in the illusionistic representation of space and perspective, and in a careful depiction of the idealised human figure, recalling ancient Greek values of physical and moral beauty. Such painters as Nicola da Urbino (*c.* 1480–1538) and Francesco Xanto Avelli (*c.* 1486–1544) pioneered this trend in painted *istoriato* wares with the depiction of historical, Classical, mythological and allegorical themes.

An important contributing factor to maiolica imagery of the time was the proliferation of engravings in the mid-15th century. These were widespread, and often served as models for figurative *istoriato* imagery. Scenes from popular prints were adapted freehand to suit the circular ceramic format, or even copied directly, by making prick patterns into the actual prints and then dusting them lightly with charcoal directly against the glaze surface (pouncing). The fine dots would then be joined up to form the prerequisite drawing outline. Examples of pin-pricked engravings have been found, and certainly 'pouncing' was a well-established technique for creating complex repeat border patterns.

Even if not used as actual templates, the engraved works of such artists as Albrecht Dürer, Martin Schongauer and Marcantonio Raimondi were freely used as inspiration for painted maiolica istoriato imagery. We see an example of this in Figure 21 in Francesco Xanto Avelli's magnificent plate of 'The Abduction of Helen' (*c.* 1534). It is an almost literal visual translation of Marcantonio Raimondi's engraving of 'The Abduction of Helen' (*c.*1510–20) after Raphael, as seen in Figure 20. If one examines the two images side-by-side, the central figures on the plate of the Trojans and Helen (with an attendant clutching at her garments) are identical to the figures in the engraving. The only actual differences between the two occur in some of the landscape and background details. All the human figure activity is virtually identical and proportionate in both images.

The story of the abduction of Helen is of course one of the most familiar in Greek mythology, and the catalystic event to the great Trojan war as described by the poet Homer in the *Iliad*. Paris, prince of Troy, is approached by the three goddesses Hera, Athena and Aphrodite, and bidden to choose the most beautiful among them by giving her a golden apple. Hera offers him wealth and kingship, Athena's reward is great wisdom and virtue, and Aphrodite's prize the possession of the world's most beautiful woman. Paris (unwisely perhaps) chooses the latter, and thus ensures the permanent enmity of Hera and Athena against himself and his entire country. The most beautiful (and unavailable) woman happens to be Helen, wife of King Menelaus of Sparta, and her abduction by Paris and the Trojans (with Aphrodite's help) sparks the great ten-year siege and final downfall of Troy.

This epic tale makes wonderful reading and has provoked a great deal of imagery throughout the ages. Personally, I have always wondered what would have happened if Paris had given the apple to some else. I'm afraid I still see a no-win situation — there would still have been two angry and rejected goddesses, but might only Paris have suffered the consequences, and Troy been spared? Would the *Iliad* then never have been written, or would Homer have written another epic entirely? Delicious speculations . . .

OPPOSITE PAGE

FIGURE 20 (above)
Engraving of 'The Abduction
of Helen,' c.1510–20,
by Marcantonio Raimondi
(Italian, c.1480–1534), after
Raphael (Italian, 1483–1520).
26.9 x 42.4cm (11⅝ x 16¾ in.).
Courtesy of Graphische Sammlung Albertina,
Vienna

FIGURE 21 (below)
Plate with image of 'The
Abduction of Helen',
Francesco Xanto Avelli
(c.1486–1544). Italy,
Urbino, 1534.
Tin-glazed earthenware,
ht: 6.3cm (2½ in.),
dia: 46.1cm (18⅛in.).
Courtesy of The J. Paul Getty Museum,
Los Angeles
Photograph: Jack Ross

THIS PAGE

FIGURE 22
Detail of dish with image of
'The Rape of Europa', Italy,
Faenza, 1537.
Tin-glazed earthenware,
dia: 47cm (18½in.).
Gift of George and Helen Gardiner
Courtesy of The Gardiner Museum of
Ceramic Art, Toronto

The popularity of thematic imagery borrowed from Classical Greek mythology at this time is again evident in Figure 22, in this detail of a dish from Faenza, dated 1537, depicting the 'Rape of Europa'. It shows a progressive narrative by the simultaneous depiction of several chronological scenes of the abduction of Europa by Zeus, taken from Ovid's *Metamorphoses*.

The philandering god-father Zeus appears to Europa, daughter of the king of Tyre, in the form of a gentle white bull in a meadow. Seduced by the animal's apparent docility, Europa climbs onto his back, and he forthwith plunges into the sea with her. He carefully takes her to the shores of Crete, where he assumes mortal form and does indeed seduce her. The unhappy girl is abandoned by the fickle god, but Aphrodite, goddess of love, appears to her, explains the seduction and that (small reward) the continent that now harbours her will henceforth be called Europa.

Certainly the *istoriato* maiolica wares of the Italian Renaissance must be acclaimed as one of the truly great ceramic narrative traditions of all time. They are perhaps rivalled only by the great Attic vase paintings of ancient Greece. The narratives of both traditions seem to have had a lasting impact on all Western culture, and some of these potent narrative themes will crop up again in my examination of 18th- and 19th-century porcelains, and much later on 20th- and 21st-century ceramic narrative works.

Italian Maiolica: The della Robbias

A separate category of tin-glazed narrative work, and one unique for its time, was the use of clay and glaze for the creation of monumental ecclesiastic sculpture by the della Robbia family in the 1400s. The transition from marble to tin-glazed clay with a minimal colour palette and exquisite modelling was an entirely new invention which captured the public imagination.

Luca della Robbia (*c.* 1399–1482) born in Florence, was well-known for his sculptures in marble and bronze. It is a testimony to a strong and serene character that in his long life he managed to stay out of the notorious back-biting milieu of Florence's internal politics and devote himself solely to his work. He was highly esteemed by such contemporaries as Leon Battista Alberti, who in his *De pictura* praises Luca alongside the artists Donatello, Brunelleschi, Masacchio and Ghiberti.

Luca's nephew Andrea della Robbia (born *c.*1435) continued his uncle's ceramic workshop tradition, and was also known for his prolific production and his mastery of this new medium. The image I have chosen here in Figure 23, called the *Alessandri Crucifixion*, was realised in 1480–81, alongside a cycle of similar works for the Chapel of the Stigmata, at La Verna near Arezzo. This work represents a new typology unprecedented even in paintings of the time, in that it is a unitary altarpiece consisting of a single scene. The work takes up the entire rear wall of the chapel and was a replacement for existing previous frescoes. The sacred representation of the Crucifixion is enclosed by a double frieze with winged heads of cherubim and a symmetrical arrangement of fruit and leaves. To illustrate the dramatic event, Andrea makes use of all the iconographic elements associated with it: the pelican feeding its young with blood from its own breast (seen over the head of Christ); the skull of Adam (below); and the grieving sun and moon above the cross. The golden rays of the sun recall the symbol of St. Bernardine, but also draw on Classical mythology in evoking the snake-like curls of Medusa's head.

I have mentioned earlier in the Introduction that narratives change with each retelling, and that imagery can be seen to adapt to a particular time, place and narrator. As a point of interest, one might briefly compare the *Alessandri Crucifixion* to the Crucifixion scene slip-carved on a later Venetian plate (see Figure 1, facing the Introduction on page 7). The story of course is unchangeable, but those aspects of the story that each artist chooses to depict are entirely distinct and personal in each work.

As a birthday present while in Italy, I was taken to visit the Chapel of the Stigmata at La Verna. Most of the church was decorated with ceramic narrative Bible scenes by Andrea della Robbia, and the experience was a very moving one. The six major works of the chapel must surely be considered remarkable among all ecclesiastic church sculpture. Later works by Francesco and Giovanni della Robbia, although continuing the tradition of sublime craftsmanship, tend to be more ornate and far more colourful, and to my own eye, do not have the same profound and contemplative impact of the works of their predecessors.

OPPOSITE PAGE

FIGURE **23**
Wall relief *Alessandri Crucifixion* by Andrea della Robbia (1435–1525).
Italy, Arezzo, La Verna, Chapel of the Stigmata, c.1480–81.
Tin-glazed earthenware, 600 x 420cm (236¼ x 165⅓in.).
Courtesy of Scala, Art Resource, New York

Dutch Delftware

The tin glaze tradition entered the Netherlands from Antwerp in Flanders in the mid-1500s. Initial ceramic models in Dutch factories were based more on polychrome Italianate styles, but by the 17th century the blue-and-white colour scheme had come to predominate. The city of Delft, with its many ceramic factories, became the leading proponent of this type of work, especially after the importation of blue-and-white *kraak-porselein* (a Dutch term for late Ming blue-and-white porcelains shipped to Europe in a merchant vessel called a carrack). These were introduced by the Dutch East India Company in 1602, and became immediately sought after. Following a decline in Far Eastern imports due to internal domestic troubles in China at the time, the Dutch potteries were stimulated to produce similar imitative wares at lower temperatures. This they did with great success, using a light clay body with cobalt-blue surface painting under a transparent glaze. By the 1630s a richer tin glaze was in use with cobalt in-glaze painting and a light *kwaart* (*coperta*) transparent glaze coating, which closely imitated the much desired Chinese blue-and-white Ming porcelain surfaces.

Chinese-inspired motifs and painting styles remained prevalent up to the mid-18th century, alongside Italianate compositions taken mostly from engravings of landscapes and hunting scenes. Truly 'Dutch' imagery began to emerge in the form of landscape and seascape imagery that probably drew inspiration from the strong painting and etching works of such local artists as Rembrandt van Rijn and Jacob van Ruisdael. The city of Delft remained one of Holland's premier tin glaze production centres, perhaps because it was a well-established centre for painters and engravers, and skilled labour and imagery were close at hand.

By the late 1600s, Chinese *famille verte* ('green family' porcelain, usually characterised by a brilliant green enamel), and Japanese Kakiemon and Imari enamelled imports were inspiring more and more factories to produce colourful polychrome ceramics. Plaques with Chinese-type figurative decoration, serving dishes, garniture jar sets and pictorial plates embellished with land- and sea-scapes and religious illustrations — these were the popular order of the day. Elaborate flower holders and *tulipières* in complex stacked shapes were very much in demand by 1700, and by this time the Dutch tile industry was also in full swing. Tiles were being produced in vast quantities for interiors, not only at Delft but also at Makkum in Friesland, and in Rotterdam and Amsterdam. These highly-specialised tile factories produced decorative tiles for domestic interiors as wall and stove coverings. The strong blue-and-white tradition maintained its prevalence alongside polychrome imagery, and a simple style of manganese-purple imagery on a white ground was also popular.

Narrative Dutch delftware is to my mind best illustrated by some of the more devotional religious imagery that was often to be found on tiles, particularly in the 18th century. Figure 24 shows a tin-glazed tile, *c.*1750, from Amsterdam. It was

FIGURE **24**
Dutch delftware tile with image of the Resurrection
Amsterdam, *c.*1750.
Tin glaze with cobalt painting
13 x 13cm (5⅛ x 5⅛in.).
Author's collection
Photograph: Jan Thijs

probably part of a wall covering, one tile among many, as can be assumed by the four corner ox-head motifs, which serve as connecting patterns to adjoining tiles. They can also be seen in the earlier English delftware tile panel of the 'Popish Plot' in Figure 25 on page 75, and obviously were a standard pattern convention.

The scene on the Amsterdam tile depicts Mary Magdalene and Joseph of Arimethea by Christ's empty tomb, after His Resurrection. The angel is informing them of this momentous event, and the stance and serious facial expressions of the two figures on the left (Mary and Joseph) reflect the solemnity of the occasion. The fresh and simple repetitive brushwork leads us to imagine that such a tile was painted with great speed and verve, and yet the careful placement of the figures and their immobility might remind us that this is indeed a devotional image. Every onlooker would know this story from the Bible and be moved to contemplation by its profound content. For interest's sake, at this time another version of this same Bible story can be seen in the earlier maiolica tile plaque in Figure 18 at the beginning of this chapter. Here the Resurrection (or Entombment?) is dealt with in more 'iconic' terms, with Christ rising from His tomb. He is shown displaying stigmata on his hands and chest, wearing a crown

OPPOSITE PAGE

FIGURE 25
Nine-tile panel depicting
'Popish Plot,' attributed to
Jan Ariens van Hamme.
England, London, Vauxhall,
c.1679–80.
Tin glaze with cobalt painting
Each tile approx. 12 x 12cm
(4¾ x 4¾in.).
*Courtesy of V&A Images, Victoria and Albert
Museum, London*

of thorns and surrounded by the symbols of the Crucifixion: nails, hammer, ladder, sponge of vinegar, and the crowing cockerel.

Beyond images of religious content, narrative representations in Dutch delftware seem to be relatively limited. In general after 1750, Dutch delftware declined, not so much in productivity, but in the originality of its images. Itself a copy of Chinese porcelains, it had been copied by others such as Japanese and European porcelain manufactories. By the end of the 18th century Delft potteries had been superseded in the European marketplace by porcelain factories across the Continent and by new popular English whiteware producers.

Early English Delftware

English delftware had its origins in the Flemish/Dutch tin glaze tradition, and can most likely be traced back to around 1567, to master potters Jasper Andries and Jacob Jansen, both from Antwerp, who had settled near London. The earliest English tin-glazed works closely followed those Italianate and Orientally-inspired models popular in the Netherlands. In fact initially, early English delftwares were indistinguishable from contemporary Dutch and Flemish prototypes. They were in time characterised by a recognisable verve and even eccentricity of style quite unlike the more 'refined', or elegant continental wares. This naivety of style may have been due to several factors. English tin-glazed wares neither benefited from an exalted patronage nor from the established technical finesse of Dutch and French manufacturers. Potteries tended to be more lowly and less lucrative in the absence of a strongly-developed export market or a local moneyed clientele. It seems that English tin glaze potters were of a humbler caste, and the buyers of their products less wealthy than their Continental compatriots.

The use of brightly-coloured enamels, and of the brilliance-enhancing *kwaart* or *coperta* was also absent in the early English delftwares. Colours were more subdued and less brilliant, but nonetheless suitable for the wide range of domestic objects being produced. Mugs, dishes, ewers, posset-pots and a variety of bowls were standard items. London potteries, such as those at Southwark and Lambeth, were the initiators of English tin-glaze production, but by the mid-1600s were followed by Brislington near Bristol, and Liverpool. The latter became pre-eminent over the next century, and was considered to be the most technically advanced of English tin-glaze manufactories.

A more English iconography became visible in time, perhaps based on Elizabethan embroidery patterns and decorative wall paintings. These new images, mostly on large plates, were in the form of vigorously executed floral and fruit patterns (such as tulips and pomegranates) which were bold and naive in style, and certainly unlike the previously-known precise and more refined

The Plot first hatcht at Rome by the Pope and Cardinalls &c

The Conspirators Signeing y Resolve for killing the King.

Father Connyers Preaching against y Oathes of Alejance & Supremacy.

D Oates discouereth y Plot to y King and Councell.

C Bedloes discoverer of the plott.

Cap Bedlow examind by y Secret Comitee of the house of Commons.

Pickerin attempts to kill y K. in S Iames Park.

Pickerin Executed.

S William Waller burning Popish books Images and Relitues.

Italianate and Oriental motifs. After the mid-1600s a new type of figurative plate decoration came into being outside of the functional repertoire. Two popular types of imagery were portraits of reigning rulers and their consorts, and 'Adam and Eve' images.

Figure 25 exemplifies the rather narrow range of narrative iconography associated with early English delftware. This is a nine-tile panel, very much in the Dutch blue-and-white tradition depicting the 'Popish Plot', a fictitious Catholic conspiracy to kill Charles II, which the Reverend Titus Oates claimed to have uncovered in 1678. (It should be remembered that at this time there was much dissension among rival Catholic and Protestant religions.) The nine tiles in chronological order, with detailed written captions, unravel the entire story from beginning to end. (They should be read from left to right, and from top to bottom.)

The tiles were made in London around 1679–80, and are attributed to Jan Ariens van Hamme, who arrived from Delft in 1676 and established a pottery at Vauxhall in London. An English ban on Dutch tile imports had spurred on local tile production, and by the early 1700s English tile manufacture was widespread, mostly for use on fireplace surrounds. The use of tiles for entire wall coverings was not as popular in England at this time as it was in Holland and in Portugal.

The second image that to me is typically narrative is seen in Figure 26. This is a tin-glazed shallow bowl from Brislington, *c.*1680 (artist unknown) which rather typifies the naive and eccentric English style I mentioned earlier. The image is the popular one of the period, of Adam and Eve before their expulsion

FIGURE 26
Dish depicting 'Adam and Eve'. England, Brislington, *c.*1680.
Tin-glazed earthenware, ht: 6.3cm (2½in.), dia: 33.5cm (13¼in.).
Gift of George and Helen Gardiner
Courtesy of The Gardiner Museum of
Ceramic Art, Toronto

from the Garden of Eden. The story of man's fall from grace would of course have been familiar to everyone in the Christian world at that time.

The figures themselves, although extremely badly drawn (certainly by Italian *istoriato* standards), nonetheless exhibit the kind of innocence and gusto of interpretation that characterises most early English delftware and makes it so endearing. Adam on the left is modestly covered by a seemingly accidental and self-adhesive leaf (a popular convention in painting, often seen in the works of Abrecht Dürer and Lucas Cranach). Eve likewise is modestly wrapped in a convenient swirling swath of her own hair, while nonchalantly accepting an apple from the serpent. Adam is eager to receive the apple with one hand, while the other hand seems to be about to drop his leaf . . . A careful effort (unsuccessful) has been made to deal with Adam's foreshortened leg, and over-heavy shading on both figures demonstrates our painter's keen desire to show off his grasp of volume, light and shadow.

Nevertheless, despite its many artistic shortcomings, the image is lively, and to my eye exhibits all the charm of a child's drawing. Compared to the more sophisticated tile panel of the 'Popish Plot' conceived at the same time, I would have to conclude that the 'Adam and Eve' painter was local, and lacking the professionalism of his Dutch *confrère* van Hamme. The latter's Delft background likely encompassed more rigorous drawing and painting skills, yet to me both works exemplify the narrative imagery of early English delftware.

Portuguese Tiles

In the early 16th century the Italian maiolica *istoriato* style of painting was introduced into Triana, Seville, in Spain. The Islamic practice of tile facings in an architectural context was already well established there, and the *istoriato* style permitted the decoration of altar frontals, tomb walls and interior church wall panels. By the 1570s, craftsmen from Antwerp had settled near Seville and were working in the Italo-Flemish tradition. Tiles from Valencia and Seville were imported into Portugal for facings on such prestigious buildings as the Old Cathedral at Coimbra and the Royal Palace at Sintra. The taste for elaborately painted pictorial tile panels began to grow in Portugal from the mid-17th century onwards following the War of Restoration, in which independence from Spain was reasserted.

The use of decorative tile facings for interiors and exteriors became more widespread in Portugal than in any other country at that time. Lisbon, Oporto and Coimbra became the leading centres of tile manufacture, and by the early 18th century, tiles were adorning most major public buildings, churches, schools, monasteries, palaces and residences of the wealthy. They were an important integral feature of all architecture, and were being widely exported to all other areas

of Portuguese influence, such as the Azores, Madeira and Brazil. In the mid-1600s, threatened by the influx of imported tiles from the Netherlands, a ban was declared on such imports, which allowed local manufactories to expand and develop. The popularity of blue-and-white over polychrome imagery remained prevalent, and by the early 1700s a variety of imagery was being exploited by such artists as António Pereira, Manuel dos Santos and António de Oliveira Bernardes.

As in Spain, religious subjects for altars and church walls were still popular, but by 1750 more secular imagery came into use, illustrating courtly vignettes, hunting scenes and landscapes (often copied from engravings), as well as allegorical and mythological images. Theatrical figurative scenes were set within frameworks of *trompe l'oeil* pilasters, caryatids and other architectural ornaments. Rich borders of foliate rococo motifs in purple, yellow and green created frames for the ubiquitous blue-and-white central figurative panels. All this tilework was unprecedented in terms of scale and lavishness on both interiors and exteriors of most buildings, and reflected the taste and wealth of the merchant and professional classes.

After the Lisbon earthquake of 1755, tile decoration became more restrained and small-scale, in keeping with the more sober style of reconstructed buildings. By the early 19th century Portuguese tile manufacture had radically declined, yet in Brazil it had been maintained with great vigour. In the late 1800s an influx of Brazilian immigrants revived the Portuguese tile industry and the manufacture of industrially-produced tiles for architectural embellishment came into being again.

Figure 27 shows a large tile panel from the gardens of the Quinta dos Azulejos in Lisbon, *c.*1740, depicting the story of 'Apollo and Marsyas'. The scene derives from an etching by Michel Dorigney, after works by Simon Voulet for the Hôtel Séguier. The retelling of Greek myths was very popular in narrative scenes of this type; Thomas Bulfinch's *Mythology* gives us the following version: the goddess Athena, having invented the flute, played upon it to entertain the gods. The mischievous urchin Eros laughed at the queer faces made by the goddess while playing, and in a pique she flung the instrument to earth. It landed at the feet of the satyr Marsyas, who was so enraptured by the sounds he drew from it, that he unwisely challenged the god Apollo to a musical contest. The god of course triumphed, and Marsyas was punished for his presumptuous challenge by being flayed alive.

Fortunately, the most gruesome aspects of this story are left to the imagination, and the panel focuses more on the scene of Marsyas' dejection, with the broken flute before him, and a triumphant Apollo on the left. The narrative was of course meant to be enjoyed in a garden setting, reinforced by the pleasant sound of running water, and framed by an elaborate rococo colourful frieze. The panel typifies both the lavishness of mid-18th-century Portuguese tile painting in its heyday, and an exuberance of style and execution on a scale seldom surpassed in the art of tile painting anywhere else.

OPPOSITE PAGE

FIGURE 27
Tile panel with illustration of 'Apollo and Marsyas', from an etching by Michel Dorigny after works by Simon Vouet for the Hôtel Séguier. Portugal, Lisbon, Gardens of the Quinta dos Azulejos, c.1740.
Tin glaze with cobalt, manganese, ochre and chrome pigments, ht: 272cm (108in.).
Courtesy of V&A Images, Victoria and Albert Museum, London

5

European Porcelains

Background, History and Manufacture

It was possibly Marco Polo who first coined the phrase 'porcellana' (or porcelain). The great merchant traveller had returned to Italy in 1296 after a long sojourn in China and was in fact describing that country's high-fired whitewares similar in surface to the white *porcellana* cowrie shells being used there as ornaments and currency of exchange. Porcelain has since become a broad term describing Chinese, Korean, Annamese (North Vietnamese), and Japanese high-fired whitewares, as well as the later products of such European manufactories as Meissen, Sèvres, Du Paquier, Chelsea, and so on.

True porcelain (or 'hard paste') as first developed by the Chinese was basically a mixture of white kaolinitic clay and *petuntse* (a type of feldspar), that when fired to above stoneware temperatures (1400°C or 2552°F) became highly vitrified to the point of translucency. Porcelain clay allows for a full range of modelling and casting techniques, and this versatility of process combined with its fired density and whiteness, has ensured its popularity. It has always been considered the most 'noble' of ceramic materials, as well as being the most imitated, the most collected and the most documented.

As mentioned in Chapter Three, the initial development of porcelain can be traced back to Tang dynasty China (AD 618–907), based on high-firing techniques dating back even further to the 3rd century AD. Porcelain technology was transmitted to other parts of Asia, and we have seen in preceding chapters how influential and far-reaching Oriental porcelains were in affecting Middle-Eastern and European tin-glaze traditions.

The inspirational and aesthetic development of European porcelains is directly linked to European and Far-Eastern trade history. As early as the mid-1500s, the Portuguese had been importing the blue-and-white Chinese porcelains

FIGURE 28
Detail of *The Canada Bowl*, painting attributed to Johann Gregor Höroldt (1696–1775). Germany, Meissen, c.1725. Hard-paste porcelain with overglaze and lustre, dia: 15.5cm (6⅛ in.).
Gift of George and Helen Gardiner
Courtesy of The Gardiner Museum of
Ceramic Art, Toronto

81

from the East, and by the early 1600s other concerns such as the Dutch East India Company were also actively trading with China. By the mid-17th century Oriental porcelains had achieved a high visibility and popularity in the European marketplace, and blue-and-white porcelains, as well as colourful enamelled wares, were highly prized.

I should mention at this point that the European porcelains under discussion in this chapter differ in techniques of manufacture from previously discussed work. Most of the *istoriato* earthenwares, as well as Dutch and English delftwares, were thrown on the wheel and/or combined with occasional pressmoulded components for added details. Glazing and painting were of course done by hand, and all production took place in workshops, as had been the case for centuries.

The later, more mechanised 18th- and 19th-century European porcelain manufactories worked on a much larger scale, and with an emphasis on mould-making and casting techniques to facilitate increased production. The individual artistry of the mouldmaker and modeller was really most apparent in the creation of the initial prototypes. Great expertise went into the modelling of these, and there was extensive and precise labour in the dissecting of the moulded objects, the joinery, the addition of details, and in the glazing and final hand painting. Since most porcelain bodies were white in colour, they tended to be covered with a transparent glaze, sometimes over underglaze patterns, and often with the addition of third-firing enamels and/or gilding.

Before the advent of true hard-paste porcelains (high-fired and closer in composition to Far-Eastern types), there were some brief attempts in Europe to create 'soft-paste' porcelain, made from white clay and frit, and lacking the all-important ingredient of kaolin. Soft pastes were fired to a much lower temperature of about 1100°C (2012°F). In the late 1500s Francesco de' Medici, Grand Duke of the Florentine Republic in Italy, encouraged the development of porcelain, and the first European soft pastes were produced. Although some translucency was achieved, the hard body characteristic of true Chinese porcelain was lacking. Medici porcelain output was extremely limited, and ended with the death of the Grand Duke in 1587.

The next venture into soft-paste porcelains occurred almost a century later at Rouen in France, under the patronage of Louis IV. The Poterat brothers, Louis and Michel, developed a type of soft paste, but again production was limited, and the secrets of manufacture were lost with the death of Louis Poterat in 1696. Both the Italian and French early soft pastes, although virtuosic technical achievements for their time, did not achieve the brilliance of colour and surface, nor the hardness and delicacy of the true Oriental hard pastes, or of the later high-fired Meissen porcelains.

The study of the history of European porcelain is an all-encompassing one and has been explored by many experts in the field. The scope of possible study material is enormous. For example, by the late 1700s there were literally dozens of porcelain manufactories throughout most of Europe. To name just a few of the better-known ones; in Germany: Meissen, Berlin, Nymphenburg, Frankenthal, Fürstenberg and Höchst; in France: St. Cloud, Chantilly, Vincennes and Sèvres; in Italy: Venice, Capo di Monte and Doccia; in England: Chelsea, Bow, Derby and Worcester; and in Russia, Scandinavia and America, many others too numerous to mention, let alone to examine in detail. Most of the above factories employed varying techniques of decoration and were known for creating speciality wares, and of course many of them created works that embraced narrative imagery.

To that end I would like to concentrate on just four European porcelain manufactories with relevant examples of narrative works that I find particularly engaging: namely Meissen, Du Paquier, Chelsea and Sèvres.

Meissen and The Canada Bowl

The first true hard-paste porcelains came into being at Meissen near Dresden in Germany in the early 1700s. Three people in particular were directly responsible for this development: Augustus II (The Strong), Elector of Saxony and King of Poland (1670–1773), a powerful prince and ambitious collector and patron; Count Ehrenfried Walther von Tschirnhaus (1651–1708), a nobleman-scientist; and Johann Friedrich Böttger (1682–1719), a young alchemist.

Von Tschirnhaus, having examined and found negligible the French St. Cloud soft-paste porcelains that claimed to vie in quality with the high-fired Oriental models, was consequently determined to create hard-paste porcelain in Saxony. In collaboration with Böttger under the Elector's patronage, a hard red stoneware was first produced that somewhat emulated the qualities of porcelain. After von Tschirnhaus' death in 1706, Böttger continued his researches and in a report to the king dated March 28, 1709, he claimed that he could make 'good, white porcelain with finest glazing and painting in such perfection as to at least equal if not surpass the Eastern production'.

His discovery led to the establishment of the Meissen factory in 1710 and the first production of true hard-paste porcelains in Europe. Both stoneware and porcelain manufacture progressed at Meissen, and Chinese-inspired shape models and motifs were gradually replaced with a more indigenous German style. Baroque vases, richly modelled teapots and dinner wares were embellished with foliate patterns in enamels and lustres. These became the order of the day, along with the gradual inclusion of figure production somewhat later.

Böttger died at the early age of 37, but fortunately the talented painter Johann Gregor Höroldt (1696–1775) was introduced from the Du Paquier factory in Vienna in 1720. Höroldt developed an enriched colour palette at the Meissen factory and popularised the painting of *chinoiserie* and narrative themes.

FIGURE 29
The Canada Bowl, painting
attributed to Johann Gregor
Höroldt (1696–1775).
Germany, Meissen, c.1725.
Hard-paste porcelain with
overglaze and lustre,
dia: 15.5cm (6⅛in.).
Gift of George and Helen Gardiner
Courtesy of The Gardiner Museum of
Ceramic Art, Toronto

With its expanded colour and image repertoire under Höroldt's energetic direction, Meissen became Germany's premier porcelain manufactory and its products became the inspiration for many subsequent porcelain producers.

The first Meissen piece I would like to discuss as an example of porcelain narrative is a charming bowl especially close to my own heart in the collection of the Gardiner Museum of Ceramic Art in Toronto. It tickles both my German and Canadian roots. Figures 28 and 29 show *The Canada Bowl*, *c.*1725, with painting attributed to Johann Gregor Höroldt. He was the first painter at Meissen to look to engravings for inspiration. This particular piece, as the earliest known depiction of Canada on porcelain, shows a scene of Hudson's Bay traders. The imagery on the bowl was based on an engraving in Carel Allard's *Orbis Habitabilis Oppida et Vestitus* (Cities and Costumes of the Inhabited World, Amsterdam, *c.*1695). Sketches for the two Canadian scenes on this bowl survive in the *Schulz Codex*, a collection of drawings made by Höroldt and other artists between 1720 and 1730. In describing the depicted figures on *The Canada Bowl*, ceramic historian and curator Meredith Chilton provides us with some insights into the 'artistic licence' employed by the bowl's painter:

> [...] the costumes drawn on the prints and on the bowl are most likely the products of lively imaginations combined with some accurate details about furs worn by Aboriginal peoples in the Arctic.
>
> Obviously puzzled by the appearance of the beaver and the arctic fox that appear in the engravings, the artist at Meissen decided to transform them both

into red-coated foxes when he painted the bowl [see Figure 29]. [...] the identity of the animal with the long, straight horns remains a mystery.

The figures that appear in the 'Canada' scene may be allegorical. Laden with her basket of fruit and surrounded by the abundance of the New World, the female could be interpreted as an image of plenty, more typically shown at this time as the goddess Flora or as the personification of spring. As such she would have symbolised the bountiful resources of the New World. What is certain is that the Meissen artists had no concern about the geographic harmony of their images. Imagery of China and Canada are freely mixed, because both places represented wonder, mystery and curiosity.

Meissen and the Commedia dell'Arte

Meissen was as famous for its individual figure and group figure production as it was for its dinner services, breakfast sets and ornamental tureens. The most famous of all figure modellers at Meissen was a young sculptor, Johann Joachim Kändler (1706–1775), who was employed by the factory in 1731 to collaborate with modeller Johann Gottlob Kirchner in the production of ambitious large-scale porcelain sculpture for Augustus II's Japanese palace. Most of these were life-sized figures of animals and birds, which were technically more difficult to execute.

The early small-scale figures at Meissen were made in red stoneware and copied *blanc de chine* models or European baroque sculpture. Kändler's particular *forté* was the delicate modelling of such figures as dwarves and artisans, and most notably his extraordinary recreation in porcelain of the stage characters of the Italian *commedia dell'arte*. Kändler very likely had noted and copied costumes from performances seen at the court at Dresden.

In the introduction to her book *Harlequin Unmasked; The Commedia dell'Arte and Porcelain Sculpture*, Meredith Chilton 'sets the stage' immediately by stating the following:

> Wily and agile Harlequin, pensive Pierrot and flirtatious Columbine are vibrant theatrical characters familiar to us all today. These characters were part of the *commedia dell'arte*, a form of improvised theatre that developed in Italy by the mid-16th century. The *commedia dell'arte* was performed by companies of itinerant players who acted in different locations all over Europe, from town squares during markets and festivals, to palaces and gardens of the nobility. Spontaneous and independent, the *commedia dell'arte* could include biting political satire, gross physical buffoonery, slapstick humour and sexual innuendo. It was a comedy of opposites and the unexpected, erudite yet irreverent, full of clever repartee, yet blatant. Each actor in the company took on the role

of a special character, who quickly became identified by accent, individual costume, mask and accessories. Although major characters and their costumes became standardised, their roles and parts constantly changed. Their dramatic action might be clearly defined, but they had a wide range of interpretative possibilities. This adaptable, unpredictable form of theatre gripped the public imagination and retained its popularity for well over two hundred years, until it declined and died in the early 19th century.

The figure grouping *Mockery of Age* (Figure 30), also in the Gardiner Museum's collection, is one of Kändler's best-known models. It typifies the symbolism that would have been known to viewers at the time, in this case playing with the theme of cuckoldry. We see an elderly man relaxing at home with his young wife.

FIGURE 30
Sculpture from the *Commedia dell'Arte, Mockery of Age*, modeller: Johann Joachim Kändler (1706–75). Germany, Meissen, c.1740–41. Hard-paste porcelain with overglaze enamels and gilding, ht: 19.1cm (7½in.).
Gift of George and Helen Gardiner
Courtesy of The Gardiner Museum of Ceramic Art, Toronto

One servant (dressed as Harlequin) offers him a dish of celery, which was considered an aphrodisiac. Behind him another servant holds up cocks' feathers (symbols of cuckoldry) behind his unsuspecting master's head, while the young wife embraces her husband, with her attention over his shoulder.

The very best of Kändler's Harlequin figures and groups were created between 1736 and 1744. Certainly his impact on Meissen output was second to none, and helped to make it Europe's premier porcelain manufactory. The decline of Meissen's fortunes occurred during the Seven Years War of 1756 to 1763. However, Meissen did survive to flourish again in the 19th and early 20th centuries and remains in operation to the present day.

Du Paquier: The Romance of the Western Chamber Retold

The Vienna factory was founded by Claudius Innocentius Du Paquier (d. 1751), an Austrian court official. In 1719 Samuel Stölzel, who was Böttger's kiln master at Meissen, came to Vienna and initiated the active production of porcelains there. Unfortunately his stay was short-lived, and dissatisfaction with working conditions prompted Stölzel's defection back to Meissen in 1720, along with the painter Höroldt. As we have just seen, the latter's introduction to Meissen brought tremendous innovation and vigour to the German factory.

The Vienna concern was made an official state factory by the Empress Maria Theresa after the expiration of its imperial patent in 1774. Some of the Du Paquier porcelains resemble the early Meissen Böttger works, but are often slightly bluer and smokier in colour. They also tend to be somewhat more imaginative and unusual in shape from standard Meissen wares, being more baroque and using more black and gold lustre colour schemes. Around 1730, even before Meissen, European flower themes were popularised at Du Paquier alongside standard *chinoiserie* imagery and landscape paintings inspired largely by Japanese Imari wares. Some of the better-known painters included Anton Schulz and later C.D. Busch and J.G. Klinger from Meissen. Figure modelling was also perfected at the Vienna factory with J.J. Niedermayer and Anton Grassi in particular being pre-eminent modellers.

Maria Theresa died in 1780 and was succeeded by her son Joseph II. With little interest in the arts, he attempted unsuccessfully to sell off the factory. Finally, Konrad von Sorgenthal was appointed manager, and the introduction of popular neo-classical imagery by Grassi brought the Du Paquier factory considerable international repute. Unlike many others, the Vienna factory survived the Napoleonic wars, but after the deaths of von Sorgenthal and Grassi in 1805 and 1807 respectively, the factory's best and most innovative period production was over, and it finally closed in 1864.

A particularly fine example of *chinoiserie* and Chinese-inspired narrative porcelain can be seen in Figure 31 in a Du Paquier hard-paste tureen, with underglaze blue, overglaze enamels and gilding. The piece dates from *c.*1725, and is typical of the eclecticism of Du Paquier's designs. The shape is based on Chinese porcelain, the handles are derived from European silver and the enamel-painted motifs are copied from designs from lacquer. The blue-and-white narrative scene is from the Chinese play the *Romance of the Western Chamber* (frequently depicted on 17th-century Chinese porcelains, see Figures 11 and 12 in Chapter Three).

In an article published privately in 1999 (from *Mélanges en souvenir d'Elisalex d'Albis 1939–1998*, Paris), Meredith Chilton describes the scene here entitled 'Beauty's Enchantment', Part I, Act I, of the play:

> [The scholar] Zhang Sheng is being guided around the monastery by the monk Fa Ts'ung, but he is completely distracted by his first unexpected glimpse of the lovely Cui Yingying who is accompanied by her maid. Enchanted, Zhang Sheng sings:

> 'My eyes are bedazzled, and speech fails me, my soul has soared to mid-heaven …'

FIGURE 31
Covered tureen with illustration from the Chinese *Romance of the Western Chamber* story. Austria, Vienna, Du Paquier Factory (1718–1864), *c.*1725. Hard-paste porcelain with underglaze blue, overglaze enamels and gilding, ht: 22.5cm (8⅞in.).

Gift of George and Helen Gardiner
Courtesy of The Gardiner Museum of
Ceramic Art, Toronto

'Slowly advancing, she arrives at her threshold,and at that short distance, she purposely turns round to look ...'

'Leaving behind her only the willows wrapped in mist and the chirping of the birds.'

This poignant moment in the drama has thus been captured and retold, in this case for the fascination and pleasure of European viewers, ready to embrace the exoticism of the Orient.

English Porcelain: A Chelsea Teapot

Whereas German and French porcelain manufacture had already been well established in the early 1700s, it was not until the 1740s that such English factories as Chelsea, Bow, Limehouse and Vauxhall in London, really came into their own. The popularity of tea drinking in England had encouraged the importation of Oriental porcelains by the East India Company and the first imitators of such porcelains (at Bow in particular) tended to copy the popular blue-and-white Oriental wares, and eventually supplanted the less refined and less durable English delftwares.

Unlike their continental counterparts, before 1790 the English porcelain manufactories tended to specialise more in soft-paste (lower-fired) porcelains. Some innovations were made to the existing soft-paste bodies, which included the addition of bone ash to the clay body. The new body was stronger and more heat-resistant and less likely to collapse during firing, a recurring hazard in the manufacture of soft-paste porcelain.

Another important technical development occurred at Bristol and at Worcester some ten years later around 1750, namely the addition of soapstone (steatite) to the clay body, which made it impervious to sudden changes in temperature. This was of course crucial in the manufacture of heat-resistant tea wares. 'True' hard-paste porcelains had been developed successfully at Plymouth by 1768 after extensive research, but finally it was 'bone china' (a hybrid modified porcelain with the addition of calcined bone, acting as a flux) that was to be the more standard and commercially viable type of tableware in England, even to the present day.

The Chelsea factory holds a unique place in the history of 18th-century English porcelain by being the only one to cater primarily to a high-end, luxury market. A Huguenot silversmith from Liège, Nicolas Sprimont, was the initial proprietor and also its guiding spirit. He maintained the high profile of the factory's production output by means of his influential contacts and by encouraging the development of a wide variety of glazes, shapes and pattern types.

During its peak production period, from about 1745 to 1769 when it was finally closed down, Chelsea's production can be divided into four major periods, each of them being identified by a different mark. The Incised Triangle Period porcelains are most noted for restraint of colour, moulded plant decorations and a predominance of 'all-white' wares that reflected in line and shape Sprimont's earliest creations in silver. The Raised Anchor Period is considered by some to be Chelsea's most successful period in artistic and commercial terms, especially between the years 1750 and 1756. It is best known for its more colourful wares inspired by Japanese Kakiemon motifs of floral designs, figure and landscape scenes, Oriental birds, and so on. Some of these tended to emulate Meissen's tastes, or were reminiscent of the brilliant palette and almost botanical detail of French Vincennes porcelains.

A particular Chelsea speciality at this time was the depiction of fable narrative subjects, principally drawn from engraved illustrations by Francis Barlow (1612–1704) of *Aesop's Fables*, published in London in 1666. My example of Chelsea narrative porcelain is a delightful teapot with painting attributed to Jefferyes Hammett O'Neale (1734–1801), an accomplished miniature painter who endowed his fable creatures with a particularly whimsical humour. Figure 32 shows a Chelsea teapot (*c*.1752–55) with Aesop's *Fable of the Horse and Ass*. The fable goes as follows:

> A Horse, proud of his fine harness met an Ass on the high-road. As the Ass with his heavy burden moved slowly out of the way to let him pass, the Horse cried out impatiently that he could hardly resist kicking him to make him move faster. The Ass held his peace, but did not forget the other's insolence. Not long afterwards the Horse became broken-winded, and was sold by his

FIGURE 32
Teapot with Aesop's *Fable of the Horse and Ass*, painting attributed to Jefferyes Hammett O'Neal (1734–1801). England, London, Chelsea Porcelain Manufactory (1744–69), *c*.1752–55. Soft-paste porcelain with overglaze enamels, ht: 13cm (5in.).
Gift of George and Helen Gardiner
Courtesy of The Gardiner Museum of Ceramic Art, Toronto

owner to a farmer. One day, as he was drawing a dung-cart, he met the Ass again, who in turn derided him and said, 'Aha! You never thought to come to this, did you, you who were so proud! Where are all your gay trappings now?'

This particular version of the fable comes from a translation by V.S. Vernon Jones from 1912, with an introduction by G.K. Chesterton (author of the Father Brown mysteries), and some wonderful illustrations by Arthur Rackham.

In the 1750s, the Raised Anchor Period at Chelsea also saw the production of sculptural figures, birds and animals, adapted from Meissen and created by principal modeller Joseph Willems. His creations were less biting caricatures than some of the German prototypes, and conveyed a more gentle satire. Colours were more restrained and sparing, and the Chelsea models of the mid-1750s are considered to be among the finest of all English figure production.

The subsequent Red Anchor Period at Chelsea is most noted for its variety of vessel shapes and highly-naturalistic botanical and animal imagery, again with Meissen overtones, often copying popular botanical illustrations. Finally, the Gold Anchor Period introduced the use of heavy gilding on Sèvres-inspired opulent rococo and neo-classical vases and garniture sets. Bird and floral motifs still remained highly popular, as well as fanciful *chinoiserie* figures in the manner of Watteau. The Gold Anchor Period at Chelsea ended when Sprimont sold the factory in 1769, to the proprietor of the Derby factory. Its output was then known as Chelsea-Derby, until it was shut down entirely in 1784, and its remaining moulds removed to Derby.

Sèvres Porcelain

Early French porcelain factories such as those at Rouen and St. Cloud had been successful in the development of soft pastes. In the early 1700s the discovery of deposits of kaolin (the essential component of true hard-paste porcelain) had given Meissen the edge in this field. In France however, it was not until the late 1760s that kaolin deposits near Limoges began to be exploited.

The Vincennes factory opened in 1740 as an experimental venture producing soft-paste wares. Under a royal charter it was given the exclusive right to manufacture 'porcelain in the style of Saxony [Meissen], painted and gilded and depicting human figures'. The workshop at Vincennes was the first in France to produce a clay body of perfect whiteness, with a fine, transparent glaze. By the mid-1750s, Vincennes was producing a large variety of tablewares, colourful and gilded, with Orientally-inspired motifs, Meissen-influenced patterns and later, with figurative scenes in the style of François Boucher.

In 1756, the factory was relocated to a purpose-built site at Sèvres, a village ideally situated between Paris and Versailles, and taken directly under royal administration in 1759. The first years of porcelain production at Sèvres were a continuation of the work carried out at Vincennes. Louis XV and his mistress Madame de Pompadour became patrons of the factory, and Sèvres porcelains branched out into a great variety of baroque and later neo-classical vases, urns, dinnerware and figurative sculpture.

Vases from garniture sets began to display strong solid background colours, such as the famous *rose Pompadour* and *bleu céleste*, framing elaborately painted scenes. Sèvres's painting was highly specialised. Some examples include the painting of naval scenes (J.L. Morin), pastoral and mythological scenes (Ch.N. Dodin and Ch.E. Asselin), and the depiction of children or small lively landscapes (A.V. Vielliard). Many other painters specialised in bird imagery, in *chinoiserie* and in various gilding techniques.

After the introduction of hard-paste porcelains in the late 1760s both soft- and hard-paste porcelains were produced until 1804, when soft paste was finally abandoned. Towards the end of the 18th century, enamelled and gilded tablewares, vases, urns, furniture and clock accoutrements, as well as figurative sculpture, all formed part of the Sèvres repertoire intended for a prestigious luxury market. Louis XV and Louis XVI made a habit of presenting sumptuous Sèvres services and ensembles to other European royals and dignitaries, so that the perfection of the French arts could be displayed around the world. The kings of France also organised exhibitions of Sèvres wares every year at Versailles, thus giving the factory an opportunity to display and sell its most recent creations.

Although much of Sèvres' output would have to be classified as 'decorative', there were a large number of narrative works produced as well, many dealing with Greek-inspired mythological themes. Figure 33 shows a vase from a garniture pair, *c.*1770, with the story of 'Jupiter and Antiope' from E. Fessard's engraving of 1758 after Carle van Loo. The image shows Jupiter in the guise of Pan (with pan pipes, a satyr's mask, tambourine, cornet, basket of grapes and a chalice) about to seduce the sleeping Antiope.

The ancient Greek legend has Antiope, Queen of Thebes and daughter of the Boeotian river god Asopus, seduced by Jupiter in the guise of the god Pan. She later gives birth to twins, Zethus and Amphion, who are exposed at birth on Mount Cithaeron, where they are found and fostered by shepherds. Their mother Antiope had been treated with great cruelty by Lycus, the usurping king of Thebes and his wife Dirce. However (in the tradition of Greek revenge drama) — the adult twins finally oust and slay Lycus, and Dirce is tied to a bull by her hair and dragged to an ignominious death. Justice triumphant, Amphion becomes King of Thebes and fortifies the city with a great wall. It is said that when he played his lyre, the stones moved into place of their own accord.

Like so many European porcelain manufactories, Sèvres's history (and

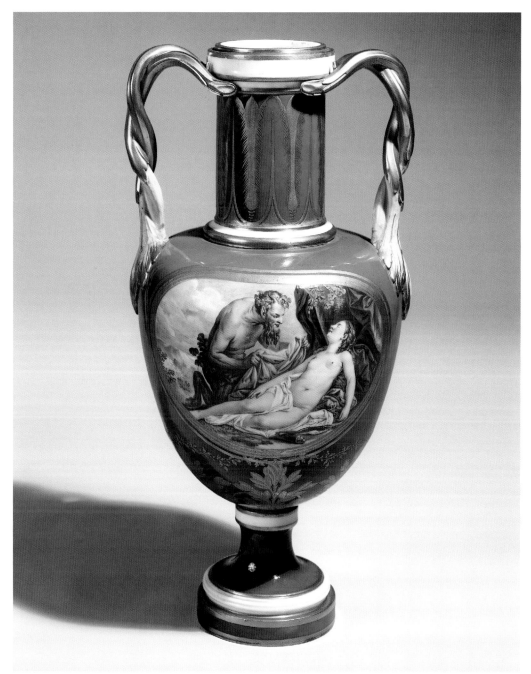

FIGURE 33
Vase (from a garniture pair)
with the story of 'Jupiter and
Antiope' from E. Fessard's
engraving of 1758 after
Carle van Loo. France,
Sèvres, c.1770.
Hard-paste porcelain with
overglaze enamels and gilding
ht: 31.2cm (12⅛in.),
w: 15.6cm (6⅛ in.).
*Reproduced by kind permission of the
Trustees of the Wallace Collection, London*

production) reflect the shifts of politics, power, patronage and the financial swings of fortune. For example, the factory did survive the French Revolution (Louis XVI alas did not — he was guillotined on January 21, 1793). Despite the suspension of the monarchy, the declaration of national bankruptcy and of course the loss of aristocratic patronage, Sèvres still managed to survive as a national property, but only under the most difficult circumstances. Perhaps its saving grace was that it could still produce objects and imagery that promoted those symbols of prestige that succeeded Louis XVI, from Napoleon to the Second Empire. The factory is still in active production to this very day.

6

The 20th-century Ceramic Narrative

Some Precursors and Pioneers

by David Whiting

The 20th-century ceramic narrative has essentially been a continuation and reinvention of the various commentaries and symbols that have covered ceramics, in various forms, for thousands of years. Pots, after all, have long been as much about metaphor and message as everyday use, an integral part of their ritualistic and celebratory role. But much of the early initiative in this modern liberation, a **new** sense in studio practice — that the message was as important as the medium — came from the fine arts, and a new interest in clay among late 19th- and early 20th-century painters and sculptors. Narrative has never been entirely absent from the mainstream ceramic creativity in factories and city and country workshops. However, for that specifically 20th-century invention, the self-conscious artist potter, it was the new intellectualised cross-fertilisation of visual and expressive ideas, that by World War II had created such a powerful new impetus.

Henri Matisse (1869–1954), the father of Fauvism, was primarily drawn to the decorative sensuality of the human form in his art, and it played the central rhythmical role in his ceramics as well. The chapel of the Rosary at Vence, completed in 1951, was in some ways an architectural summation of his concerns, a pure synthesis of line and colour. These starkly linear biblical murals drawn on ceramic tiles, show the act of figurative storytelling at its most abstract and refined. Meanwhile, by the time of Matisse's death three years later, potters in

FIGURE **34**
Viola Frey (United States).
Tile painting, 'Western
Civilisation' series, 2000.
228.6 x 180.3cm (90 x 71in.).
*Courtesy of Rena Bransten Gallery,
San Francisco*

FIGURE 35
Marc Chagall (France).
Plate, *Poisson et Amoureux de Vence*, 1955.
30.8 x 48.5 cm (12 x 19 in.).
Courtesy of Museum of Contemporary Art, 's-Hertogenbosch, the Netherlands
© Estate of Marc Chagall / SODRAC (Montreal) 2005

Europe, America and beyond were rediscovering that illustrated vessel surfaces could again be implicit in the objects' meaning, and not just a means of elaboration or a method of creating formal unity.

Matisse was artistically indebted, among others, to Paul Gauguin (1848–1903), an artist whose inventively integrated symbolism was also expressed in ceramics. These projects were truly pioneering. Collaborating with the potter Ernest Chaplet from 1886 onwards, Gauguin borrowed from ancient cultures such as Japan and Pre-Columbian America, elaborating on the ancient ritualistic and ceremonial role of clay. His wheel-thrown and constructed totem forms were imbued with the same search for meaning that drove his painting. Matisse, along with fellow Fauves such as Maurice de Vlaminck (1876–1950) and André Derain (1880–1954) went on to work with the potter André Metthey (who had already worked with Impressionist and Symbolist artists). Using tin-glaze, *faïence fauve* artists added painterly life and expressive verve to the figurative connotations of the vessel. They were also excited by the new spatial dimension that ceramics offered. Georges Rouault (1871–1958) also worked with Metthey, exhibiting *faïence* and then lead-glazed pottery along with his painting, intrigued as he was by the combination of line and colour in-the-round. The vehicle of traditional form created a liberating three-dimensional ground for painters to work on without becoming exclusively sculptural. The illustrated pot may always have been there — from the Mycenaean bowls of 3000 years ago to the 17th-century slipware of Thomas Toft — but there was a true sense of rediscovery now in the subjects which could be portrayed in clay.

FIGURE **36**
A.R. Penck (Germany).
Bodenvase, 1997,
100 x 65cm (39⅓ x 25½ in.).
*Courtesy of Museum of Contemporary Art,
's-Hertogenbosch, the Netherlands*

A crucial instigator in the new relationship between painters and clay was the Catalan potter Josep Lloréns Artigas (1892–1980). A maker of pure undecorated bottles, Artigas' collaborations with other artists could not have been more different. Moving to Paris in 1924, he made early experiments with Picasso, and then an important series of pieces with the colourist Raoul Dufy (1877–1953). In Dufy's vibrantly painted pots, tiles and architectural forms, the Classically-inspired figure, swimming and dancing in air, was a predominant theme. But Dufy's poetics were an exception. Other projects — like Albert Marquet's landscapes on tile — were lame and diluted. It was only by the 1940s and '50s, with the investigations of artists like Miró, Picasso and Chagall, that a quite new spirit in representational ceramics had arrived.

Joan Miró (1893–1983) another Catalan, had a more intimate hands-on feeling for the clay. Not only painting Artigas-thrown bottles and jars, but making large murals, plaques and freestanding amorphous sculptures through the 1950s and '60s, he explored the primitive surreal and mythological imagery he had made his own. Far more than token, Miró's ceramic projects were those of a true artist-potter, whose preternatural iconography seemed to grow organically out of the material. Clay was not merely a canvas. Neither was it for Pablo Picasso (1881–1973), the artist who exerted the most important single influence not only on modern clay narrative, but on the whole sculptural direction of ceramics after World War II. In 1946 he had visited the Ramie's Madoura Pottery at Vallauris and, much intrigued by the work he saw, began to embellish some pots. So excited was he by the plastic and painterly possibilities of the medium that he returned to Vallauris in 1947 for a much longer spell, continuing to work frequently at Madoura until 1955, and thereafter still regularly collaborating with the Ramies. At Madoura the pieces were thrown by Jules Agard, and subsequently transformed by Picasso through alteration and decoration. As well as more conventional dishes and vases, he worked on sculptural assemblages and complex composite and constructed forms, animating them with brush, resist, relief and incised drawing. In clay, Picasso had a substance with which he playfully improvised and combined his abilities as painter and sculptor. With their gestural expressive glazing, these ceramics were a richly pliable and fluid means by which he could further investigate the transformative, biomorphic and mythological world of his art in general. The more familiar conventions of ceramic form gave him a new kind of pictorial frame, populating vessels with a repertoire of bullfights and acrobats, classical dramas and sexual encounters. Like Miró, his tales in clay went beyond the surface, embracing a medium that could, in Picasso's more surreal anthropomorphic configurations, truly transmogrify subject and shape.

The Russian Marc Chagall (1887–1985) may have been more conventional in his early use of ceramic form, with paintings applied mainly to plates, vases and tiles, but with a rare ability to align the characters of his ethereal poetic stories to the abstract contours of pottery. Floating across the surface, his luminous lovers carried some illusion of depth despite their stylisation (see Figure 35 on page 96). Chagall had begun to work with clay in 1949 and went on to produce over 200 pieces, working with, for example, the Ramies at Vallauris and Madame Bourreau at Antibes. Scenes from the Bible, Greek myth, modern life and love were expressed with a colouristic richness that echoed his projects in stained glass as well as oil. His forms soon became more baroque in their figurative

FIGURE **37**
Mimmo Paladino (Italy).
Vessel, untitled (from 'Vasi
Eremitici' series), 1993,
26 x 19cm (10¼ x 7½in.).
Courtesy of Museum of Contemporary Art,
's-Hertogenbosch, the Netherlands

allusion, and were often modelled by Chagall himself, who liked a more direct involvement with clay than many artists. Of making ceramics he said, 'one delves into a mystical and symbolic world in which there is no concept of time'. Certainly Chagall's works in clay, like all his art, have a lyricism which is essentially spiritual — and timeless — in nature. Meanwhile, the versatile painter Fernard Léger (1881–1955) worked on a greater scale. His abstracted and vivid figurative ceramic sculpture and giant relief murals with their monumental stylisation were ideally suited to architecture.

The impact of these new artistic forays into clay — particularly by Picasso — made a big impression in London. The influence was strong among those narrative potters associated with the Institute of Education and the Central School: William Newland, Margaret Hine and Nicholas Vergette were even dubbed 'the Picassettes' by Bernard Leach. However, they were as indebted to other exemplars — ancient Mediterranean ceramics for example — as to developments across the Channel. The slipware, tin glaze and terracotta of William Newland (1919–1998) had a freshness and expressive spirit that was still rare in British pottery. With its gallery of mythical and animal characters, there was something both cosmopolitan and bucolically British about it, an ambitious and witty reinvention of slipware and maiolica traditions. Nicholas Vergette (1923–1974) later took his narrative and figurative ideas to the United States, where he became an influential teacher. A contemporary of Newland's at the Central School was Eric James Mellon (b. 1925). Experimenting with a variety of ash glazes, Mellon remains one of the most individual of British narrative

FIGURE **38**
William Newland (United Kingdom). Shallow bowl, *Europa and the Bull*, c.1965, dia: 60cm (23⅝in.).
Courtesy of Jeremy Newland

potters, using his bowls, vases and platters to explore a number of principally Classical themes, with deft and lively brushwork. Subjects like Daphne and Apollo, the sons of Saturn, Europa and the Bull, Pluto and Persephone — as well as scenes from modern literature and fragments of autobiography — are represented in a kind of compressed theatre (see Figures 49 and 50 on page 117). Both Newland and Mellon have demonstrated the continuing currency of the old stories — of how pots could also express the eternal truths of the great myths, here reinterpreted through and for modern experience. In Mellon's case, these subjects continue to be conveyed with a poetic life and intimacy that gives them a precious domesticity.

In Australia, painters like Arthur Boyd (1920–1999) and John Percival (1923–2000) have also used ceramics to reinterpret the great stories, partly as a means of addressing modern Australian experience. Boyd, the son of the potter Merric Boyd, set up a pottery with Percival after World War II. The original intention was to make decorative wares that would subsidise their painting, but they were also excited by the freedom of clay and made bold functional pieces with energetically painted religious and mythological episodes, much indebted to the maiolica collections in the National Gallery of Victoria and the 16th-century works of Breughel and his contemporaries. Boyd went on to use clay as a frame, in a major series of so-called 'ceramic paintings' that investigated more grand themes: love and despair, life and death, cruelty and compassion, explored through the fables of the Bible and the Classical world. Boyd's primitive figuration was developed in a number of sculptural pieces as well.

In the United States *émigrés* and shorter-term visitors made a significant impression on the new direction of clay. The Austrian-born Valerie Wieselthier (1895–1945) moved to the United States at the height of her career in 1929. Taught in the figurative tradition of Michael Powolny and the Wiener Werkstätte, Wieselthier went on to make increasingly large, and eventually giant-sized female sculptures, superficially Art Deco in style, but with an expressive sweep that seemed a far cry from the decorative milieu in which she had trained. They showed to progressive circles in America just what clay was capable of, freed from earlier forms of function and ornament. The British surrealist and potter Sam Haile (1909–1948) went to the United States in 1939. His period there was short but the impact he made, through his ceramics and his teaching, was considerable. Haile's pots, essentially a three-dimensional extension of his painting, and immersed in the transformative world of Mediterranean and British myth and symbolism, were also ingenious integrations of form and narrative. His energised slip-decorated earthenware and painted stoneware created a new ceramic pictorial space several years before Picasso started work at Vallauris. When these were exhibited in New York in the early 1940s, American potters were very excited, a mood compounded by Haile's inspired teaching at New York

State University's Alfred College and the University of Michigan. Haile returned to England in 1944, and was tragically killed only four years later, but his artistic legacy was lasting.

The United States, with its pioneering art teaching and progressive outlook, was a hotbed of ceramic exploration after the War. It was hungry for ideas, for new creative routes. 'Picasso suggested a wider range for ceramics', said the potter Stanley Rosen, one of many who followed the European developments in the leading American craft journals. There was the catalyst of new sculpture and painting (much of it, like Picasso's, being regularly exhibited in the American museums in the 1950s), but also a growing engagement with the graphic surface of clay — the use of carving, painting, sgraffito and so on. Integral to this process was the potter Peter Voulkos (1924–2002). An important teacher, Voulkos (whose own early pots had narrative elements) initiated a whole new physicality of approach, closely associated with the new material freedom of the Abstract Expressionist school. Robert Arneson (1930–1992) stated that Voulkos had encouraged him to move away from traditional pottery to a much freer expressive style, and this soon developed into a quite new and distinctive language of his own — Funk. The Dada-inspired Funk school, centred on the University of California, came to define the new artistic excesses of the early 1960s in its eclectic referential style. Funk was bizarre and irreverent, and very different from the passive, cool objectivity of Pop. Arneson concerned himself with the trappings of modern American culture, his brash in-your-face sculpture viscerally engaged with the unattractive complexities of a frenetic, greedy, alienated but also exciting era. The familiar was treated in an unfamiliar way. As Paul S. Donhauser wrote, 'working in clay allowed Arneson to explore more fully the parody of everyday objects and their witty associations… poignant reminders of human activities'. Making crude use of hobby craft materials, Arneson's symbolic visual/verbal puns resulted in a quite new type of totem/object, remote from the world of the vessel. Deeply disturbing, his use of garish colour and imagery was also voluptuous, sensuous and strangely optimistic.

A colleague of Voulkos' at the Archie Bray Foundation, Rudy Autio (b. 1926) was, like Arneson, very receptive to the advent of Abstract Expressionism. 'It initiated', he said, 'a new freedom from the sometimes rigid discipline of the potter's wheel', enabling him to make the vessel into a fluid and amorphous ground for his vibrant studies of the intertwined human figure. Autio's economic and emphatically linear brushwork created a painterly rhythm across the restless undulating outline of his pots (see Figure 45 on page 112). It was an approach taken up by the much younger Akio Takamori (b. 1950). Like Autio, Takamori has been attracted to mythological subjects, but he is even more interested in drawing **with** the contours of the clay than drawing **on** them. Influenced in part by Japanese woodblock printing and Paleolithic art, Takamori has transferred the same kind of graphic economy to his ceramics, but the stories he tells, brilliantly foreshortened and spatially dramatic, are full of intense action and sexual drama. More recently he has been concentrating on figure sculpture (see Figures 134–136, on pages 185–6).

Autio and Takamori have used line rather than colour to narrate. The remarkable Viola Frey (1933–2004) had more in common with Robert Arneson. Much attracted to Arneson's abrasive trophy-making, Frey also turned to the everyday object for her eclecticism. Again using the imagery of mass culture, much of it shaping her own childhood, she was a *bricoleur*, an erudite collector and re-assembler. She made figures in the form of slipcast tableaux and free standing sculptural monoliths (see Figures 121–3 on pages 177–8), inspired in part by the flea market figurines that she habitually hoarded. Almost excessive overglaze painting heightened the element of kitsch, but her work, like that of Arneson, was full of expressive charge — celebratory on one level, but question-ing of America's modern fast-food values on another. A close friend of Frey's, Howard Kottler (1930–1989), whose mysterious silhouette haunted a series of plates she made in the 1970s, was also attracted to the world of bric-a-brac. A teacher at the University of Washington, Kottler controversially distanced him-self from the craft and mechanics of clay, using arm's-length industrial tech-niques and commercial components for his equally commercial imagery. A mas-ter of *trompe l'oeil* modelling and assemblage, Kottler's style was 'supermannerist', influencing the growth of the so-called 'superobject', using commercially avail-able ceramic decals on his vividly coloured glazes to make satirical and witty visual puns about art, politics, sex, religion and other topics. Iconoclastic and dif-ficult to define, Kottler's super realism had distinctly Dada traits, and despite his premature death, his mark on ceramic 'post modernism' is indelible.

In the hands of Ken Price (b. 1935) the superobject remained very charged — but its actual meaning seemed more oblique. As one of Voulkos' leading stu-dents at the Otis College of Art and Design in Los Angeles, Price's work had become very sculptural by the 1960s. Employing a style of extraordinary control and precision (the antithesis of the gutsy Funk) he made finely crafted biomor-phic egg shapes with brilliantly painted and glazed surfaces. The relationship between primordial form and intense synthetic colour was disturbing and unex-pected, the object seemingly imbued with a remote ritualistic significance. By the end of the decade he had moved on to a series of surreally playful cup forms, functional familiarity subverted by glossy 'vividly' coloured surfaces — both seductive and unsettling in the true tradition of the 'Fetish-Finish' school. One of Voulkos' last pupils at Otis was Michael Frimkess (b. 1937). Along with Price and other Voulkos *protégés*, his early gestural style led to inclusion in the 'Abstract Expressionist Ceramics' exhibition at the University of California in 1966. By the late '60s, however, he had moved on to a repertoire of Classical

FIGURE **39**
Michael Frimkess (United States). Lidded jar, *Visit to Club W.O.C. E.K. (The Band)*, 2004, 44.5 x 38cm (17½ x 15in.).

Photograph: Leroy Lucien

Greek and Chinese forms, decorated with colourful overglaze painting. The shapes were archaic but the imagery very contemporary — cartoon-like illustrations that dealt, like Arneson and Frey, with his own cultural perceptions and concerns. Frimkess has worked effectively with the stereotypes and clichés of modern life and living, illustrating in a dispassionately controlled style a myriad of sexual, musical, ecological and racial issues, as well as the legacy of Pop.

The complex cultural issues that Frimkess and his American contemporaries first investigated so forcefully in the 1960s and '70s, still set much of the narrative agenda today — ceramics with a social and political conscience. In Britain alone figures like Grayson Perry, Philip Eglin and Stephen Dixon show the continuing currency of work that bites. Perhaps there is something about the domestic scale and familiarity of ceramics — its sheer approachability — that makes it such a potent platform for modern observation and storytelling. Pottery is now a central part of the political, satirical, spiritual and self-examining tool of modern art, a pluralist condition really shaped in the cultural flux that followed World War II. Using forms and materials based in the long history of clay (and others since borrowed from other visual disciplines), these objects come into our space saying quite new things. On another level, the 20th-century narrative in clay is simply a regeneration of what it has long been — the pot as ornamental image, a mirror of the society and the values that produced it.

Copyright © 2006 David Whiting
David Whiting of the United Kingdom is a critic and a writer on studio ceramics and the applied arts. He has curated exhibitions and contributes regularly to such magazines as Crafts *(United Kingdom) and* Ceramics: Art and Perception *(Australia).*

Contemporary Narratives:

Mythologies, History and Archetypes Re-Explored

7

The work presented in this chapter, although entirely contemporary, draws its inspiration largely from the past and from existing thematic models. I have previously discussed the recurrence over time of particular narratives that, retold and reinvented, attest to an ongoing relevance and fascination. 'Europa and the Bull', and 'Adam and Eve', are just two examples of such recurring narratives taken from mythologies. Other references to pre-existing models might be historical allusions to past places and events, or deliberate stylistic inspirations from existing ceramic and painting traditions. I should reiterate that few works fall into just one simple descriptive category. However, for the sake of some kind of chapter organisation, I have attempted to place artists' work into thematic contexts and most often have let the artists choose those frameworks themselves. I would like to think that as narratives shift and change with retelling, so might also the contextual framework be changed, according to the responses of the viewer and the reader.

Marino Moretti – Italy

Moretti's predominant influences have their roots in the imagery and shape repertoire of mediaeval Orvietan ceramics. He in fact grew up in Orvieto surrounded by the extensive mediaeval ceramic collection of his father and grandfather, namely 500 pieces that included early ceramic works, not only from Umbria, but also from Tuscany and Alto Lazio. He states:

OPPOSITE PAGE

MARINO MORETTI (Italy)

FIGURE 40
Detail of plate, *Spinaciona*, 2004.
Earthenware with coloured glazes and oxides, fired in oxidation, dia: 55cm (21⅗in.).
Photograph: Marino Moretti

107

MARINO MORETTI (Italy)

FIGURE 41
Detail of plate, *Dialogue*,
2004.
Earthenware with coloured
glazes and oxides, fired in
oxidation, dia: 25cm (10in.).

Photograph: Marino Moretti

OPPOSITE PAGE

FIGURE 42
Vase form, untitled, 1999.
Tin-glazed earthenware
with coloured glazes, stains
and oxides, fired in oxidation,
ht: 27cm (10⅝in.).

Photograph: Luigi Moretti

I remember when my grandfather and father dedicated entire afternoons to restoring mediaeval ceramics from their collection. This was the beginning; the shapes, the iconography, the glazes, the oxides — all left an indelible impression on my memory. At present, through continuous research and interpretation of tradition I try to go beyond these, creating my own personal idiom, while being aware of the many and complex manifestations which are found in the contemporary art movement.

Further studies in art and art history in Rome have made themselves felt in his work as well. *Spinaciona* (Figure 40) shows a plate detail strongly inspired by naive figurative painting of the 16th century from the now-destroyed town of Castro. Similar stylistic references can be seen in the plate detail of *Dialogue* (Figure 41), where Moretti recreates a conversation between himself and a deceased beloved cat.

Another type of imagery, usually satiric in content, can be seen painted on a traditional Orvietan vase form (see Figure 42). The biomorphic creatures, both masculine and feminine, are engaged in a dispute for an invisible prize. The primary influence for this type of imagery comes from a number of sources: *Il Mediovoevo Fantastico* (Mediaeval Bestiary) of Jurgis Baltrusaitis; The *Manuel de Zoologia Fantastico* of Jorge Luis Borges; the anonymous 14th-century *Luttrel Psalter* (again, a mediaeval bestiary); and the work of such painters as Hieronymus Bosch.

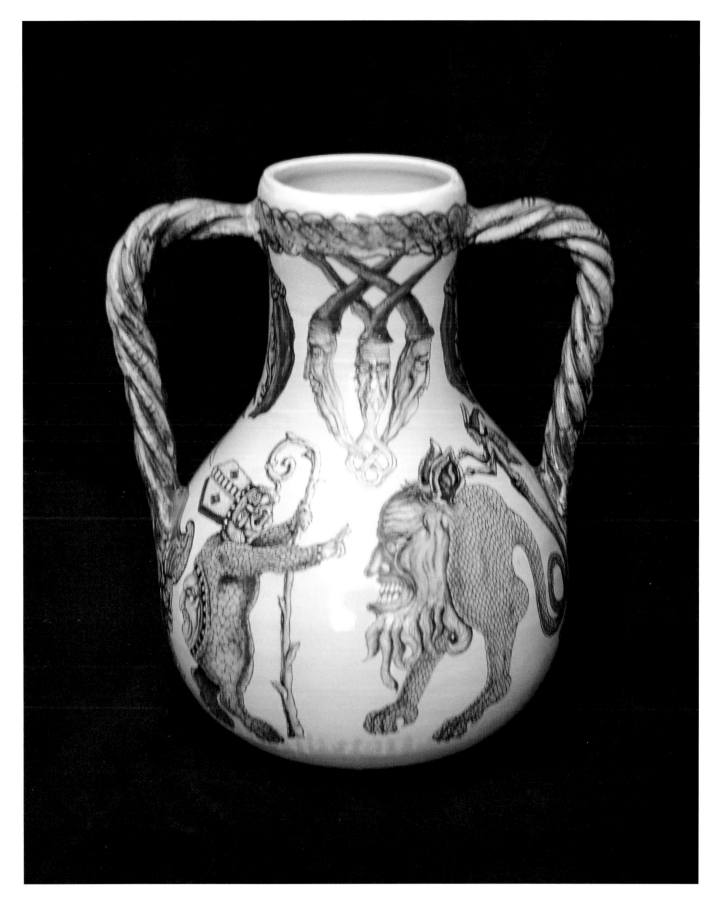

Philip Eglin – *United Kingdom*

In this series of works, Philip Eglin has drawn inspiration from the Victoria and Albert Museum's collection of northern mediaeval woodcarvings which were displayed alongside his own ceramic works in an exhibition in 2001. In describing his work *The Virgin and Child* (Figures 43 and 44), Eglin states:

> I made a series of polychrome Madonnas, initially inspired by a V&A Museum publication — Paul Williamson's *Northern Gothic Sculpture 1200–1450*. Its illustrations gave equal prominence to the backs and fronts of these carvings. I was particularly fascinated by their backs, which had been deliberately left roughly hewn and hollowed out, as they were never intended to be seen from behind. With this in mind on my large clay versions of these forms, any purposefully subversive or irreverent imagery was presented on their backs. I wanted their surfaces to be deliberately complex and confused, full of contradictory messages and symbols drawn from a range of disparate sources.

The exhibition's curator, Alun Graves, sheds further light on Eglin's 'Madonna' series:

> In this series of works, Eglin has captured something of the robustness and solidity of the carvings, their quiet insistent demand for attention, their beauty and grace. If he has observed with sensitivity the aesthetic qualities of these most exceptional works, he has, however, equally understood their nature as damaged artefacts. For these works are survivors; damaged, mutilated even, but enduring. There is in fact something almost defiant in Eglin's recognition of the damage as vital components of their form. The loss of the Virgin's nose, the reduction of the Infant Christ to a mere stump — such features, when assimilated into Eglin's own works, seem to lend them a history of their own and to increase their feeling of timelessness.

Rudi Autio – *United States*

In speaking of major developmental work periods, Autio underlines his work and studies at the Archie Bray Foundation in Helena, Montana. He was first introduced to clay at Montana State College under Frances Senska in the early 1950s. In discussing important visual and pictorial influences, Autio reveals the following:

> I fondly recall the work of Picasso, Moore, Marini, Tamayo, Noguchi and Rivera. Of special interest was an artist I met briefly in the early 1950s named Hank Meloy. Matisse influenced me also, as did Munukata's energetic wood

OPPOSITE PAGE

PHILIP EGLIN (United Kingdom)

FIGURE **43**
Sculpture (front view), *The Virgin and Child*, 1999. Slab-built earthenware with pressmoulded additions, added coloured slips, stains and oxides, and low-fired transfers, fired in oxidation, 86 x 46 x 25cm (33¾ x 18 x 10in.).
Photograph: Andrew Pritchard

FIGURE **44**
Sculpture (back view), *The Virgin and Child*, 1999.
Photograph: Andrew Pritchard

block prints. In ceramics Hamada was the first major artist who magically made clay into high art 'by letting the clay speak', as he would say to an audience watching him work. There is no question that the influence of the abstract expressionists – DeKooning especially – affected my work and left a permanent imprint. So did the charismatic vigour of my friend Peter Voulkos.

Odyssey (Figure 45) makes obvious reference to Homer's great narrative. Autio has combined the figures of women and horses so familiar on ancient Greek Attic wares, and adapted them to an entirely contemporary 21st-century ceramic form.

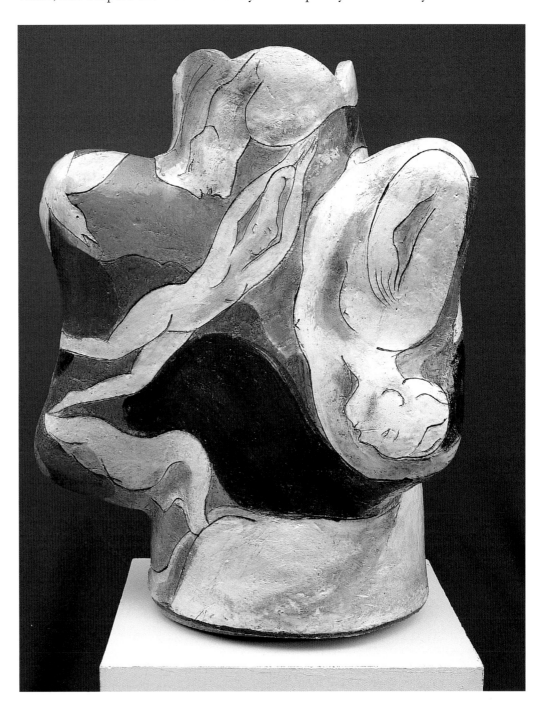

RUDI AUTIO (United States)

FIGURE 45
Sculpture, *Odyssey*, 2000. Handbuilt low-fired stoneware, with incising through coloured slips and underglaze colours, transparent glazes, multiple firing, fired in oxidation, 80.6 x 55.8 x 70cm (31¾ x 22 x 24in.).

Photograph: Chris Autio

ALEXANDRA COPELAND
(Australia)

FIGURE 46
Platter, *Italian Jugs with Green Lemons and Locquats*, 1999.
Wheel-thrown earthenware (Roberto Domiziani) with tin glaze and painted metallic oxides, fired in oxidation, dia: 55cm (21⅝in.).
Photograph: Andrew Clarke

Alexandra Copeland – *Australia*

Copeland discusses her narrative imagery with the same freshness and gusto that characterise the images themselves:

> I love pots. I grew up in a community of potters who espoused the Bernard Leach Japanese aesthetic and philosophy. Books on Japanese graphic art that I was fortunate enough to see as a child fired my imagination.
>
> Nature provides symbols related to our lives. The brevity of life is one of my preoccupations. Blossoms and fertility fade. Friends have been struck down in their youth, and ageing parents bring feelings of sadness.
>
> My own symbolic language includes images of the moon for female fertility, and autumn berries and insects with their busy short lives. Pots from earlier times and cultures refer to an eight-thousand-year-old line of painters of pots. Pots endure far longer than flowers or potters.
>
> There have been regular returns to the circus. Most artists can identify with the little dog valiantly jumping through a hoop, or with the lion tamer alone in the lion's den with a chair and perhaps a paintbrush as defense.

Italian Jugs with Green Lemons and Loquats (Figure 46) makes reference to a

ALEXANDRA COPELAND
(Australia)

FIGURE 47
Platter, *Camellia Garden*, 2000.
Wheel-thrown earthenware (Roberto Domiziani) with tin glaze and painted metallic oxides, fired in oxidation, dia: 55cm (21⅔in.).

Photograph: Andrew Clarke

sojourn in Deruta, Italy in 1993. Copeland recaptures the humorous and historical scenes painted on mediaeval jugs. Shards of old wine jugs found in the dirt around the town's walls evoke painters and revels long-gone. *Camellia Garden* (Figure 47) evokes other memories:

> In Central Asia women believe that the moon governs their fertility. In China bats symbolise happiness. Moths can fertilise flowers and can be eaten by bats. Camellias are hardy Chinese shrubs which I associate with polite conservative Melbourne suburbia. If you touch a camellia you will mark the fleshy petal. In China, I once ate a delicate custard flavoured with red camellia petals.

Tiburcio Soteno Fernándes – Mexico

The tradition of constructing ceramic 'Trees of Life' in Mexico may date to the time of the Conquest by the Spanish in the early 16th century. It is possible that the metal candelabras and incense burners used by the Catholic clergy may have been the original source of inspiration. Certainly in Pre-Classic Mesoamerica, early pictographic expressions make reference to trees that appear repeatedly over time in various forms of mythology and art.

The following information was taken from an interview with Cloë Sayer in London as quoted from 'A Lover of Clay: Tiburcio Soteno Fernándes' (*Artes de Mexico*, No. 30, 1995–96). Fernándes belongs to a large and important family of ceramic artists. His native town of Metepec near Mexico City is famous for the scale and exuberance of its ceramic production. Soteno specialises in the creation of 'Trees of Life', and has passed his knowledge and skill on to his sons. His mother, a noted local ceramic sculptor, remains an important source of inspiration.

The *Tree of Life* seen in Figure 48 depicts the conquest of Mexico. It was

TIBURCIO SOTENO FERNÁNDEZ
(Mexico)

FIGURE 48
Sculpture, *Tree of Life*, 1992. Hand-modelled earthenware clay, with added wire and industrial paints, fired in oxidation, ht: 100cm (39⅓in.).
© copyright the Trustees of the British Museum, London
Photograph: David Lavender

made in 1992 during a residency at the Museum of Mankind in London, in conjunction with the exhibition, 'The Skeleton at the Feast: The Day of the Dead in Mexico.' (1992 was Columbus year and this work commemorates the encounter of the New and the Old Worlds with the discovery of Aztec civilisation by the conquistadors in 1519.)

Some of the imagery reads as follows: (top) Spanish galleons displaying the Christian sign of the Cross; (centre) the Aztec Sun Stone (or Calendar Stone) where victims as messengers to the Gods had their hearts cut out; (clockwise) Tenochtitlan was founded when the Aztecs entered the valley of Mexico and saw the promised sign of an eagle on a prickly pear cactus; corn (or maize) which formed part of the staple diet of Mesoamerican civilisation. Then as now it was ground on a *metate* (grinding stone).

The brilliance of conception of this *Tree of Life* refutes Soteno's own modest appraisal of his abilities: 'I'd like my work to last forever. I believe that I haven't yet become an artist and probably not even a potter, just a clay-lover, always fooling around with clay'.

Eric James Mellon – *United Kingdom*

In a biographical statement Mellon describes the motivating forces behind many decades of narrative ceramic imagery:

> I trained as an artist using various media, and like the mediaeval English craftsmen I needed to decorate surfaces. In painting on pots, I wanted to illustrate my responses to contemporary social events and to human behaviour and relationships.
>
> The well-known Greek myth of the abduction of Europa to Crete by Jupiter offers a subject rich in details for decoration. The visual images include a bull, Jupiter's eagle, a dog made for Jupiter by Vulcan and given to Persephone, the peacock (Hera's favourite bird), and Persephone, a beautiful woman. To this I added the figure of a maiden observing the event, reclining against a tree. She comes from the 15th-century painting, *The Annunciation of the Virgin*, by Carlo Crivelli. In his painting the maiden is a young girl looking at the Angel and Virgin. In my decoration she is some years older but is continuing the theme of a spectator's curiosity in unexpectedly observing an event of importance.
>
> In my composition, first drawn in water colour [see Figure 49], I use the figure of a young woman looking at the bull and of Persephone and above her the peacock to give a compositional diagonal from top right to bottom left. The left to right diagonal is fixed by the eagle (top left) to the prancing dog (bottom right). In the European tradition we write from top left to bottom right, but the artist,

in using space, tries to avoid this over-familiar positioning of subject matter. In placing subject matter on a ceramic form the decoration must embellish and not destroy the form [see Figure 50]. It must also conform to the compositional solutions used and developed by European artists during the past 500 years. This solution uses a grid made up of diagonals together with verticals and horizontals, applying the use of space as defined in the principles of Classical composition taken from the Greek Golden Section. Rembrandt used this method in all his compositions both in preliminary drawings and in finished paintings. The drawing requires modification to fit around a cylinder that can only be seen in its entirety by turning the piece. The figures and motifs are drawn with slight diagonal movements as in handwriting. This allows the eye to flow around the pot.

ERIC JAMES MELLON (United Kingdom)

FIGURE 49 (left)
Watercolour sketch maquette for cylinder, *Europa and the Bull*, 1974, ht: 19cm (7½ in.).
Photograph: Beaver Photography

FIGURE 50 (right)
Cylinder, *Europa and the Bull*, 1974.
Wheel-thrown stoneware with underglaze cobalt and iron oxide painting, elm tree ash glaze, fired in reduction, ht: 19cm (7½ in.).
Photograph: Beaver Photography

Karen Koblitz (United States)

FIGURE 51 (above)
Vessel, *Homage to New Jerusalem*, 2004.
Thrown and handbuilt white earthenware
with coloured underglazes and transparent
glaze, fired in oxidation, ht: 42cm (16½in.),
w. 33cm (13in.).

Photograph: Susan Einstein

Karen Koblitz – *United States*

My work references historical pieces and various ethnicities, an interest encouraged by my love of travel and reading. A trip to Russia in 2002 as an Art Ambassador and a guest of the United States Department of State's 'Art in the Embassies' program has introduced me to the rich history of the arts in Russia.

While touring the environs of Moscow in 2002, I was taken to the site of the 16th-century Russian Monastery at New Jerusalem. The richly-colored and textured tiles of the exterior and interior of this church were truly inspirational. I noticed the imagery of the angel as a recurring theme throughout the complex.

Homage to New Jerusalem [shown in Figure 51] has four narrative areas, separated by four wings. Three of the four narratives on this piece present different views of this amazing architectural wonder; the fourth has an image of a Phoenix rising from the ashes. In World War II, the Nazis occupied this church for 21 days and blew it up with dynamite upon their retreat. The site is being completely restored, with a ceramic workshop on-site. The patterns and colours on the wings and base reflect some of the tile designs one finds on the walls of New Jerusalem.

Dalia Laučkaitė-Jacimavičienė – *Lithuania*

My works are influenced by the history of art and architecture. Art history is my real fascination, especially old Netherlandish painting with its love for details, and its sometimes obsessive precision. I combine architectural constructions with references to classical painting. In the manner of Postmodernism, I blend 'high' art (Madonnas of Ghirlandaio and Lippi) with shapes of functional wares. In one and the same work I present angels and bugs, and cows and church towers, which in contrast to their natural and symbolic order are shown equal in size.

Many of my narrative images come from mythology or, through old painting, from Catholic iconography. However, I never try to retell these narratives (stories?) or to logically interpret them; I use them intuitively, combining them with personal histories and images. My favourite personage, a woman-bird, is deeply rooted in ancient mythology. I like it as a poetic and very polysemantic, humorous and tragic icon.

Dalia Laučkaitė-Jacimavičienė (Lithuania)

FIGURE 52 (left)
Plate, *Animals Talking*, 2003.
Slab-built porcelain with transparent glaze, enamel painting, lustres and transfers, fired in oxidation, dia: 32cm (12½in.).
Photograph: Vidmantas Ilciukas

FIGURE 53 (right)
Wall sculpture, *Talking about St. Jacob's Church*, 2003.
Slab-built and pressmoulded earthenware with transparent glaze, enamel painting, lustres and transfers, fired in oxidation, 83 x 73 x 2.5cm (32⅔ x 28¾ x 1in.).
Photograph: Vidmantas Ilciukas

The plate *Animals Talking* [Figure 52] has some references to the story that animals talk on Christmas Eve. I wanted to make this piece mysterious and luxurious — with much gold and ornamentation. The tiled floor is an old painting convention. I like playing with illusion, and the perspective of a tiled floor gives a good illusion of space. I do not try to make it perfect however, but rather I prefer to suggest some ambiguity in the image.

The composition of *Talking about St. Jacob's Church* [Figure 53] has come from a *Virgin and Child Enthroned with Saints*. Old architecture of my native city, Vilnius, is an important source of inspiration. I can see St. Jacob's, one of the beautiful Vilnius baroque churches, through the window of my workshop. I have made a series of works containing views of this church. They depict a scene that is very familiar to me, but on the other hand I invest it with some strange personages, thus making it surrealistic and dream-like. The personages on the side panels have my and my son's faces — the idea has come from old paintings, when masters used to incorporate their self-portraits or the portraits of their family members somewhere in a corner of the composition.

GEORGES JEANCLOS (France)

FIGURE 54
Sculpture, *Barque Saint-Julien*, 1991.
Slabbed, handbuilt and pressmoulded grey terracotta, fired in oxidation,
ht: 51cm (20in.).
Courtesy of the Gardiner Museum of Ceramic Art, Toronto

Georges Jeanclos – *France*

In an article entitled 'The Sculpture of Jeanclos' appearing in *American Ceramics* (Vol. 10, No. 3, Winter 1993), Anne McPherson describes the monumental and moving clay sculpture of Georges Jeanclos as follows:

> What animates Jeanclos's works are memories from childhood so painful and invasive that they have continued to affect his life. Laying these grim ghosts to rest has been part of his artistic goal ever since he began to work in clay.

Particularly haunting were war memories of survival in France in 1944, living wild in a forest with his family, in order to escape Nazi persecution. The memory of the decimation of the European Jewish community was summed up in one simple phrase: 'My tears still water the clay I work'. In further describing the inspirational sources of Jeanclos's work, McPherson continues:

> The process by which he makes his figures has deep metaphorical meaning as well. He throws slabs of clay onto an inclined surface so that they stretch out

and become thin. Thrown on the ground in the same manner, they become marked with striations and impressions caused by dust, pieces of clay, and other vestiges of peoples' passage. [...] With this method in which change plays a large part, Jeanclos is able to restore the history of the clay, the significant moments of his biography and of Jewish history, while giving all of these particularities a universal meaning.

Finally, Jeanclos himself discussed his approach to his work as follows:

> Clay holds memories of every act upon it. It is the bearer of its own form, texture, language. It reveals by its structure what truly belongs to itself. By compressing the block and by these marks, one tries to make the interior memory of the clay appear. I don't try to tame the clay to force a form; it's rather a marriage with the material.

Barque Saint Julien (Figure 54, opposite) illustrates the legend of St. Julien the Hospitalier. He is shown here embracing a leper, an illustration of the redemptive power of love over personal suffering and that of all humanity. This powerful story recounted in Gustave Flaubert's *Three Tales* (Paris, 1877), mirrors the suffering and horror as well as the heroism of World War II. In the story St. Julien is redeemed for the murder of his own parents by living a life of Christian self-sacrifice. His final act of mercy is the succour of a leper, whom he warms with his own body.

Susan Thayer – *United States*

I grew up in a drafty Victorian summer cottage that my family lived in year round. The house overflowed with cats, dogs, gerbils, hamsters, rabbits, brothers and sisters. Amid the tumult, hidden in a dark closet lit by a single bare bulb, we kept our family treasure: a cylindrical Chinese teapot, smuggled out of the mainland by my uncle in 1949; my silver baby cup, dented by the reckless jaws of our English mastiff; and a blue Wedgwood pitcher that was the subject of my mother's first oil painting.

The objects in this closet were never used. Though designed to be practical participants in the life of a household, their preciousness interfered with their utility, until at last the passage of time gave them new purpose as relics, fragile half forgotten links to the stories that defined us as a family.

My experience with ceramic objects as prompts that elicit the recollection and invention of stories is central to the narrative aspect of my work. [...] As an artist I enjoy learning about the variety of responses elicited by the images I've assembled. I don't want to deprive myself of that experience by constructing an overly literal narrative to accompany the work.

SUSAN THAYER (United States)

FIGURE 55
Teapot, *Crystal Ball*, 2001.
Slipcast porcelain with
carving, transparent glaze,
stains and oxides, and
overglaze enamels,
fired in oxidation,
38 x 23. 8 x 102cm
(15 x 9 x 4in.).
Photograph: Denis Purdy

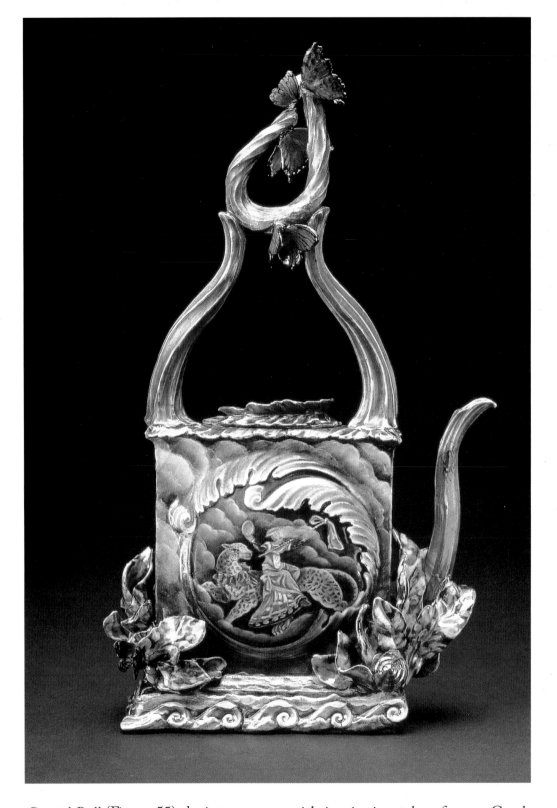

Crystal Ball (Figure 55) depicts a teapot with inspiration taken from a Greek mosaic portraying Dionysus riding a leopard through a night sky. The image is meant to evoke a sense of animal grace, and the subtle anxiety produced by a moonless night and the unfathomable depth of the ocean.

Matthias Ostermann – *Canada*

My ceramic narratives are of two types, essentially concerned with human figure activities. The first and perhaps most accessible type of narrative deals with story- or myth-inspired imagery; in this instance the retelling of ancient Greek myths or a Bible story. Another type of narrative (and perhaps more suitable for Chapter Ten) — is that which concerns issues of human behaviour, morals and our interaction with one another. In these stories, human figures are often combined with gestures and abstract symbols that might provoke a thought response in the viewer.

These particular studies of human behaviour are of course already familiar to us from the Greek myths. In Figure 56, I retell the story of Atalanta and Hippomenes (another Renaissance *istoriato* version of this story occurs on page 219, in the book's Conclusion). In the myth, the proud and undefeated princess Atalanta obliges prospective bridegrooms to race her. The losing of the race culminates in their death. However, the wily Hippomenes deliberately lets fall three golden balls during the course of the race, and greedy Atalanta, in stooping to retrieve them, loses the race and is obliged to marry (perhaps not the very best foundation for a happy marriage, in my view . . .).

MATTHIAS OSTERMANN
(Canada)

FIGURE 56 (left)
Wall plate, *Atalanta and Hippomenes*, 2002.
Slab-built earthenware with maiolica glaze, painted and smudged stains and sgraffito, fired in oxidation,
25 x 25cm (10 x 10in.).
Courtesy of Prime Gallery, Toronto
Photograph: Jan Thijs

FIGURE 57 (right)
Vessel, *Circë*, 2004.
Thrown and distorted earthenware with vitreous engobes and copper sgraffito, fired in oxidation, ht: 20cm (8in.).
Courtesy of Prime Gallery, Toronto
Photograph: Jan Thijs

MATTHIAS OSTERMANN
(Canada)

FIGURE 58
Plate, *Adam and Eve*, 2004.
Slab-built earthenware with
coloured vitreous engobes
and copper sgraffito, fired in
oxidation, w: 25cm (10in.).

Photograph: Jan Thijs

Figure 57 retells the story of Odysseus' landing on the Island of Aeaea, the home of the sorceress Circë. Beguiling the tired mariners with a feast, she transforms them into beasts (perhaps those which lurk in every man). Odysseus alone resists her magic by the use of an herb called *moly*, given to him by the god Hermes. He obliges Circë to undo the magic and restore his men to their natural forms. This she does, and in friendship sends Odysseus and his men onward on their long and troubled journey home.

Figure 58 recounts the familiar story of 'Adam and Eve', although in perhaps a more terse form than the innocent English delftware image portrayed in Figure 26 (see page 76), or the more tender version seen in Figure 59 (see page 125). Nonetheless, I do believe that these ancient narratives can still be read as contemporary parables for our own times.

Sigrid Hilpert-Artes – *Germany*

Hilpert-Artes, apart from her work as a ceramicist, is also a painter whose skills are much sought after in the restoration of old frescoes.

My mother was a painter, and I grew up with many artists in the city of Dresden, in itself a beautiful place, full of great treasures. All of this encouraged

SIGRID HILPERT-ARTES
(Germany)

FIGURE 59 (left)
Coffee pot, *Adam and Eve*, 2003.
Wheel-thrown earthenware with maiolica glaze and painted oxides, fired in oxidation, ht: 25cm (10in.).

FIGURE 60 (right)
Fish Jar with Venus, 2003.
Thrown, altered and modelled earthenware with maiolica glaze and painted oxides, fired in reduction, w: 30cm (11¾in.).
Both photographs: Martin Schreiber

me to be perpetually drawing and to choose a career in the visual arts. Painting seemed less practical than potting, so ceramic studies took precedence, and maiolica happily combines the two.

Some of the things that touch and inspire me are Arabian fairytales — lively, erotic and delicate; ethnic fabrics and carpets and wood carvings; stones, insects, butterflies and all kinds of plants; and the painters Matisse, Chagall, Picasso and Gauguin. All of these serve as food for inspiration. I have no desire to portray darker contemporary realities — the daily media surely provide us with enough of those. I would prefer to counterbalance them with optimisic and uplifting imagery, with narratives that can evoke the past as well as more eternal themes.

Figure 59 depicts the theme of love and union, but this time in reference to the ever-popular theme of 'Adam and Eve.' In *Fish Jar with Venus* (Figure 60) we see the goddess of love being transported on the back of a fish toward the shore. This image might echo the famous Botticelli painting *The Birth of Venus*, where the goddess is being carried to land on a seashell.

Contemporary Narratives:

Re-shaped Icons and New Idioms

8

T he ceramic objects presented here make strong reference to 20th- and 21st-century icons, or popular cultural imagery. In a way this predisposes most of this work to echo Chapter Eleven's theme of political and social commentary, but I feel that here these references are less direct, and that the intent of the narrator is rather to re-invent and rework popular cultural themes of our times to create a new thought-provoking genre of imagery expressing relevant ideas. These ideas might have a political bias, but might also incorporate themes of memory and personal history, reflecting the artists' own experience. Once again, I feel that these descriptive categories can remain somewhat fluid, and that an interesting study of comparison and cross-reference between this and other chapters could be made.

John de Fazio – United States

Much of my artwork draws from childhood memories of a poor working-class factory town, fuelled by canned spaghetti, Philly cheesecakes, candy, television, violence, Religion and Bad Art. Dominated by a strict Italian Catholic tradition, our home contained a crucifix in every room and Technicolour illustrations of bloody Martyred Saints sharing the pain of poverty.

De Fazio relates that in his childhood in the late 1960s and early 1970s he often passed by a neighbourhood 'kitsch' factory, selling moulds for 'do-it-yourself' painting. There were Liberty Bells and Betsy Ross for July 4th; shamrocks and elves for St. Patrick's Day; hearts and cupids for St. Valentine's Day; Baby Jesus

OPPOSITE PAGE

JOHN DE FAZIO (United States)

FIGURE 61
Sculpture, *Pop Tombstone*, 1996.
Handbuilt and slipcast earthenware with multi-fired glazes, china paints and decals, fired in oxidation, 116 x 60 x 35cm (45⅔ x 23⅔ x 13¾in.).
Photograph courtesy of Banff Arts Centre

JOHN DE FAZIO (United States)

FIGURE 62
Sculpture, *Dada Throne*,
2001.
100 slipcast and glazed
objects attached with
epoxy to a new pink
toilet from Home Depot,
127 x 76 x 81cm
(50 x 30 x 32in.).
Photograph: Joe Major

nativity dioramas, Santa Clauses for Christmas, and so on. He spent years tracking down old and dusty moulds for re-use in the assembly of his composite sculptural imagery. He states quite simply that 'this codified vocabulary of sentimental objects, both sacred and profane, served as aggregates for my sculpture'.

Figure 61, *Pop Tombstone*, was created during a three-month residency at the Banff Arts Centre in Canada, and explores the topic of pop, mass- and sub-culture.

> My initial idea was to pun the word 'headstone' by combining a typically shaped gravestone with a detachable head on top, cast from a medical school autopsy mannequin. The head on this 'tombstone' resembles the crushed head of the heroic cyborg Arnold Schwarzenegger from the sci-fi classic 'Terminator 2.' Half a head in profile on the front slab reveals the skin peeled back, with the bottom jaw removed to show tongue and taste buds. Only the ear and the eyeball remain intact for use in the afterlife, and a decorative display of roses on the skull serves as a toupee.
>
> Caspar the Friendly Ghost with a third eye of enlightenment floats playfully around both sides of the sculpture as guardian. Providing sustenance for the afterlife is an Angelic Bottle of Coke, a universal symbol of refreshment, and decal of a Budweiser beer label symbol, a cheap high. A decal image of Jesus and Mary stretch over the base, then reappear on a smaller scale, implying an Ascension of prayers while alluding to mass-produced Christian iconography.

Dada Throne (as seen in Figure 62) was commissioned by Garth Clark in 1994 as part of a charity benefit to commemorate the original *Dada Ball* by Marcel Duchamp nearly a century ago, at the same location of Webster Hall in New York. De Fazio's idea was to create a tribute to Duchamp's notorious 'Fountain' exhibit at the Armoury Show of 1917. This work caused a revolution in the art world at that time by demanding that a ready-made toilet should be viewed as 'art'.

In describing the contrast in concept between the white, sanitised Duchamp toilet with his own excessively-encrusted-with-souvenirs toilet (albeit still functional), de Fazio states: 'I wanted it to appear that a mysterious magnetic force was attracting the various ceramic detritus of Pop culture into a suicidal gesture of elimination. I also wanted the sculpture to appear as an exuberant Baroque Throne depicting tripping Pop mythologies for an MTV generation'.

Léopold L. Foulem – *Canada*

> Usually heroes, gods, and goddesses represented in art and artefacts are unknown to today's uninitiated viewer. However, it is likely that when they were made, a good number of people could recognise them at once. Santa Claus and Colonel Sanders are used as substitutes for long forgotten personages.

LÉOPOLD L. FOULEM (Canada)

FIGURE 63 (left)
Mille Fleurs Effigy Stirrup Vessel in the Form of Santa Claus, 2002.
Slab-built and pressmoulded earthenware, with commercial glazes, fired in oxidation, 33 x 15 x 21cm
(13 x 6 x 8¼ in.).
Courtesy of Galerie Lieu Ouest, Montreal
Photograph: Pierre Gauvin

FIGURE 64 (right)
Santa and the Colonel as Wedding Cake Decorations, 2002.
Slab-built and pressmoulded earthenware with commercial glazes, oxidation, 33 x 21 x 14.2cm
(12¾ x 8½ x 5½in.).
Courtesy of Prime Gallery, Toronto
Photograph: Pierre Gauvin

These figures taken from popular culture actualise the content of the pieces and turn upside down the hierarchy of importance and the status of icons. The ceramic narrative is emphasised by the appropriation of prototypes and the idiosyncrasies proper to ceramics per se.

Mille Fleurs Effigy Stirrup Vessel in the Form of Santa Claus (Figure 63) transposes the popular Christmas icon to an existing vessel prototype, namely the ancient Moche stirrup spout bottle. The over-the-top floral decoration might well be an allusion to tasteless 1960s' fabric patterns, or *millefiori* (mille fleurs) might be a visual and word pun referring to coloured *millefiori* glass techniques, or brightly coloured candies.

Figure 64, *Santa and the Colonel as Wedding Cake Decorations*, combines two popular 20th-century icons and evokes the lavish (and again over-the-top) decorations of traditional North American wedding cakes.

Ole Lislerud – *Norway*

The *Graffiti Wall: God is Woman* at Oslo University's Faculty of Divinity (see Figure 65) is described by artist Ole Lislerud as follows:

Graffiti texts or one-liners are quick and to the point, creating an emotional, philosophical or political counterpoint in contrast to what can be expected from academia. The graffiti texts at Domus Theologica (the Faculty of Divinity) are related to religion in one way or the other.... 'Everybody wants to go to heaven, but nobody wants to die' ... 'live until you die' ... 'www.jesusonline.com' ... Others are more provocative: 'Was Mary raped', ... 'Jesus loves the little children — is he a pedophile?'...

The *Graffiti Wall* project includes an LCD flat-screen monitor that enables students to be online with God at all times, and also to receive updated daily information from the University administration. *Graffiti Wall* represents the secular world and is a visual contrast to the intellectual studies at the Divinity Faculty. In terms of contextualising new theology, the *Graffiti Wall* is a reminder of the real world outside of academia.

The *Graffiti Wall* is an abstract composition with texts and calligraphy. The composition also deals with issues of information and identity. By combining computer icons with tagging and airbrush techniques, a visual expression dealing with protests was created. The composition represents a mixture of contradicting information with statements and questions without any answers.

One of the dominant elements in the composition is the text 'God is Woman' and the airbrushed image of Marilyn Monroe. She is the ultimate female icon of the 20th century and a natural choice to symbolise the female God.

OLE LISLERUD (Norway)

FIGURE 65
Graffiti Wall: God is Woman, 2000.
Pressmoulded porcelain tiles, PhotoShop-processed silk-screened imagery and air-brushing, fired in oxidation, 50sq. m (538sq. ft).
Courtesy of University of Oslo
Photograph: Glen Hagbru

DANIEL KRUGER (Germany)

FIGURE 66
Dinner service, *Maria Callas*,
2000.
Drape-moulded earthenware
with third-firing transfers and
lustres, fired in oxidation.

Photograph: Eva Jünger

Daniel Kruger – *Germany*

This dinner service made in 2000 [see Figure 66] consists of 6 dinner plates, 6 fish plates, 6 soup plates, 6 side plates, 6 desert bowls, 1 large oval platter, 2 small oval platters, 2 dishes, and 2 covered dishes. Each individual object has a different image. The bottom/outside surfaces are glazed ox-blood red, the inner surfaces are glazed white, and the decor is deep pink, with black china paints, burnished gold, and transfer images.

It is an homage to Maria Callas, the last diva of the opera. The pictures are taken from newspapers and magazines. They document her in the roles she made famous and her glamorous social appearances. Ox-blood red, gold and black, pink and white — the colours of the opera stage, of passion and of sensuality.

We remember her uniqueness as an artist and as a personality that tolerated no one at her side, uncompromising in all respects, and the glory and solitude that these standards bring with them. Her little dog 'Toy' remains her faithful companion and is the one figure that accompanies her. As on the tomb of a mediaeval Lady, he guards over her memory and symbolises her allegiance and service to art.

Bill Stewart – *United States*

These are narrative pieces created utilising assembled information obtained from innumerable sources over an extended period of time. Images may be derived from or contain, in some convoluted way, social, political, or social commentary or they may be strictly fictional, a total product of my imagination.

The piece tells a story. The story has no beginning or end, it exists somewhere in between. An observer can move forward or backward, up and down. A non-linear chronology exists, a jigsaw puzzle that must be assembled. The pieces are fragmentary, they consist of some objects and images that are not totally or easily recognisable. A hypersensitive surface forces the viewer to absorb much more information than under normal circumstances. The story can be narrated or observed on a visceral level.

Body decoration and costuming relative to popular and primal cultures has provided the foundation for some of my work [see Figure 67]. Ideas obtained from objects such as toys, games and a variety of new and primitive artefacts are occasionally salvaged and used as source material and assimilated into the work [see Figure 68]. I am particularly fascinated by images and objects produced by children, folk- and outsider-artists. Their ability to communicate without being encumbered by skill and technique, yet with such honesty and passion, is exemplary.

This assimilated information integrated with a working approach based on intuition and a spontaneous response to the magic of the imagination, hopefully produces objects that have an eccentric energy. The objects are somewhat on the edge; off centre, humorous, weird, absurd or irreverent.

BILL STEWART (United States)

FIGURE 67 (below left)
Sculpture, *Man Balancing a Greek Vase*, 2000.
Handbuilt and moulded earthenware with multiple-fired slips and glazes, fired in oxidation, 71 x 23 x 76cm (28 x 9 x 30in.).
Photograph: Bruce Miller

FIGURE 68 (below)
Sculpture, *Off to See the Wizard*, 2001.
Handbuilt and moulded earthenware with multiple-fired slips and glazes, fired in oxidation, 109 x 63 x 43cm (43 x 25 x 17in.).
Photograph: Bruce Miller

Richard Milette – *Canada*

Ceramicist and author Léopold L. Foulem describes the work of Richard Milette as follows:

> Richard Milette has been re-examining prototypical Greek vessels in various series of works for more than a decade. Not only does he question again the

RICHARD MILETTE (Canada)

FIGURE 69
Vessel, *Bilingual Pelike*, 1996.
Pressmoulded, thrown and
handbuilt earthenware with
coloured glazes, fired in
oxidation, 51.5 x 28.5 x 28.5cm
(10¼ x 11¼ x 11¼in.).

Photograph: Raymonde Bergeron

'museum status' of broken Greek pots, but also the notion, role, and value of narration in art. Milette's appropriated 'Classical' Greek forms have now lost their 'true' (real) historical narrative content because the original storytelling image (the 'art') has been painted over, and therefore erased. The theatrical arena, the territory where the 'real narrative' based on recognisable representations was initially located, has now been invaded by a discontinuous text [see Figure 69]. By cutting text and words randomly, both lose their veritable meaning, thus annulling the narrative.

The artist is not here replacing images with words, as was the case in one of his previous series, 'Words of Love and Hate' (1994). Rather, he stresses the fact that narrative and content are neither synonymous nor interchangeable. When Robert Rauschenberg erased De Kooning's drawing, it was an iconoclastic gesture. Milette's erasure is as political, but probably not as nihilistic. He does not totally destroy the icon itself, so much as drastically modifying the status of the narrative.

By abstracting the most fetishist part of Classical Greek vases, and treating the framed area where the myths (tales) are painted as a palimpsest, the artist takes over both the art of painting and the craft of pottery. The vessel becomes a whole where all parts are components of equal importance. The ceramic object must now be re-evaluated for its own merit. In the recontextualisation process, the neo-Greek vase has now become the image of itself.

Russel Biles – *United States*

My narrative ceramic sculpture is satirical in nature. To support this perspective I rely on a high level of craft. I've always appreciated and respected craft and it's ability to transcend culture and social class, thus appealing to a broad audience. Another aspect of my work that appeals to a broad audience is my visual narrative. This narrative is influenced by my fascination with the written word, TV and film. Like the aforementioned, I use our culture's obsession with celebrity to engage the audience and to tell my story.

I grew up in a small Bible Belt town where ceramic figurines were my only exposure to sculpture. To honour this significant influence I created a body of figurines. The 'Seed Receptor' series comprises four of these figurines [see Figures 70 and 71]. This series is based on the biblical belief that the redemption of women in our culture is founded on their ability to procreate. The two [out of four] biblical women represented here are from the lineage of the Christian Messiah mentioned in the first Book of Matthew (1:3-7). The function of these women was to perpetuate the lineage of King David. Coincidentally they all had questionable erotic experiences while achieving this function.

I first chose women of celebrity that I admired for their struggles and triumphs

RUSSEL BILES (United States)

FIGURE 70 (left)
Sculpture, 'Seed Receptors' series; *Rahab (Judy Garland)*, 2001.
Coiled and modelled earthenware with underglazes and transparent glaze, fired in oxidation,
42 x 13 x 18cm
(16½ x 5 x 7in.).
Courtesy of Leslie Ferrin Gallery, Lenox, Massachusetts.
Photograph: Tim Barnwell

FIGURE 71 (right)
Sculpture, 'Seed Receptors' series; *Ruth (Josephine Baker)*, 2001.
Coiled and modelled earthenware with underglazes and transparent glaze, fired in oxidation,
43 x 20 x 20cm
(17 x 7¾ x 7¾in.).
Courtesy of Leslie Ferrin Gallery, Lenox, Massachusetts
Photograph: Tim Barnwell

to portray in a contemporary context. Next I redeemed them through reproduction and safeguarded them with cherubs. Each woman processes a Christian icon and is depicted with references to her biblical counterpart. The flower portrayed is from the mandrake plant, which is traditionally known as an aphrodisiac and is mentioned in the Bible.

Keiko Fukazawa – United States

Originally from Tokyo, Fukazawa received her BFA in painting from Musashino Art University in Tokyo, and her MFA in ceramics from Otis/Parsons School of Art in Los Angeles in 1986. Under the grants from the California Arts Council, Fukazawa has taught ceramics in the California State Prison system for more than eight years, and perhaps her dedication to this work has shaped her personal work more than any other force. Fukazawa describes the act of literally breaking her vessels as her way of escaping traditional limitations of form and process. She describes this collaborative body of work, as seen in Figure 72, as follows:

This artwork is from the series called 'Art & Deviation' which was based on the collaborative effort between juvenile inmates within a correctional institution and myself. Fusing ceramics with the aesthetics of graffiti, the project was designed to bring to the foreground the voices of incarcerated young adults through their writing and graffiti. These works are an original and authentic collaboration with incarcerated gang members.

The bisque ware is broken and given to inmates to write their stories or to create images. I then add my work to the remaining pieces. All pieces are reassembled into a 'Reborn Piece'. The glue holding the broken shards serves as a metaphor for the kids from broken homes trying to hold their lives together. The act of breaking a mould is also a metaphor for those inmates attempting to break the mould of their old reality and to find positive and creative ways of representing themselves.

KEIKO FUKAZAWA (United States)

FIGURE **72**
Plate, *Nothing Lasts Forever*, 2000.
Broken and re-assembled white stoneware bisque shards, with oil-based marker painting, ceramic glue, and polyurethane coating, dia: 69cm (27⅛in.).
Photograph: Anthony Cunha

STEPHEN DIXON (United Kingdom)

FIGURE 73
Vessel, *Apocalypsis*, 2000.
Slab-built and modelled
T-material clay with slips,
transparent glaze, in- and
onglaze photocopy decals,
fired in oxidation,
51 x 39 x 30cm
(20 x 15⅓ x 11¾ in.).
Photograph: Joel C. Fildes

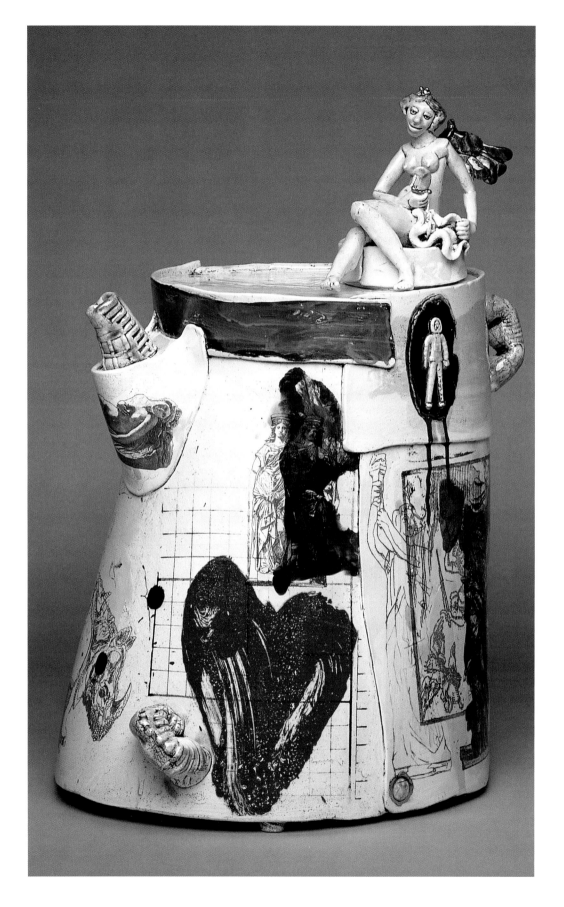

Stephen Dixon — *United Kingdom*

Garth Clark, in *The Potter's Art* (Phaidon Press, 1995) comments upon this artist's work:

> Dixon's subject matter is political, and seeks to make sense of the anarchy he finds around him. His strongest inspiration comes from the figurative art of the German Expressionists, as well as from the political satirists of the mass media.

In his own words, Stephen Dixon describes the motivation behind his work, as seen in Figure 73:

> The vessel *Apocalypsis* represents a body of work which explores the universal theme of 'Beauty and the Beast', using both visual and literary metaphors. The figurative/narrative elements within the work seek to examine the duality of human nature, to question our attitudes and values, and to challenge assumptions of the moral superiority of contemporary Western society.
>
> Adorning these ceramic forms, iconic images of Classical sculpture rub shoulders with 'pop' and media imagery, contrasting the high and low points of a culture equally capable of producing the Renaissance and the Holocaust, the Sistine Chapel and the cluster bomb. The vessel itself embodies an additional metaphor, referencing the forms and textures of oil barrels and petrol cans, alluding to the focus of current global conflicts.
>
> *Apocalypsis* examines attitudes to war and warfare, mixing the familiar Winged Victory of the war memorial with apocalyptic visions of the Four Horsemen, Star Wars and the sugary sentimentalism of the valentine heart.

Matt Nolen — *United States*

> I grew up in Alabama, the land of azaleas, fried green tomatoes and George Wallace. I consider myself to be primarily a storyteller, and attribute my growth and development in this regard to the rich tradition of oral and written storytelling in the South.
>
> It was clear to me from the beginning that my two loves, architecture and painting, could be married through ceramics. My pots are for me 'rooms' in clay where issues of function become integral to the process of making, as they do in the designing and making of architecture. Painting on a three-dimensional ceramic form and the fusion of the surface to that form through fire, proved to be an infinitely more dynamic, challenging, and rewarding process than the flat, square canvas could provide.

MATT NOLEN (United States)

FIGURE 74 (below)
Detail (three sinks) of a functioning men's restroom for the John Michael Kohler Arts Center, *The Social History of Architecture*, 1998–99.
Slipcast tiles and fixtures of vitreous china clay, with onglaze painting, double firing in oxidation,
w: 270cm (9ft),
l: 7.2m (24ft),
ht: 4.2m (14ft).
Courtesy of John Michael Kohler Arts Center

OPPOSITE PAGE

FIGURE 75
Detail of restroom (three urinals).

Sources of inspiration have come from ceramic history: the pots of ancient Greece, Italian Renaissance maiolica, the 18th-century porcelains of Sèvres and Meissen. The works of Giotto, Matisse, and of such surrealists as de Chirico and Magritte have moved and inspired me as well.

The theme for *The Social History of Architecture*, a men's restroom for the John Michael Kohler Arts Center in Wisconsin (see Figures 74 and 75), is described by artist Matt Nolen as follows:

Restroom users experience going back in time through a narrative history of architecture beginning with modernism just inside the door, to ancient Egypt in the back of the space. A social history of man is also related through text and images that appear in the sinks, urinals and toilets that occur in each 'architectural zone.' Each restroom user assumes the identity of the highest male role model for each period, as each fixture is carefully labelled with the appropriate title: e.g., CEO for modernism, PHARAOH for ancient Egypt, etc.

A frieze of text from Goethe wraps around the entire space uniting the social history with the built form of historical architecture: 'Whatever you can do or dream you can — begin it, for boldness has genius, power and magic in it.'

Contemporary Narratives:

Personal Visions, Private Stories and Memory

T he narratives examined in this chapter are perhaps the most intimate. As the chapter heading suggests, the ceramic images presented here are reflections of the artists' own lives and experiences, stories they tell about themselves. Some stories deal with the theme of inner growth and conflict, and as such are more autobiographical in nature. Yet other narratives tend to be more idea-based, extrapolating upon personal histories, events and memory, and placing these into a broader human context. Much of the imagery in this chapter can be related to Chapter Ten, since it predominately portrays human figure imagery, and that portrayal is the most potent of all when it comes to self-revelation and self-exposure. I feel that this may also be considered the most courageous work on the part of any artist, since it demands great introspection and a public sharing of very private information.

Anne Kraus – United States

Garth Clark makes the following observations in his catalogue entitled *Anne Kraus: A Survey*:

> Not all of Kraus' works are dark in their content, but many cut into the psyche with the quickness and sharpness of a scalpel. The drawings and texts present narratives — some complete and some fragmented like jagged shards — that deal with private moments, the hauntings of past failures, the exhaustion of hope and the bitterness of rejection. What redeem the works is that they are not nihilist. There is always a commitment to survival: a tiny glimmer of light at the end of the darkest corridor, or a door slightly ajar that suggests relief or respite.

OPPOSITE PAGE

ANNE KRAUS (United States)

FIGURE 76
Tile panel, *I Can't Sleep*, 1998.
Painted underglaze stains under transparent glaze, whiteware, fired in oxidation, 74.9 x 54.5cm (29½ x 21½in.).
Courtesy of Garth Clark Gallery, New York
Photograph: Noel Allum

ANNE KRAUS (United States)

FIGURE **77**

Teapot, *I Look for a Door*,
1999.
Painted underglaze stains
under transparent glaze,
whiteware, fired in oxidation,
ht: 23.5cm (9¼in.),
w. 27.9cm (11in.).
Courtesy of Garth Clark Gallery, New York
Photograph: Anthony Cunha

Other works approach life more philosophically and objectively. They are neither optimistic nor pessimistic. They are the observations of a poet who wrestles with life and at times finds islands of calm and perspective. But these perspectives are not linear. They take their shape mainly from dreams so there is always a surrealist edge and a trafficking in symbol and metaphor. One first reads them and then passes through the drawings into landscapes and events. What the viewer draws from the work may be different to what the artist intends; it is, nevertheless, difficult to spend time with one of these pieces and come away unmoved or unchanged in some way. [...]

The large tulip vases, oversize teapots [see Figure 77] and other over-scaled pieces do not encourage [...] hands-on contact. In these works, Kraus deals with a more sculptural, shrine-like presence. In the latest *trompe l'oeil* tile panels, she creates idealized settings for her bowls, vases and jars [see Figure 76]. This allows her to extend the environment that her art inhabits, sealing her carefully orchestrated world of objects and emotions in clay and glaze.

Edward S. Eberle – United States

Eberle discusses the inspiration and content of his work as follows, as seen in Figures 78 and 79:

Generally, my work is about bringing together my love of form and drawing. The painting and the form are interdependent, supporting each other. The content or subject matter largely comes by way of a stream-of-consciousness process where one thing leads to another. The materials and the process allow the intermingling to take form. The work contains matters of imagination, soul, the collective unconscious, symbology, mythology, the unknown, dynamic symmetry, pattern, the human condition, birth-life-death, past-present-future, texture, and so on.

A press release from Garth Clark Gallery in New York provides further insight into Eberle's narrative imagery and influences:

> The artist's voluminous, lidded porcelain vessels draw vague allusions to houses and architecture. His elaborate sgraffito imagery narrates, with lively parades of people, the interior life of his 'houses'. Eberle's imagery fluctuates deftly between tonal representation of bodies in space, and graphic surface pattern that serves to reinforce the pot's formal structure. Many influences can be found in his work from the black and white Mimbres pottery to painting and decoration on early Greek vases. Eberle directs the eye between the lavish, lyrical narrative imagery, and the two-dimensional line of the form they move around.

EDWARD S. EBERLE (United States)

FIGURE 78 (left)
Vessel, *Black Water*, 2000. Black-and-white painted terra sigillata, porcelain, fired in reduction, 43 x 43cm (17 x 17in.).
Collection: Sprint Art Collection
Courtesy of Garth Clark Gallery, New York
Photograph: Edward S. Eberle

FIGURE 79 (right)
Vessel, *Added Trio*, 2001. Black-and-white painted terra sigillata, porcelain, fired in reduction, ht: 70cm (24in.), w: 45.7cm (18in.).
Courtesy of Garth Clark Gallery, New York
Photograph: Edward S. Eberle

NEIL BROWNSWORD (United
Kingdom)

FIGURE 80 (left)
Sculpture, *Drifting in Circles*,
2003.
Thrown, hand-formed and
cast components with metal
armature and epoxy, varied
clays and glazes, fired in
oxidation, ht: 39cm (15½in.).
Photograph: Neil Brownsword

FIGURE 81 (right)
Sculpture, *Something So
Pure Just Can't Function No
More*, 2003.
Thrown, hand-formed and
cast components with metal
armature and epoxy, varied
clays and glazes, fired in
oxidation, ht: 43cm (17in.).
Photograph: Neil Brownsword

Neil Brownsword – *United Kingdom*

The reason why clay continues to be a medium central to my creativity is deeply rooted within my personal history. Being born in Stoke-on-Trent and raised in neighbouring Newcastle Under Lyme, it was difficult to ignore the fact that the ceramic industry was a key source of employment for the majority of the local populace. The surrounding landscape, which bears the scars of hundreds of years of industrial activity, has remained embedded in memory since childhood. Spoil heaps from the collieries, which supplied fuel to the pottery kilns, and marl pits from which clay has been mined, litter the area. Nineteenth-century factories still stand, and in some cases are still working; there is a constant reminder that this was a great centre for pottery production that paralleled China. Family and friends have or still work in the ceramic industry. At sixteen, I was apprenticed at the Wedgwood factory initially as a trainee mould maker.

Working in a factory of this magnitude and experiencing the futility of some peoples' working lives has, and to a large extent still does, influence the concepts behind my narrative structures. The objects are a form of social documentary, and try to articulate through gesture, title and symbolism personal situations witnessed first hand [see Figures 80 and 81].

A compulsion to convey emotional experience through object making, has been fundamental to my creative practice. Subject matter has tended to draw upon many aspects of human anxiety; low self-esteem, disillusionment with the lack of control we are able to register upon our lives, and flawed expectations of relationships. Dealing with issues like these not only serves as a means of catharsis, it helps to concentrate my need to question and reinforce a deeper understanding of why these intimate feelings arise. This embodiment of emotion has frequently manifested itself in a semi-figurative guise, in the hope that recognisable gestures will extend the empathy of others. Narrative structures are also poignantly outlined and made accessible through titling — often inspired by the lyrics of pop songs, these seem to succinctly encapsulate the thoughts aroused.

JEANNIE MAH (Canada)

FIGURE 82
Vessel installation, *Revolution and Family: From Mao's House to Our House*, 2001. Slab-constructed porcelain with photo transfers, fired in oxidation, 152 x 30.5 x 61cm (59¾ x 12 x 24in.).
Courtesy of Art Gallery of Calgary.
Photograph: Edward Jones

Jeannie Mah – *Canada*

The exhibition 'Cineramics' in 2001 allowed me to indulge in my greatest loves — cinema, museums, and travelling. By using family and holiday photos on parchment-like porcelain, I approach social history, family

history, and ceramic history, by way of cinema. Snapshots on pots arranged on a mantle, are given 'meaning through montage'. I have borrowed my methodology from Russian film-maker and theorist Sergei Eisenstein, who believed that if two images were seen one after the other, we will make an intellectual connection; Christian Metz added that we will create a narrative. My subjective narrative is held together by ideas about art, cinema, history, and ceramics.

This work [see Figure 82] makes references to geographical sites, but such sites and metaphorical distances are traversed by way of montage and imagination. My 'essays in perspective' refer to acts of seeing, but also to our relationship with social history and iconography.

Revolution and Family: From Mao's House to Our House, shows photos of my father and brothers in front of our family grocery store and home in Regina, Canada, and of my parents as tourists in front of the house where Mao was born in China. They are flanked by photos of the paintings of Mao by Andy Warhol, in museums in New York and St. Etienne, France, where I am a tourist. Onto floral patterned Song-like celadons, I usurp the troupe of Chinese people on pots, as seen on Export wares, and replace the palatial vistas with common family photos, to make visible the influences of politics and economics on the migration patterns of people and ceramics over the centuries.

Thomas Werneke – *Germany*

My father was passionate about the great storytellers and encouraged us children to be lucid and inventive in our own narrative efforts. We studied Homer and Ovid in their original versions and I grew up with the idea of the narrative as 'a linear progression'.

We moved to the country, and I spent long roving afternoons becoming a dreamer with eyes wide-open. We were constantly drawing – in cafés and parks during the summer, and in museums during the winter. Face to face with the works of the Michoaca Indians, the Yoruba potters, and great Renaissance sculptors, I discovered even beyond their religious and mythological content, the joys and pleasures of both making and storytelling.

I dream in clay. I do not necessarily create 'stories' in the strict sense, but rather three-dimensional 'frozen moments' that might allude to a narrative in the context of broader life experiences. The viewer can then respond and extrapolate from his or her own experiences, and the viewed narratives can become highly intimate and personal [see Figures 83 and 84].

My figures often seem to evoke a sense of loneliness in the crowd, the expectation of something sought-for and forever elusive, perhaps the desire for communication, for sharing, and for community.

Thomas Werneke (Germany)

FIGURE 83 (above)
Installation, untitled, 2003.
Earthenware with painted
slips and sgraffito, fired in
oxidation, 20 x 40 x 12cm
(8 x 15¾ x 4¾in.).
Photograph: Toni Ott

FIGURE 84 (left)
Installation, untitled, 2004.
Earthenware with painted
slips and sgraffito, sawdust
and electric firing, fired in
oxidation and reduction,
25 x 50cm (10 x 20in.).
Photograph: Toni Ott

149

ANITA MCINTYRE (Australia)

FIGURE 85
Vessel, *Kimberley Boat*, 2001.
Pressmoulded earthenware
with sgraffito through
transferred slips, bone china
and terra sigillata, fired in
oxidation, 38 x 20 x 6.5cm
(15 x 8 x 2½in.).
Photograph: Wendy Lamb

Anita McIntyre – Australia

I first came to clay as a medium from a painting background, and my first tentative works were in the nature of sculptural forms. As I studied further and gained an understanding of the medium, I was fascinated by the scope of expression inherent in the material, and the diversity of objects that could be created, from the domestic to the sculptural.

In 1999 my husband and I travelled in the far North Kimberly region of Western Australia and spent some time with an indigenous family. The impact of this experience on my work has been significant. From abstract pictograms, my work has moved to incorporate a strong narrative element that continues to inform my practice [see Figure 85].

The family led us to many good fishing spots near where we were camped. One memorable experience was when the head of the family and his six grandsons travelled to an island three hours distant from their camp to hunt for turtles. The group was caught by the tide and did not return until the following day.

They had caught two very large turtles and a smaller one. The latter was released and the others were cooked and offered to us for dinner. This caused a serious cultural dilemma for my husband and myself. It was considered a great honour to be offered turtle meat: as a token of esteem and recognition of the friendship between us and our indigenous hosts, and as a source of great pride to the hunters in demonstrating their skill and hunting prowess. On the other hand, the death of these wonderful creatures was not something easily accepted by ecologically conscious white Australians from an urban background. Nevertheless we ate the gift and shared the hunters' pride in their catch.

When we returned to Canberra the imperative to express this experience in my work was such that I developed the boat form both graphically and sculpturally, as an image and form that evoked memory, place and the intersection of cultures.

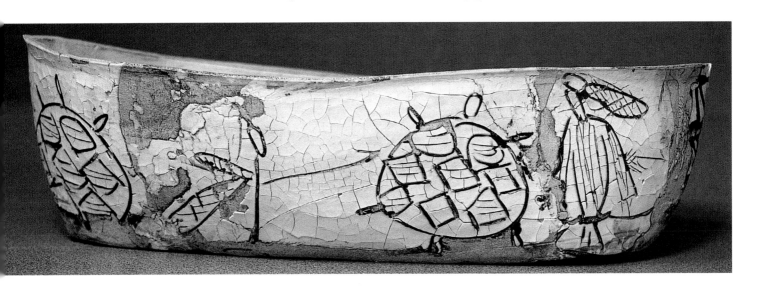

Cindy Kolodziejski – *United States*

My work is an attempt at bending the boundaries of Western decorative arts, ceramic tradition, painting, and good taste for the purpose of inducing complex narratives. Some of the conventions I play with include various periods of Western Art from Classical to baroque to contemporary. While I see value in violating conventions, doing so in the service of psychological narratives is the essence of my work. My medium exists between painting, ceramics, and sculpture, aiming at a kind of conceptual drama. I work with composite forms, imagery, and implied narratives, pushing these into the realm of extremes. I have always felt that painting on traditional two-dimensional canvases was too limiting for my ideas of expression, and found the curvaceousness of the vessel body a more accommodating form. I have currently been exploring vintage chemistry glass forms and their metal support structures. These forms I have slipcast into clay and underglaze paint images as diverse as landscapes, human organs, or pelvic bones that appear to float inside the vessels like pickled specimens. I enjoy these forms and the myriad of associations that develop when combining art and science.

CINDY KOLODZIEJSKI (United States)

FIGURE 86 (left)
Sculpture, untitled, 2001. Slipcast earthenware with underglaze painting, transparent glaze and mixed media support, fired in oxidation, 72.4 x 27.9 x 16.5cm (28½ x 11 x 6½ in.).
Photograph: Anthony Cunha

FIGURE 87 (right)
Sculpture, *Crane-Necked Separatory Funnel*, 2002. Slipcast earthenware with underglaze painting, transparent glaze and mixed media support, fired in oxidation, 66 x 22.8 x 27.9cm (26 x 9 x 11in.).
Courtesy of Frank Lloyd Gallery, Santa Monica
Photograph: Anthony Cunha

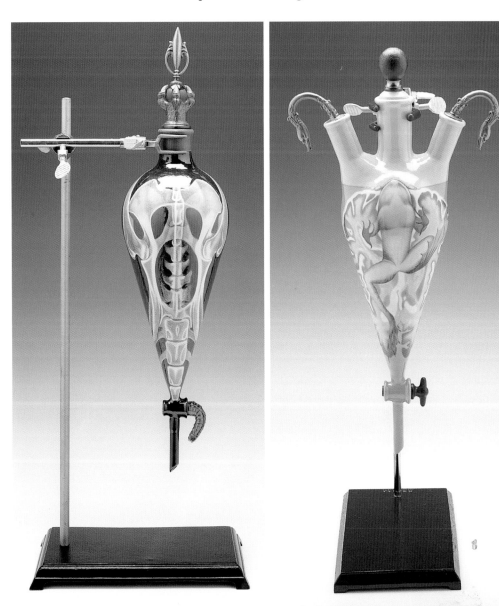

The untitled image with elongated skull [as seen in Figure 86] shows an image of a dog skull. The shape of the skull and the separatory vessel are similar and the skull can seem suspended within the shape. I like the play of the X-ray image of the skull and the abstractions that occur within that image, abstractions that can look like trees in the woods, among other things. There is also the obvious association with death and a skull image. What I find appealing is that a dog skull is not so easily recognisable, and although one knows it is a skull one is not certain what kind it is.

Crane Necked Separatory Funnel [Figure 87], shows an image of a frog swimming to the surface of a liquid and taking air. Behind the frog is a sliced section of a brain. The colors of the brain are orange and purple and are recognisable as a brain but also seen as an abstract painting. The separatory funnel shape suggests a scientific process and the association of the thousands of frogs being dissected in the name of science.

Kurt Weiser – United States

For years the work I did in ceramics was an effort to somehow express the beautiful nature of the material. As interesting as this exploration was, I always had the vague feeling that the best expression of the material only came as a gift of nature — problem was, nature and I never got along that well. Somewhere in the midst of this struggle I realised that the materials are there to allow you to say what you need to say, not to tell you what to say. So I gave up trying to control nature and decided to use what I had learned about the materials to express some ideas about nature itself and my place in it.

The ideas and subjects of these paintings on the pots are for the most part just a collection of my own fantasies, built the same way we dream — a central idea and a cast of other characters and environments that just seem to show up to complete the picture.

In his gallery catalogue *Kurt Weiser*, Garth Clark gives us further insight into some of the stylistic influences that might have shaped Weiser's particular image repertoire, as seen in Figures 88 and 89:

Stylistically the work stands somewhat alone [...] the work's unabashed opulence and romanticism strains even the promiscuous freedoms of postmodernism. Some see references to outsider art such as Rousseau. Others see Hick's *Peaceful Kingdom*. Yet Weiser is too informed and connected to be an outsider, even if he is a bit of a loner. Rather, his work evokes the spirit of Magic Realism, a term coined in 1925 by the German critic Franz Roh to describe a style of painting identified by sharp focus detail. However, the work fits even better with

KURT WEISER (United States)

FIGURE **88** (left)
Double vessel, *Roulette*,
2002.
Slipcast assembled porcelain
with transparent glaze and
painted enamels, fired in
oxidation, 39 x 45cm
(15⅓ x 17¾in.).
Photograph: Kurt Weiser

FIGURE **89** (below)
Vessel, *Orbit*, 2002.
Slipcast assembled porcelain
with transparent glaze and
painted enamels, fired in
oxidation, 43 x 39cm
(17 x 15⅓in.).
Photograph: Kurt Weiser

a slightly later American manifestation of the style characterized by an inventive soft-core surrealism that flowered in the late 1930s and early 1940s in the work of Paul Cadmus, Jared French and George Tooker [...] the subject matter of [these painters] is very different from Weiser's, but it communicates the same mood of sexual dream states and the same precision of technique.

Stephen Bowers — *Australia*

Since the early eighties I have been working as a visual artist — mostly in ceramics but also in other visual art media. I am motivated by the brilliant clarity available with ceramics and love the vitrified medium because of its transformation by fire into enduring objects, where images are forever transfixed by the alchemic action of heat. There is a strange quality about images and marks preserved under glaze — so close you can hold them in your hand, but under that lens of the glaze you can never touch them. If someone makes a pot they can tell a story, make a mark, a gesture or a statement that can still be read long

STEPHEN BOWERS (Australia)

FIGURE **90**
Monkey Plate, 1999.
White earthenware with painted coloured slips, oxides and stains, transparent glaze, fired in oxidation, dia: 33cm (13in.).
Photograph: Michael Kluvanek

after the original act of the making has been lost in time. On a personal level, I present imagery snapshots of narratives and give a kind if vitrified voice to echoes of imaginings and memories of things I have seen. Often things are out of context, juxtaposed like the surprising glimpses so brilliantly and tantalisingly evoked by fragments and shards.

In a piece like *Monkey Plate* [Figure 90], the viewer might well ask, 'What is happening here?' The underglaze pictures painted on my ceramics always invite a question. I like my pottery to stake out a claim on the imagination. Just what are those images about and what are those characters lurking just below the surface up to? The story of our lives is something of a collage and mosaic, but life also has some definite form, shape and (we hope) purpose. This is very much like a pot, in fact.

Ann Roberts – *Canada*

My memories, growing from child to adult in Africa, contain much-loved narratives told and retold. I learned at a young age to read from books that were always set in other countries, never in Africa. While the written stories that fed my youthful imagination were peopled with English children in a green and verdant land that I had never seen, the oral stories told by Africans were peopled with animals that spoke and spirits who intervened in the lives of humans. They controlled the earth, sky and rivers and were capable of holding the regenerative power of a springtime rebirth or conversely, the calamities of drought, famine and death. Their beliefs were interwoven in my mind with biblical and folk tales of shifting populations and eternal migrations.

The use of a dog as the protagonist in my work has been intermittent in the past [as can be seen in Figure 91, *Last Waltz*]. My interest in canine intelligence and their total integration into the human world of gestured poses of affection was awakened when my grandchildren acquired puppies in 2003. The *Last Waltz* work is part of an ongoing depiction of full, sensual, somewhat aged or timeless images of mythic relationships and interdependency. As I face my own ageing, I wish to continue to confront my viewers with their personal relationships, by drawing on the common ground shared by humans and animals in their struggle for survival.

ANN ROBERTS (Canada)

FIGURE 91
Sculpture, *Last Waltz*, 2003. Hand-modelled earthenware with soluble salt surface, fired in oxidation, 48 x 26 x 24cm (19 x 10 x 9½in.).
Photograph: Ann Roberts

Maruta Raude – *Latvia*

Table in the Grass [Figure 92] is a piece about memories, and there is light sadness in this story. A table is for gathering people around, for sitting, reading books and contemplation. There is a drawer under the tabletop to hide various items. This is a table from my grandmother's country house where my relatives gathered a couple of times each summer. Various things and items were kept in the drawer.

That particular house no longer exists, but the place where it stood still keeps the memory of it. Grass covers the basement of my grandmother's house today and the table has since found another home, where I spend my summers with my family. This is now a log house built on a hill that is marked in maps as an ancient fortification, and a place where I feel that I belong.

Grass can cover desire, feelings, and activity, and can also be seen as a symbol of rejuvenation. My little son opens the drawer of the table and looks for funny things inside. There is a small world inside the drawer — my memories and stories? Perhaps ....

Striped Bowl with French Pines [Figure 93] tells another story. This is one of my larger bowls; I like the symbolic meaning of these — the bowl or sacred cup of plenitude, of joy and festivity, or a bowl as vessel to store valuable and dear things.

The painting is arranged in stripes in a kind of divisional logic, each stripe with a story. Some of the stripes are connected by ladders, offering the possibility to move from one level to another. This particular story is about French pines. One year our family went to the south of France, where my husband studied, and I took care of our two-year old boy. In a remote park there were beautiful French pines. Frequently there were other people picnicking, playing sports or just sitting relaxing under the trees. The pines were enormous (much larger than our Nordic pines) and their forms were sheltering. Pines, sunsets and turbulent light appeared to me exactly as they do in French impressionist paintings.

Rimas VisGirda – *United States*

My work in ceramics started in the 1960s and has changed considerably up to the present — more so in my art-formative years and less so in later years as I developed my own visual vocabulary, philosophy, and technology. One of my fundamental beliefs is that experience affects everything one does; sometimes immediately and sometimes not until years later. In retrospect I can see my experiences from childhood and early adulthood entering, re-entering, and coloring my vision of my work.

In my sophomore year at California State University in Sacramento, I stumbled into ceramics and took easily to the wheel and was rewarded by some quick successes. I liked the activity so much that I managed to find the time for a ceramics

MARUTA RAUDE (Latvia)

FIGURE **92** (left)
Installation, *Table in the Grass*, 1999.
Porcelain, wooden table and grass, 90 x 90 x 65cm (35½ x 35½ x 25½in.).
Photograph: Aigars Jukna

FIGURE **93** (below)
Vessel, *Striped Bowl with French Pines*, 2002.
Slipcast porcelain with transparent glaze and painted enamels, fired in oxidation, ht: 23cm (9in.).
Photograph: Aigars Jukna

RIMAS VISGIRDA (United States)

FIGURE 94
Vessel, untitled, from 'Subway' series, 2003. Porcelain, with underglaze pencil shading, overglazing, enamels, decals and lustres, fired in oxidation, 20 x 15 x 15cm (8 x 6 x 6in.).
Photograph: Rimas VisGirda

OPPOSITE PAGE

SUNKOO YUH (South Korea, United States)

FIGURE 95
Sculpture, *Bed-Time Story*, 2002.
Handbuilt porcelain with multiple coloured glazes, fired in oxidation, 67.5 x 50 x 42.5cm (25½ x 19⅔ x 16¾in.).
Courtesy of Helen Drutt Gallery, Philadelphia
Photograph: Larry Dean

class each term until I graduated. From Robert Arneson I learned about ideas — they need to come from the inner self, either as an expression of emotion or as the internalisation of observations and a regurgitation through personal vision.

In the mid-to-late '70s I started to visit London and I went there a number of times. These travels were a visual delight. I found the Rocky Horror Show playing at a theater on the Kings Road, and was intrigued by the punk movement and it's visual versatility and vitality. I was delighted by all the sights and sounds so different from where I lived. I became more interested in erotica, fashion, and sub-cultures of all sorts. In particular, I remember an experience in London that persists to this day [see Figure 94]. I was on one of those very long, very steep and narrow (wooden?) escalators in the underground during rush hour. I remember looking at the escalator adjacent (going the other way) and there was this never-ending parade of profiles moving across from me; each face was of course different, but they were all similar.

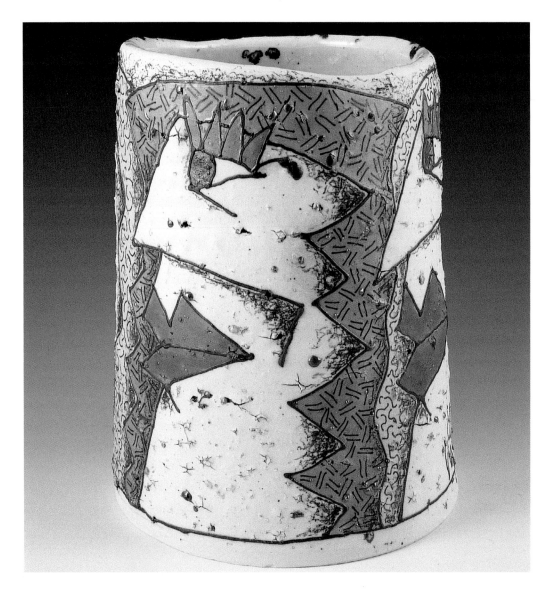

Sunkoo Yuh — *South Korea, United States*

In a recent exhibition catalogue entitled *Cultural Order/Natural Chaos: The Known and the Unknown in the Ceramic Sculpture of Sunkoo Yuh*, Tony Marsh describes the work of Sunkoo Yuh as follows:

Sunkoo Yuh is an artist who is caught between the very real differences in the

SUNKOO YUH (South Korea, United States)

FIGURE 96 (left)
Sculpture, *Inspiration JP*, 2003.
Handbuilt porcelain with multiple coloured glazes, fired in oxidation, 58 x 43 x 36cm (22¾ x 17 x 14in.).
Courtesy of Helen Drutt Gallery, Philadelphia.
Photograph: Larry Dean

FIGURE 97 (right)
Sculpture, untitled, 2002.
Handbuilt porcelain with multiple coloured glazes, fired in oxidation, 42 x 38 x 38cm (16¾ x 15 x 15in.).
Courtesy of Helen Drutt Gallery, Philadelphia.
Photograph: Larry Dean

histories, values and assumptions of two powerful cultures. Over the years he has slowly come to understand the depth and grace of the artistic heritage of his homeland Korea. This appreciation plays against the backdrop of an arts education in the States that is built on a comparatively shallow art history — one that stresses invention and a lack of reverence for artistic canons and promotes artistic freedom [...] — you [thus] have a powerful paradox in the hands of a tireless worker.

Sunkoo Yuh himself talks about the sources of inspiration and meaning of his work (as seen in Figures 95–97):

> In the past, there was an ambiguous indication of time in most of my works. I made a series of pieces called 'self-portrait', but I could not figure out what tense I was using. There was no past, present or future. I felt like my work was just flowing or waiting to move in some direction. I have always felt art has to have a universal meaning, such as the meaning of life or the meaning of existence as an artist.
>
> I'm trying to understand myself. As soon as my wife became pregnant, my interest shifted from questions about my personal identity to issues concerning my everyday life. Recently, I have started to see universal issues such as life and death through my daughter's birth. I think I know now that everything can have both universal and personal meanings. Making art may be a quest in search of broad meanings or answers, but it may be expressed through the small, mundane awareness of daily life.

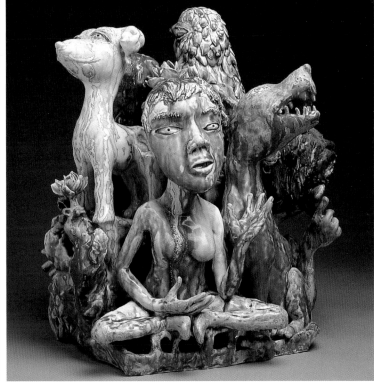

Stephen Benwell — *Australia*

I started making ceramics in the early 1970s. It was one of those 'end of painting' moments (or so I thought). I liked to paint (and still do) in a figurative style. But as I thought this was not much appreciated, I took up ceramics. I felt I could paint what I wanted in the less rigorous and historically 'decorative' way of that medium. I spent a year in Paris in 1984 where I saw the figuration of neo-expressionist work, which added to my own inclination for figuration and narrative.

Now I continue to use the vase as a surface on which to paint [see Figures 98 and 99]. My work is a bit of an oddity in that respect, it is as though paintings that may have been on a wall have instead drifted onto a piece of pottery. In these works the narrative revolves around a naked male figure. He stands for the 'beautiful youth' as depicted throughout Western art since antiquity. In this guise he is also a homoerotic image and a protagonist in episodes of cruising in the open air. He is a sort of neo-classical, physique-pictorial naturist who is also a Romantic from the mould of Wordsworth, wandering in an idyllic landscape with his head full of alternately ecstatic and elegiac thoughts.

The landscape he wanders in is a mixture of the Australian outback and Claude Lorrain's Arcadian visions. Bare, desert-like plains change into grassy plots with tombstones. These juxtapositions are the result of samplings from the nostalgia of art history, a process that I employ for developing the work.

STEPHEN BENWELL (Australia)

FIGURE 98 (left)
Urn, untitled, 2003.
Handbuilt porcelain with painted underglaze stains and transparent glaze, fired in oxidation, 40 x 27cm (15¾ x 10⅝in.).
Photograph: David McArthur

FIGURE 99 (right)
Bowl with handles, untitled, 2004.
Handbuilt porcelain with painted underglaze stains and dolomite glaze, fired in oxidation, 24 x 31cm (9½ x 12¼in.).
Photograph: David McArthur

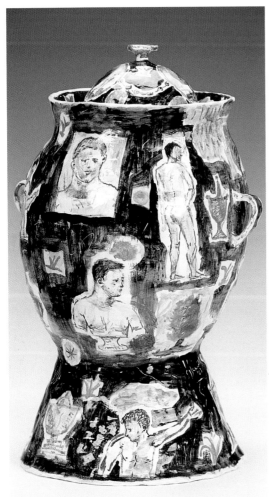

EDOUARD JASMIN (Canada)

FIGURE 100 (left)
Wall sculpture, *L'épluchage de patates*, 1981.
Hand-modelled earthenware with painted coloured slips and glazes, fired in oxidation, 29 x 21 x 6cm
(11½ x 8¼ x 2⅓in.).
Author's collection
Photograph: Jan Thijs

FIGURE 101 (right)
Sculpture, *Le cheval est aussi cher...*, 1981.
Hand-modelled earthenware with painted coloured slips and glazes, fired in oxidation, 17 x 17 x 13cm
(6⅔ x 6⅔ x 4¾in.).
Author's collection
Photograph: Jan Thijs

Making artworks by daydreaming of beautiful men and Arcadian landscapes is both enjoyable and melancholic. But these themes may fail because of an excess of sentimentality. I suppose that is why I 'rough up' the painting, scratching and blurring it, or drawing in a clumsy, broken way so that the sentimentality is lessened. But despite this threat of sentimentality, I stick to my little imaginings of cute men, naked and wandering *en plein air* and with their heads full of poetry. Pygmalion-like, I am teased by their shapely legs and rounded buttocks and I imagine them stepping out of the picture to greet me.

Edouard Jasmin – *Canada*

Edouard Jasmin was a truly remarkable folk artist, and unique in Canada for creating works in clay. True to the genre of folk art, his work could be seen as naive, but was perhaps most notable for its humorous and gentle comments on daily life, mostly that of his own *québecois* culture. After retirement, Jasmin, with indefatigable energy, created many narrative ceramic works in his apartment in Montreal. In an interview with Pascale Galipeau in 1985, he stated his intentions. Loosely translated, Jasmin's philosophy might be interpreted as follows:

I enjoy these humorous little dramas. I always try to find the amusing, the pleasant side of life. If we present the dark side, then life is dark. The brighter side feels better, almost like a tonic, not bad at all [...] So I like to create fantasies and oddities, sometimes exaggerated, and if they make people laugh, then I too am happy. If they laugh at me, I like that too, because it means they are enjoying themselves — it's at my expense, but costs me nothing.

In an article from *Studio Potter* entitled 'Edouard Jasmin: Folk Ceramicist' (Vol. II, No. 2, 1982), Léopold L. Foulem and Gloria Lesser provide the following insights into Jasmin's methodology and ideas:

> Most of Jasmin's clay murals are oval in shape (selected because the eye is oval-shaped), and pressmoulded in his own fashion. Because of this, no two works are identical, and, depending upon the scenario, the depth of the mural can vary greatly from piece to piece. A favoured leitmotif of his is the surrealistic utilization of time, where past, present, and future coexist in an episode set in no specific time period, despite the fact that a scene and title have been carefully dated on the work. [...]
>
> Jasmin is a folk artist who defies categorization. His concepts are highly thought out, whereas most folk artists create in an intuitive manner. Again, folk artists often work in one concept of space, but Jasmin selects many spatial perspectives, both pictorial and symbolic. His spaces are always narrative, utilized to enhance his story. The settings for his works are mostly interior and exterior environments, situated in familiar urban surroundings or rural vicinities of Quebec [see Figures 100 and 101]. While the sites for these scenes are identifiable (characteristically he chooses street, park and church locales), he often plays with the time sequences. Some anecdotal stories allude to local folklore of a satirical nature, but Jasmin always adds a light, humourous touch in the retelling. These scenes are seldom truly documentary. Rather, they refer to a specific context and usually are personal reminiscences of events which Jasmin might have experienced and then embellished. All of Jasmin's work is characterized by two main thrusts common to the work of many folk artists: it is always narrative and figurative.

Figure 100 represents one of Jasmin's typical oval wall plates simply entitled: *L'Épluchage de Patates* (Potato Peeling). It shows a scene from a typical *québecois* farmhouse kitchen, full of homely domestic objets, with a woman peeling potatoes, and a child helping out by sampling from the potato basket.

Figure 101 shows one of Jasmin's more unusual ceramic constructions, and typically conveys his slightly off-beat humour. The piece is titled as follows: *Le cheval est aussi cher que le boeuf qui ne laboure plus — mon mari a pris la relève,* (The horse is as costly as the ox who is no longer working — my husband has taken over his shift). We see the happily retired ox peering out from the barn, and the husband yoked to the plough with the horse. The wife follows behind, and all are wearing their straw hats against the sun . . .

Ilona Romule — *Latvia*

> The reason I chose ceramics for myself was that it was possible to express my ideas in three dimensions, to decorate sculptures with drawings and paintings, and to tell my 'stories' not with words, but through the use of diverse visual arts

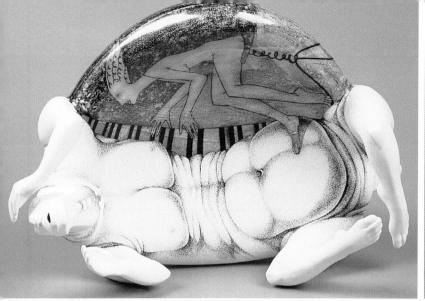 

ILONA ROMULE (Latvia)

FIGURE 102 (above left)
Sculpture, *Play*, 2003.
Slipcast modified porcelain
with transparent glaze and
enamels, fired in oxidation,
34 x 19 x 24cm
(13⅓ x 7½ x 9½in.).
Photograph: Ilona Romule

FIGURE 103 (above right)
Sculpture, *Kind of Deer*, 2003.
Slipcast modified porcelain
with transparent glaze,
enamels and lustre,
fired in oxidation,
40 x 27 x 14cm
(15¾ x 10⅔ x 5½in.).
Photograph: Ilona Romule

techniques. Of all ceramic materials I prefer porcelain as that which helps me to reach a harmony of idea, form and surface. I use the porcelain's white surface as a three-dimensional canvas.

There is no ultimate explanation of the way daily life transforms into artwork. There exists a relationship independent from me, in my surrounding life and my feelings, and the final result is the porcelain figure. The primary function of my figurative porcelain is not the creation of a pot, or a bowl, or a cup, but rather of a container which can hold ideas, emotions, sexuality, pain, and so on. The topic is the old one: the relationship between a man and a woman, and the resolution of our differences in coming together.

Play [in Figure 102] expresses the following: To my mind on the border between dream and reality came a hybrid of man and chameleon: clearing his thoughts while someone is playing jazz on the side of his body . . . the last melody before falling into the dream of Summer Time . . .

Kind of Deer [in Figure 103] talks about the roots of imagery of those dreams and fantasies found in Northern and Baltic countries, where the diversity of peoples produces a rich storytelling culture, mixing myth and mystery. I have absorbed this heritage and created a personal mythology, my own vision. I think of games, symbols and situations where the main heroes are Woman and Man, although sometimes depicted as animals or hybrids. Altogether these images translate into a personal portrait of my own feelings and fantasies.

Michael Corney – *United States*

My interest in narrative clay work is a response to my early ceramic education. As a student I looked at all the ceramic books and magazines I could get my hands on. Most of what I saw was work firmly rooted in the Asian traditions: tea bowls, teapots very Zen, very brown. At first I tried to emulate this type of work, but the aesthetics of quiet contemplation were entirely unnatural to me. I grew up in a family of four boys in southern California. Mine was a family where everybody had an opinion and at the dinner table was where these ideas and stories were expressed. It is this clash of the ritual of eating and the inter-action of ideas that inspires me to focus on ceramics.

The underlying theme of my work is chaos. It comes out of my take on con-temporary American life, with its fast-paced, information-packed, media-driven frenzy. Not one for subtleties, l tend to throw as much visual information together to create an abstract, often confusing narrative. A piece usually starts off with a general theme. I want to lead the viewer in a general direction, but not one so spe-cific that each viewer will read it in the same way [see Figures 104 and 105].

Because I am primarily interested in the image, I deliberately keep the tech-nical aspects to a minimum. I mostly work with slipcast porcelain and com-mercial stains and underglazes, fired to cone 10. My palette leans towards bright happy colors, contradicting the often dark and sinister subject matter of the imagery.

MICHAEL CORNEY (United States)

FIGURE **104** (left)
Sculpture, *Rest in Peace*, 2000.
Stacked slipcast porcelain cubes with painted under-glazes and stains, transparent glaze, fired in oxidation, 26 x 20 x 7.5cm (10¼ x 8 x 3in.).

FIGURE **105** (right)
Sculpture, *Eat*, 2002.
Stacked slipcast porcelain cubes with painted under-glazes and stains, transparent glaze, fired in oxidation, 26 x 18 x 7.5cm (10¼ x 7 x 3in.)

Both photographs: Margot Geist

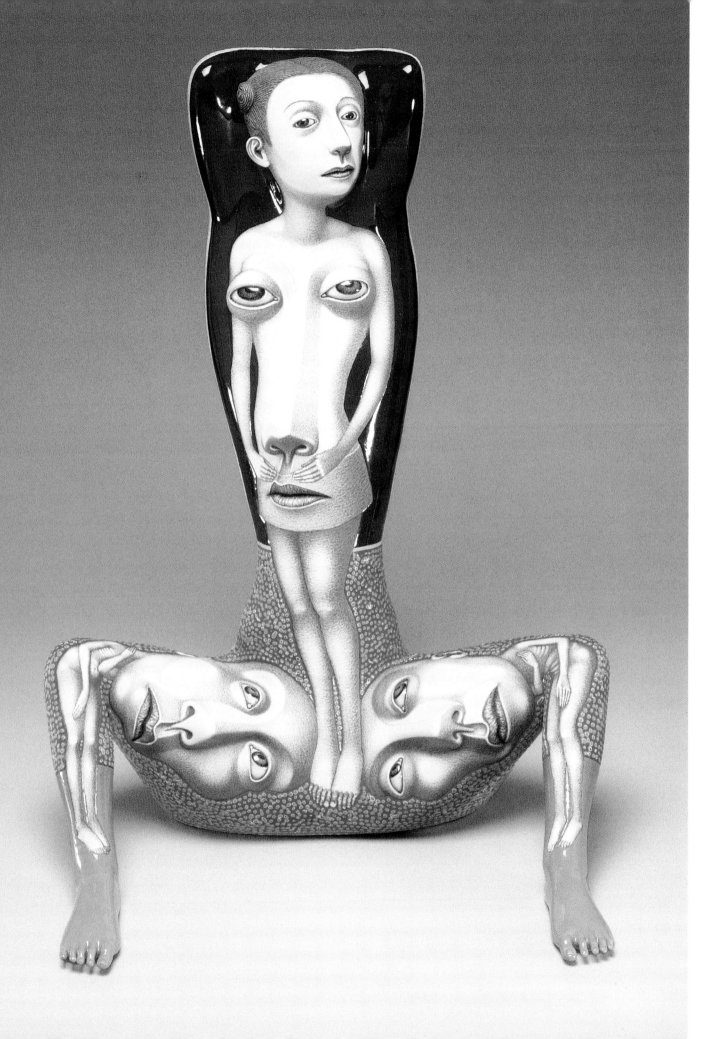

Contemporary Narratives:

The Human Figure: Aspirations, Relationships and Identity

As I have mentioned at the start of the previous chapter, the depiction of the human figure can be extremely self-revealing. Perhaps that is why it is so prevalent in most narratives, in whatever form they occur. We are the central action of all our own dramas, and of course the focus of all important questions and unsolved issues that form the basis of most narratives. In this chapter the human figure is somewhat less 'personal' and autobiographical, and tends to be more iconic and symbolic, a visual metaphor or representation, much like an actor playing out the dramas that explore life's vital questions. Kings, queens, dancers, amazons, lovers, men and women, sometimes masked, sometimes faceless — all demand introspection on the part of the viewer, and an examination of important issues. We can respond with humour, affection, discomfort or anger (as the artist may well have intended), but respond and question we must.

Sergei Isupov — United States

In *The Penland Book of Ceramics*, Estonian-born artist Sergei Isupov provides the following insights into his methodology and approach to creating the detailed imagery on his porcelain sculptures:

> I like challenges. Working in clay is really deep, and has much to interest me: philosophy, technique — so much. My own process has two stages: form, and then decoration, which is the bigger part of the work. Our minds first grasp form, and decoration is secondary, yet I pay more attention to the decoration. I like to tell stories using symbols that are universal, so that when you look at my

OPPOSITE PAGE

SERGEI ISUPOV (United States)

FIGURE 106
Sculpture, *Birth of Venus*, 2003.
Slab-constructed porcelain with painted coloured slips and transparent glaze, fired in oxidation, 55.8 x 52 x 39.4cm (22 x 20½ x 15½ in.).
Courtesy of Leslie Ferrin Gallery, Lenox, Massachusetts.
Photograph: Katherine Wetzel

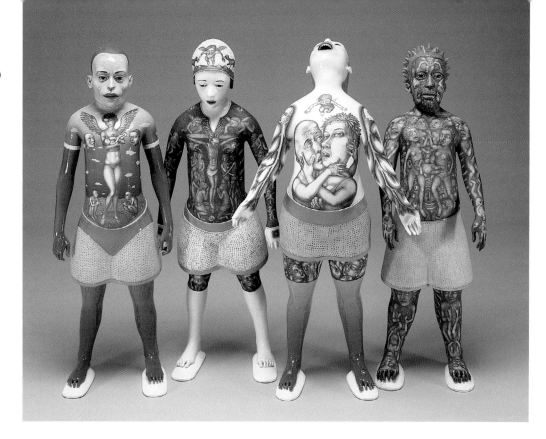

SERGEI ISUPOV (United States)

FIGURE **107**
Group of Statuettes, 2003.
Slab-constructed porcelain
with painted coloured slips
and transparent glaze,
fired in oxidation,
(each) 53.4 x 16.5 x 15.2cm
(21 x 6½ x 6in.).
*Courtesy of Leslie Ferrin Gallery, Lenox,
Massachusetts.*
Photograph: Katherine Wetzel

OPPOSITE PAGE

GABRIELE SCHNITZENBAUMER
(Germany)

FIGURE **108** (left)
Sculpture, *Jeanne d'Arc*,
2000.
Slab-constructed grogged
red clay with acrylic painting
and metal, fired in oxidation,
96 x 79 x 16cm
(37¾ x 31 x 6¼in.).
Photograph: Manuel Schnell

FIGURE **109** (right)
Sculpture, *Athene*, 2000.
Slab-constructed grogged
red clay with acrylic painting
and rope, fired in oxidation,
40 x 144 x 35cm
(15¾ x 56⅔ x 13¾in.).
Photograph: Manuel Schnell

work you can tell your own story, and interpret what you see in your own way
[see Figures 106 and 107].

Technique is not the most important thing for me. I don't want people to
look at my work and see the sweat. I want people to hear what I can say, not
how I say it. I use the nude because it appeals to a broad range of people.
Clothing goes out of fashion so quickly, but nudity is timeless. Yet I also desire
to be a contemporary artist, through the forms and the colors I use. [...]

I must draw exactly, knowing where the color goes precisely. If I don't have a
story to tell, I rely on technique. Sometimes the combination of colors tells me
were to take the decoration, but sometimes I have a story to tell, and that
guides me instead.

Gabriele Schnitzenbaumer – *Germany*

In the catalogue of Schnitzenbaumer's sculptural works from 1996 to 1998,
Engel und Amazonen (Angels and Amazons), Sigrid Weigel makes the following
observations in the article entitled 'Bricolage of Lost and Found':

The vision which finds in the leftovers of civilisation the raw material for fan-
tastic sculpture, and the eye that discovers anthropomorphic forms in useless
machines, emerges for Schnitzenbaumer from a kind of behaviour she
observed in our mothers and grandmothers: a culture of collecting, re-using
and hoarding, born of scarcity, but become a habit. Because after the war

women found literally everything valuable enough to be kept for later use, an attitude towards objects resulted which saw nothing as useless.

Her concern with the human figure deals not so much with the immediate representation of an identifiable person, but rather presents archetypal characters that epitomise those human strengths and realities that are so central to our identity and sense of being. In her sculptures *Jeanne d'Arc* and *Athene* (Figures 108 and 109), she highlights female role models from history to celebrate the universal attributes of such women; fighting, protective, submissive, nurturing, and above all, creative and rebuilding. Some of these issues arise from Schnitzenbaumer's personal childhood memories of war and privation in Germany, and the memories of recreating the identities of the bombed dead through the re-assembly of their body parts and personal artefacts. Thus the issue of identity (visible in the assembled fragmented components of her sculptures) remains a central and haunting theme for this artist.

Hylton Nel – *South Africa*

In the 1996 exhibition catalogue entitled *Hylton Nel, A Prayer for Good Governance* (The Fine Art Society, London), Tamar Garb presents the following analysis of Nel's work, in particular the sources of his narrative imagery:

> The ceramic world of Hylton Nel is resonant with allusion. His brilliantly glazed moulded plates and pots, figures and bowls [see Figures 110 and 111]

HYLTON NEL (South Africa)

FIGURE 110 (below left)
Figure grouping. (Left): *Ben Ochri figure*, (centre): *Boy with Lute*, (right): *Man Posing as Hercules*, 2003.
Hand-modelled earthenware with coloured maiolica glazes, fired in oxidation, (each) ht: 29cm (11¾in.).
Courtesy of the Fine Arts Society, London.
Photograph: A.C. Cooper

FIGURE 111 (below right)
Dish, *Life's Amazing Journey Takes You Far Away from Home*, 2004.
Pressmoulded earthenware with maiolica glaze and coloured stains, fired in oxidation, 30 x 20cm (11¾ x 8in.).
Courtesy of the Fine Arts Society, London.
Photograph: A.C. Cooper

constitute a three-dimensional clay canvas for pictorial and iconic references. His is a ceramic art with its roots in Oriental, Asian, European and English decorated ornaments and tableware, but reworked through the lens of a white African — a man immersed in the bizarre literary and linguistic sign systems of a culture in transition, with its entrenched colonial past and its vision of the future. Nel is an anglophone Afrikaner who is at once a citizen of the world, heir to its artistic and cultural traditions, and fiercely rooted in the soil and succour of the place of his birth. He straddles cultures and contexts with the glorious irresponsibility of an intrepid explorer.

There are no taboos or prohibitions in the marauding sensibility of the image raider. His own grotesque foot viewed from above; enthroned phallic totems drawn as much from the curvilinear excesses of Beardsley's *Yellow Book* as from African fetish objects; Adam and Eve waving their fig leaves provocatively in the Garden of Eden, watched by a lascivious serpent; sensual encounters between lewd young men sporting erections, matched only by their Athenian forebears; the majestic Lion of Africa, insignia of the famous Lion *vuurhoutjies* used by every South African boy scout or girl guide under the hegemonic power structures of apartheid — these are some of the bold and brilliant references to which Nel's passionate and parodic iconography refers.

In describing his own work, Hylton Nel shares the following insights:

About work, what can I say? I take both East and West as my cultural heritage. I work as best I can with the past for inspiration. Most of what I make are plates. The same shape over and over, but like people each one different. That means I don't have to think too much about the shape and can concentrate on the thing that mostly gets me going, namely colour alone or combined with other colours, lines, blotches. The subject matter comes after. It could be simply patterns or it could be

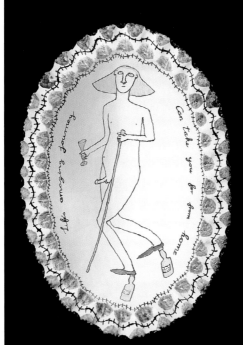

figurative. In the last case it often comes from things I read. I read almost anything. There is a bowl with the face of a Cuban writer whose book moved me. There was a series of plates using drawings of cats by Carrington. In that case I wrote her name on the plate as part of the design. There is a vase that commemorates the death of a Chilean peasant child. It is made so that somewhere, however imperfectly, he may be remembered. If I use words on a plate I prefer not to declare the source, not out of disrespect but because the naked words have their own power.

Greg Payce – *Canada*

Using the archetypal form of the ancient Mediterranean drug pot, or *albarello*, Greg Payce explores the 'human figure' spaces between carefully placed *albarello*-like shapes and confronts the viewer with a new visual premise. The 2001 exhibition 'Cineramics' at the Art Gallery of Calgary, showed the works of two Canadian artists, Greg Payce and Jeannie Mah (see Chapter Nine). In the context of this exhibition, and of thematically-related later work, Payce asks the viewer to 'Mind the Gap':

> When eyes are fooled, imaginations are thrown open wide. Realms between the virtual and the real contain unique narrative possibility. The negative spaces between ceramic *albarelli* become strange, non-dimensional, yet oddly three-dimensional images. Archetypal relationships between human and vessel form cannot help but overwhelm.
>
> In domestic contexts, pottery functions as an understated opportunity to introduce tactile, useful, visual, and intellectual experience into people's lives, often with subtle and profound effect. Approaches from within the discourse of ceramics are paramount in my work. Physically viewing static, domestic-scale ceramic objects

GREG PAYCE (Canada)

FIGURE **112** (below right)
Installation vessels,
Al Barelli, 2001.
Template-thrown earthenware with black terra sigillata, fired in oxidation,
ht: 213.4cm (84in.).
Photograph: M.C. Hutchinson

FIGURE **113** (below left)
Moving video vessel installation, *Harem*, 2004.
Template-thrown earthenware with coloured terra sigillata, fired in oxidation.
Various dimensions.
Photograph: M.C. Hutchinson

— in real time, and three-dimensional space, was the initial strategy. Virtual remediation of these ceramic forms is providing other unique possibilities for both dissemination and scale with these works.

The impetus behind *Al Barelli* [see Figure 112] was to create a larger-than-life-sized negative space figure to allow viewers to interact with a virtual figure of their own scale.

In *Harem* [Figure 113] dualities of figure/ground, positive/negative, form/surface, and object/idea, inform and develop vocabulary and grammar in the works. Point of view, syntax, and rotational speed provide a structural framework. Language evolves as ideas become more complex. Narratives construct themselves from viewers' experiences. Expansion of the discourse of ceramics in current video projects [such as *Harem*], offers time-based consideration of the dichotomy between virtual and real.

Christine Federighi – *United States*

Although I started my career making vessels, the vessels became 'canvases' for my personal journal. The important personal narratives that developed into work over the years involved poetry by my brother Ron, American Indian art

and folk art, and man and animal relationships, with the idea of the Horse, House and Rider becoming an important theme.

Two of the figurative sculptures presented here encompass several cumulative ideas. Some of the imagery concerns my interest in honouring the landscape of the West and the idea of the wrapped figure as part of this unique landscape (man and nature idea). Other imagery involves a stylisation of plant forms that reference living in tropical Florida, and I include references to house images, such as a staircase, a framing shell and a roof silhouette. In building a house/studio in Colorado, I was intrigued by the sculptural aspects of the process and the visual poetic metaphor that was fostered [see Figure 114]. As human beings we all have unseen parts of experience that contribute to our form. In my designing these personal symbols that wrap a figure form, I pay homage to the process that layers our experience. This process gives us our individuality.

The two figures in *Little Guard Dog* [see Figure 115] are wrapped in a layering. The continuing symbol narratives of landscape, leaves and house structure are partially hidden, and a wrapped dog is also part of the scene. The dog has been a guide, guardian and is considered in many cultures as a link between man and the spirit world. The wrapping of the figure occurred after the tragic 9/11 events [the terrorist attack on the World Trade Center in New York in September, 2001]. It also occurred as a response to comments about my work. I felt there was a need to pull in and protect the situation.

Scott Rench – *United States*

I represent the next generation of ceramic artists, who are combining one of the oldest traditions with today's technology. Computer-related imagery is part of my daily life and in many cases has become a part of our contemporary vernacular. I use the computer in my artwork to illustrate, manipulate and compose the elements for each piece. I also choose a more printerly approach showing the naked clay and the roughness of the medium, and use computer symbols familiar to me and to others to express some more personal thoughts. There are many layers of meaning woven into each piece, some more buried than others.

Life is a series of lessons that most often we do not understand. Some are now clearer to me and others still leave me wondering why. I find my best work comes out of the darkest moments in my life. Several years ago my work made a shift as I started to draw from my personal life.

These new themes are common to all human experience, and as such are subjects that many can relate to. Each person brings their own experiences to my work and I am continually surprised by the variety of viewer responses. In darker

OPPOSITE PAGE

CHRISTINE FEDERIGHI (United States)

FIGURE **114** (far left)
Sculpture, *Spiral Low*, 2002.
Coil-built earthenware with carving and applied parts, oil paints and sealer, fired in oxidation, 178 x 17.8 x 15.3cm (70 x 7 x 6in.).
Photograph: Bonnie Seeman

FIGURE **115** (below)
Sculpture grouping, *Little Guard Dog*, 2003.
Coil-built earthenware with carving and applied parts, oil paints and sealer, fired in oxidation, 45.7 x 20.3 x 25.4cm (18 x 8 x 10 in.).
Photograph: Bonnie Seeman

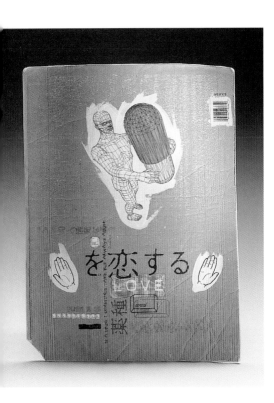

times when we feel isolated and vulnerable, I would like be able to reach out with my work and engender a sense of complicity and solidarity.

Love Is a Drug (I Sometimes Take But Always Abuse) [Figure 116] is a reflection on lost love. In many ways my imagery and work is a complex layering of semiotics. I have long been fascinated by Asian culture and its written language. I see *kanji* [Japanese writing using Chinese characters] as an art object first and its meaning as secondary. I have chosen the cardboard texture to symbolise the box I sometimes feel trapped in. It appears dirty and beaten up as if it has travelled to many places and bears all the scars of its journey. *Love is a Drug* speaks to my need to control, my loss of control and to say I'm sorry. I am torn by the extrovert who needs to express his feelings or emotions and the introvert who hides them.

Destiny: A Look at My Life [Figure 117] is a reflection on my life and the choices I have made, with regrets and mistakes. I am the figure located in the lower left.

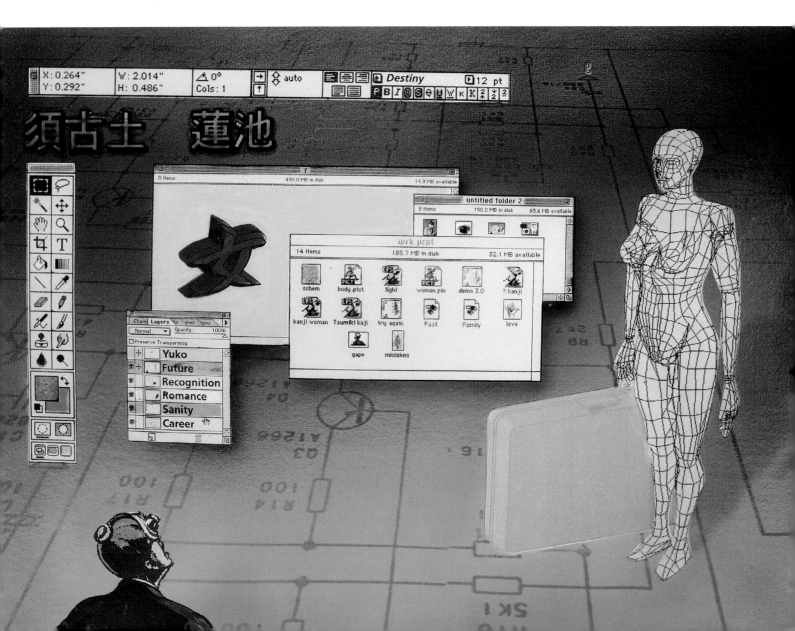

Sárka Radová – *Czech Republic*

My primary interest from the beginning has been the creation of ceramic work that deals with the issues of man and his environment, and his relationship to it. Earlier work depicted man in the context of landscapes, in conjunction with animals, and in association with various types of dwellings. All of these can be seen as 'symbolic' associations, touching upon the themes of identity, place and relationships. The latter has become more and more important in my most recent sculptural work — it is man's relationship to man that helps to identify and to place him in context with the world. It is most often through relationships that we define our own character, and our place within a community.

For the past ten years, the strength and hardness of porcelain as a material have been pivotal to the expression of these ideas in my depiction of human figure narratives. *Riders on a Saddle Roof* [Figure 118] shows us ambitious and ineffective people riding in their dreams, where there might be a danger of falling from a height but at least no need to engage with a real horse...

OPPOSITE PAGE

SCOTT RENCH (United States)

FIGURE 116 (above)
Plaque, *Love is a Drug (I Sometimes Take but Always Abuse)*, 2001.
Stoneware with nylon fibre, screen-painted slips and underglazes, fired in oxidation, 57 x 77.5 x 7.6cm (22½ x 30½ x 3in.).
Photograph: Eric Smith

FIGURE 117 (below)
Plaque, *Destiny: A Look at My Life*, 2001.
Stoneware with nylon fibre, screen-painted slips and underglazes, fired in oxidation, 81.3 x 58.4 x 7.6cm (32 x 23 x 3in.).
Photograph: Eric Smith

THIS PAGE

SÁRKA RADOVÁ (Czech Republic)

FIGURE 118
Sculpture, *Riders on a Saddle Roof*, 1997.
Hand-modelled porcelain with airbrushed oxides, fired in reduction, ht: 75cm (29½in.).
Photograph: Martin Polák

JACK EARL (United States)

FIGURE 119 (left)
Sculpture, *Scraps and Slats*, 2003.
Coiled and handbuilt earthenware with oil paints, fired in oxidation, 66 x 47 x 27.9cm (26 x 18½ x 11in.).
Courtesy of Perimeter Gallery, Chicago
Photograph: Tom van Eynde

FIGURE 120 (right)
Sculpture, *Steely-Eyed Stoneman*, 2003.
Coiled and handbuilt earthenware with oil paints, fired in oxidation, 86.4 x 45.7 x 30.5cm (34 x 18 x 12in.).
Courtesy of Perimeter Gallery, Chicago
Photograph: Tom van Eynde

Jack Earl – *United States*

Jack Earl's enigmatic human figure representations can perhaps best be summed up in his response to a letter from Lee Nordness in 1987, asking Earl to provide information for a *Studio Potter* magazine article:

> I'm using 'the figure' because since birth [...], whenever my eyes were open I was seeing figures. I think also I use the figure because I want my story to be plain and because I don't believe in magic. It is the simplest, most direct, easiest, straightest line between two points. [...] I perceive the figure with my body, mind and spirit. From an imperfect world, through an imperfect man, in an imperfect medium, my work is an incomplete and imperfect reflection [...] of what I've seen, what I know and what I feel.

From various other conversations and book excerpts, Earl further talks about himself and his clay and paint figures (see Figures 119 and 120):

> I am not a thinker. I feel things out and do them. I've never sat down and figured out intellectually what I am saying. When I do sit down to think about what I do, it's really an emotional experience. [...] One type of work that I'm doing now is making a picture three-dimensional and putting it in some kind of situation. The pictures are basically realistic, but romantic also [...]. I try to bring them down to earth to some degree and to put them in some kind of a common or normal situation. The other types of things that I make are people doing ordinary things, and the reverse of that — putting those people in an unreal situation.

 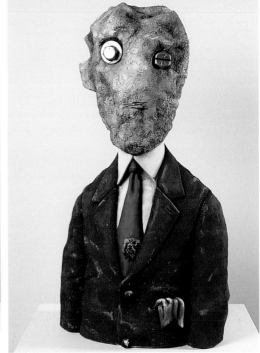

VIOLA FREY (United States)

FIGURE **121**
Sculpture, from 'Western Civilization' series, 2001. Low-fired clay with slipcast and assembled components, coloured glazes, fired in oxidation, 94 x 101.6 x 73.7cm (37 x 40 x 29in.).
Courtesy of Rena Bransten Gallery, San Francisco

Viola Frey – *United States*

The monumental sculptural work of American artist Viola Frey is perhaps best described in a number of excerpts from an essay by Paterson Sims adapted from *Viola Frey*, a brochure published by the Whitney Museum of American Art in July 1984:

> Frey's need to transform and upgrade the ordinary began in childhood. All the people on her family's rural vineyard seemed to be inveterate hoarders. They retooled for each season and crop, and abandoned machinery was left where it stopped working to be picturesquely reclaimed by nature. With her brothers, Frey dug in trash heaps filled with discarded, often despised 'Made in Japan' items. Colorful, glazed china bits were saved treasures amid the bleak solitude of the farm. These fragments and the everyday ephemera around her family's house were her visual culture. It was this kaleidoscope of childhood imagery that later became the wellspring of her mature art....
>
> Frey had first pursued clay as an artistic medium while attending community college in the early 1950s. Its three-dimensionality appealed to her, but she also perceived that clay could unify 'all the resources of drawing, of painting, of color, light, gloss, matt, of solids, of space.'
>
> Around 1979 her work achieved a new ambition. [...] She now sought, even in her still-life assemblages, a more vertical format. She began her series of single,

larger-than-life-size ceramic figures, [See Figure 123] as well as large and complex paintings. These new developments had been preceded by intricate decorated plates and assemblages of piled and painted china figures and souvenirs…. [See Figures 121 and 122.]

Viola Frey briefly provided the following answers to three topical questions concerning her work, from statements made in the late 1970s:

[On 'The Narrative']: In several series I have been interested in ceramic and plastic figurines, cheap throwaways, both the small ones and the large ones. They have a frozen presence far beyond their value. They become images from childhood, memories enlarged and scary. Among these artefacts are little animals, dogs, cats, roosters, birds, and their attendant humans. Dollies, all dollies. I decided to make them big — take them out of the crib and off the coffee table. Make them myths of childhood. I altered their poster colors using overglazes to give them alertness and vividness, to un-freeze them.

[On 'The Ceramic Medium']: Ceramic materials, clay and glaze, have several characteristics which make them increasingly effective art mediums for the coming decades. Clay and glaze can create an intimate scale, a human presence; it is also capable of large monumentality, but always with the structural division visible, such as brick and tile. They can reflect one's own self — and can record the world around. For the viewer to experience a clay form in space, to see or to hold it, to even walk across it, is to evoke a primary physical and mental response that has not changed or weakened in 5000 years.

[As an answer to 'What have I done with clay?']: I have made a record of what has been and what is. I have attempted to make a permanent whole of the transitory fragments I have seen around me. Clay has the quality of *right now*! It is able to seize this very moment under hand and eye.

Jean-Pierre Larocque – Canada

An engaging narrative will have a large measure of unpredictability built in. Writers claim that a story often begins with some characters that they keep thinking about. At this point there is a vague sense of where and how they live but there is no story. A writer writes because writing is the only way to find out what happens to those people. A story that is fully figured out lacks the drive or necessity that makes storytelling alive and vital. I feel the same way about making. I begin with a theme but without a plan and through the process I discover who that figure is. It grows into a man then it turns into a woman, I add a beard and it is an older man; I keep editing, shifting, adding, subtracting [see Figure 124].

Making is a way of thinking. Clay is suitable to the wanderings of the mind because it lends itself to quick changes. The result will be layered with evidence of what the piece has been through as an idea works itself out. A narrative, a story of its own making, is imbedded in the piece. Following clues and marks, the attentive eye is witness to the story of how a particular piece unfolds. This narrative is of a kind that is better experienced than explained.

My figures are evocative of situations and places that rubbed on them both literally and metaphorically, like refugees on a photograph with no date or caption. The things I make in clay are often evocative of a narrative of wandering and desire. They have no alibi and they reflect the changes they went through while they were becoming. They tell stories with missing pages and titles lost along the way.

OPPOSITE PAGE

VIOLA FREY (United States)

FIGURE 122 (above)
Plate, untitled, 2000.
Low-fired clay with slipcast and assembled components, coloured glazes, fired in oxidation, dia: 63.5cm (25in.), ht: 22.7cm (9in.).
Courtesy of Rena Bransten Gallery, San Francisco

FIGURE 123 (below)
Sculpture, *Seated Woman*, 2003.
Handbuilt and pinched low-fired clay with coloured glazes, fired in oxidation, 166.4 x 111.8 x 139.7cm (65½ x 44 x 55in.).
Courtesy of Rena Bransten Gallery, San Francisco

JEAN-PIERRE LAROCQUE (Canada)

FIGURE 124
Sculpture detail, *Standing Figure*, 1999.
Hand-modelled stoneware with layers of brushed and water-eroded slips, multiple-fired in oxidation, 170 x 60cm (67 x 23⅗in.).
Photograph: Andrew Neuhart

179

CHRISTIE BROWN (United Kingdom)

FIGURE **125** (below left)
Installation, *Fragments of Narrative*, 2000.
Brick and T-material clays pressmoulded from slabs, with vitreous slips, fired in oxidation, each figure approx. 170 x 42 x 35cm (67 x 16½ x 13¾ in.).
Photograph: Kate Forrest

FIGURE **126** (below right)
Installation (detail), *Minerva and Pigmalion*, with several heads from Glyptothek.
Commissioned by WPT at Wapping Project.
Photograph: Kate Forrest

Christie Brown – *United Kingdom*

My interest in the expressive use of clay began through pottery, but I quickly turned to a more sculptural use of the medium. As a result, my influences have largely come from the fine art world and figurative sculpture rather than from ceramics. Recently, connecting to the use of clay in archaic graves and burial sites, has given me a reference point within ceramic history that goes beyond the decorative or utilitarian.

Seeking to communicate something tougher than ornamentation, dealing with universal themes such as attachment and loss, fragmentation and change, I experience ceramic history either as a vital source or as heavy baggage. The use of clay in myths and narratives of origin features widely in a variety of cultures, and this is a source of inspiration.

Increasingly for me, what the work is about has become more important than the materials from which it is made. The ideas behind my work are largely informed by disciplines such as psychology and archaeology, where narratives about the human condition and material culture play a central role.

The invitation to make a body of work in response to a specific space enabled me to broaden my ideas beyond personal narratives and to increase the scale of my work. Wapping Hydraulic Power Station, a disused industrial building in London, was a challenging site, particularly in terms of size and scale. The final installation was entitled *Fragments of Narrative* [see Figures 125 and 126]. Among the works made for this show were a group of life-sized figures of

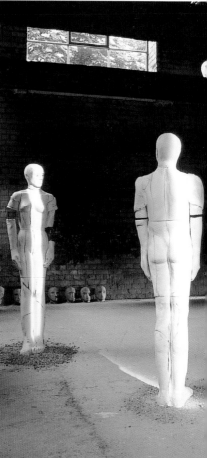

characters from myths of creation such as Prometheus, Pygmalion and The Golem. These echoed both the relationship between the legends and the ceramic material, and the original use of a space where power had once been generated. Smaller figures entitled *Helpers* were inspired by Egyptian Shabti figures who play a vital role in the afterlife. By placing the small figures in the largest space and some of the life-sized ones in the small room, ideas about the nature of scale were also explored.

Herman Muys – *Belgium*

Almost all of my sculptures relate to the existential aspects of the human condition, and therefore it is not surprising that expression plays a leading role. These expressions are not intended as figures expressing feelings, but rather as figures awakening emotions.

Over the years, artwork depicting a person (male or female) seated on a throne has become one of my favourites. Using the symbol of a throne already

HERMAN MUYS (Belgium)

FIGURE 127 (above right)
Sculpture, *Throne/Silent Observer*, 2003.
Slabbed and assembled low-fired clay with applied slips, stains and oxides, fired in oxidation, 70 x 30 x 30cm (27½ x 11¾ x 11¾in.).
Photograph: Melissa Muys

FIGURE 128 (above left)
Sculpture, *King and Queen*, 2003.
Slabbed and assembled low-fired clay with applied slips, stains and oxides, fired in oxidation,
ht: 62cm (24½ in.).
Photograph: Steven d'Haens

JINDRA VIKOVÁ (Czech Republic)

FIGURE 129
Wall sculpture (from a
cycle of twelve), *Looking
for Shelter*, 2000.
Unglazed hand-modelled
stoneware and porcelain,
fired in oxidation, 30 x 30cm
(11¾ x 11¾ in.).

Photograph: Pavel Banka

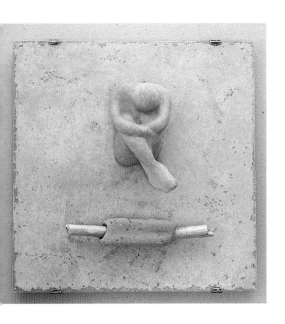

brings tension to the work and guides the viewer up to a certain level of what to expect. A throne implicitly creates the assumption of power and power evokes very strong emotions. Experimenting with the effects of having or losing power remains a constantly absorbing theme.

Throne/Silent Observer [Figure 127] shows this woman seated on her throne. With her legs crossed and her arms strategically placed on the armrests, she seems to be untouchable. Even the absent look in her eyes and the haughty expression on her face are part of a perfectly chosen pose. In this particular work power is still evident, although the first signs of decline are becoming visible.

King and Queen [Figure 128] shows two seated persons, both separated but interacting. They were originally made for a Swiss exhibition, 'Augenblicken' (Moments), but the direct translation of the word would be 'glimpse of the eye'. The two figures can be seen interacting in a moment of time, suddenly becoming aware of each other's presence.

Jindra Viková – *Czech Republic*

My work is often a metaphor for human actions, rather than the illustration of a particular concept. My own personal development in life, my maturing if you will, is perhaps now more pivotal to the work I create, and pushes me to look at the 'internal' connections between all things and objects perceived, both past and present.

Perhaps at a certain age one begins to look back and review one's life from a different perspective. This may now be less a recapitulation of past events, but rather the achieving of a sense of overview and distance from everyday experiences, which in the past I reacted to. In an earlier period, I did my best to define the imagination precisely, but have now come to the conclusion that a hint is often enough to evoke a feeling. Therefore in my current work there are more materials and the surfaces are less descriptive, but there is a greater degree of 'secrecy.'

In *Looking for Shelter*, (from a cycle of twelve wall pieces) [Figure 129], I display small fired clay figures mounted on ceramic tiles. The face is hidden and the figure is positioned horizontally. In this series I am expressing the individual connection between life's primal forces of birth, of making love, and of death. The pose of each figure expresses either the longing for protection, the basic shape of the human body immediately after birth, poses assumed

before and after love-making, or the human figure in its final pose, awaiting death.

Nan Smith – *United States*

I have always been compelled by the mysterious; things that connect us and give order to our world. I grew up in a multi-cultural city and early on valued diversity. As a child I had an overwhelming interest in religion, its history and tradition; interests which ran parallel to my love for drawing and painting. I found that my need to contribute thoughts took form during the quiet hours I spent working on my art.

As a sculptor my goal is to contribute to the recognition that spiritual evolution is a human possibility. Installation-oriented figurative sculptures reflect my perspective about the universal connection of all aspects of our world. My intent is to convey a sense of the psychology of the female attribute within consciousness. The temporal quality of human existence is an underlying theme implicit in the choice of clay as a sculptural material.

The feminine attribute in the tile diptych *In Sight* [Figure 130] is portrayed by a woman in youth (a symbol of becoming) who sees her pureness in water. In one image the female's outward gaze indicates her awareness of the outer world. In the other image she appears in profile with head uplifted and contemplative, to indicate the thought turned inward. Text overlays the linear water pattern to reveal the state of consciousness.

In the installation titled *Flow* [Figure 131], the young woman, sculpted as the corporeal body, is portrayed looking through a framed space, perhaps

NAN SMITH (United States)

FIGURE **130** (below left)
Tile diptych, *In Sight*, 1994.
Earthenware with air-brushed underglazes, stencils and PhotoShop-printed decals, fired in oxidation,
89 x 57.6cm (35 x 22¼in.).
Photograph: Alan Cheuvront

FIGURE **131** (above)
Installation, *Flow*, 1995.
Airbrushed-glazed earthenware, polychromed wood and coloured gypsum cement, fired in oxidation,
230.7 x 153.9cm (91 x 60½ in.).
Photograph: Alan Cheuvront

"Do not take life's experiences too seriously. Above all, do not let them hurt you, for in reality they are nothing but dream experiences. Play your part in life, but never forget it is only a role."

Yogananda

MICHAEL FLYNN (United Kingdom)

FIGURE **132** (left)
Sculpture, *Sleeping Saint with Two Fighting Queens*, 2002.
Hand-modelled glazed stoneware, fired in oxidation, ht: 55cm (21⅝in.).
Photograph: Michael Flynn

FIGURE **133** (right)
Sculpture, *Their New Dresses*, 2003.
Hand-modelled glazed stoneware, fired in oxidation, ht: 50cm (19⅝in.).
Photograph: Michael Flynn

mirror, perhaps portal? Within this defined space a shrouded, disembodied female gestures to her. She responds. In my vocabulary the 'empty dress' signifies the self as spirit. The multiple figures are one entity. They indicate the evolution of awareness through time.

Michael Flynn — *United Kingdom*

Any work which contains recognisable human figures immediately suggests narrative possibilities to the spectator. I am deeply committed to the human figure and to its inevitable narrative associations, but I am seeking neither to tell a story nor to illustrate one. A work is only truly finished when it is before the spectator. At this point, hopefully, the observer's personal history touches upon the narrative implicit in the piece (or vice versa) achieving a level of understanding.

An image, a text, sometimes just one word, or an everyday experience or observation, will provide a catalyst for a piece or a series of pieces. My choices of material, of scale and of form are largely intuitive but they are fostered by continuous reading and very deliberate searching for appropriate visual imagery.

Their New Dresses [see Figure 133] ostensibly has its origins in drawings made two years earlier and rediscovered in a sketchbook. They became relevant in relation to other work on the theme of 'The Decorated Self', which developed from reading Calasso's *The Marriage of Cadmus and Harmony* and Goethe's *Faust*. In this sense it is closely related to *Sleeping Saint with Two Fighting Queens* [see Figure 132], which also touches upon the themes of 'The Decorated Self' or 'Clothed and Unclothed', with perhaps a sideways look at *The Temptation of Saint Anthony*.

AKIO TAKAMORI (United States)

FIGURE 134
Sculpture, *Under the Peach Tree*, 1995.
Handbuilt and coiled porcelain with under- and overglazes, fired in oxidation, 63.5 x 78.7 x 30.5cm (25 x 31 x 12in.).
Courtesy of Garth Clark Gallery, New York.
Photograph: Akio Takamori

Akio Takamori — United States

There is a place I was born in, Kyushu Island, in 1950s' Japan. I have memories, images, stories, and sensations — collected from a childhood in the shadow of World War II. What does it mean to grow up in a culture that was itself transitioning and being rebuilt from outside factors? Who were the anonymous, who would be famous, and how would history record what I remembered?

There is the place I now live, Seattle, Washington, for the last 30 years. American culture extends to the most remote areas of the world. Its influence has altered the texture and rhythm of Japanese life. In this society, I teach, raise a family, and mature.

Somewhere between these places, I construct my own identity. The figures emerge as I am trying to come to terms with two cultures, along with my memories and humanity. My work exists in a metaphorical world where scale, proportion, and time expand and contract. It is a constantly changing place where I filter through memories. I become aware of connections to my heritage, to others, and to my present reality and perceptions. Yet despite cultural upheavals and changes, I sense a persistency in the human condition.

In *Under the Peach Tree*, [see Figure 134 on page 185] an image of fertility and family refers back to archetypal imagery of such themes found in many ancient cultures.

In *Ensemble* [Figure 135] I have juxtaposed figures from Western art with Japanese characters. For example, the central figure in the foreground [in the red cap], taken from Pieter Breughel's painting *The Peasant Wedding*, shares space with a young Japanese man reading. The arrangements of pieces create their own worlds, islands of imagery. These islands float outside reality, and, like dreams or memories are able to bring together different times and places in a single moment.

The installation *Boat* [Figure 136] recalls images from my childhood in Japan. Boats have always played a role in Japanese/American relations. Postwar Japan was in a transitional period, where a significant American military and diplomatic presence pushed the country into the modern world. Alone or in pairs, the figures maintain expressions of stoicism. Japanese peasants stand next to American soldiers. Japanese girls in kimonos are situated next to men in modern suits and work clothes. General MacArthur holds his ground in front, while the Emperor stands at the rear. Sharing the same platform, the figures seem to soberly accept the fate that has merged two foreign cultures together.

OPPOSITE PAGE

AKIO TAKAMORI (United States)

FIGURE 135 (above)
Sculpture installation, *Ensemble*, 2000.
Handbuilt and coiled stoneware with under- and overglazes, fired in oxidation.
Height range: 40.6–101.6cm (16–40in.).
Courtesy of Grover Thurston Gallery, Seattle
Photograph: Kate Preftakes

FIGURE 136 (below)
Sculpture (detail), *Sad Girl*, from installation *Boat*, 2001.
Handbuilt and coiled stoneware with underglazes, fired in oxidation, ht: 81cm (32in.).
Courtesy of Frank Lloyd Gallery, Santa Monica
Photograph: Akio Takamori

Contemporary Narratives:

Political and Social Commentary

11

The content of the work under review here is predominately political in nature, dealing with the artists' responses to the relevant problems and concerns of our times. The intent is to create specifically thought-provoking imagery that might force us as viewers to examine some of these presented issues and to question our own responses to them in turn. Such responses might include our complacent acceptance of existing cultural stereotypes (such as gender roles), our helplessness or passivity in the face of current wars or political and economic crises, our avoidance in dealing with personal and public problems, and so on. Some of this imagery is presented in mildly satiric form, some of it is ironic, some of it biting and 'in your face', even shocking, and some of it uses a more gentle, humorous approach. All of it demands examination and serious questioning on the part of the viewer.

Grayson Perry – United Kingdom

In the catalogue published on the occasion of an exhibition by Grayson Perry in November 2004 at the Victoria Miro Gallery in London, Lisa Jardine describes the artist and his work in an essay entitled 'Grayson Perry — very much his own man'. Through conversations with the artist she provides insights into his persona, his thoughts and his provocative ceramic imagery:

> Grayson Perry's work unsettles the contemporary art world. It is not simply because he chose to accept the Turner Prize 2003 in the person of his alter-ego 'Claire', dressed in the latest of his art-work 'coming out' frocks in mauve satin, exquisitely embroidered with rabbits, roses, hearts, and the words 'sissy' and 'Claire', and teamed with white ankle-socks and red patent-leather Mary-Jane

OPPOSITE PAGE

GRAYSON PERRY (United Kingdom)

FIGURE **137**
Detail of vase form,
The Soft Truth, 2004.
Glazed ceramic (unspecified),
46.5 x 33cm (18⅓ x 13in.).
Image courtesy of the artist and Victoria Miro Gallery, London
Photograph: Stephen Brayne

189

GRAYSON PERRY (United
Kingdom)

FIGURE 138 (left)
Vase form, *Wisdom Is Cool*,
2004.
Glazed ceramic (unspecified),
47 x 25cm (18½ x 10in.).
Photograph: Stephen Brayne

FIGURE 139 (right)
Vase form, *Us Against Us*,
2004.
Glazed ceramic (unspecified),
45 x 34cm (17¾ x 13⅜in.).
*Images courtesy of the artist and Victoria
Miro Gallery, London.*
Photograph: Stephen Brayne

shoes. Although, as Perry himself is quick to point out, the 'tranny' (which is how he refers to himself) does have a remarkable capacity to provoke anxiety. That, he explains, is some combination of disappointment and unease at the fragility of the illusion. The tranny does not try to 'pass' as a woman, all too clearly failing to convince, playing a part. In the street, the sidelong appreciative glances of the passers-by detect the illusion in a split second and their admiration falters. As Claire, Perry inhabits a space too close to the edge of acceptability for us — as audience — to be altogether comfortable.

What makes the art world even more nervous than Claire is the status of Perry's pots. Does a pot count as high art? Can an art vase move out of the world of craft, [...] school art rooms and evening classes? The decorated pot brings the domestic, the banal everyday, into the gallery. It blurs the boundary between familiar homely clutter and the way a gallery space strives to keep us aware of the representational strangeness of what we are looking at — the need to scrutinise it closely if we are to understand it. Is the critical anxiety generated by Perry's work a response to the fact that an exhibition of his ceramic pots all too closely resembles a department store window display of desirable consumer items set out for sale on pedestals?

[...] Grayson Perry as artist authority-figure, called upon to assign meaning to his work, is nowhere to be found. His insistence on the subordinate, inferior stance of the 'tranny potter' will not allow us to look to him for any sort of masculinist or triumphalist version of the 'meaning' of his work. 'It's no good asking me. I put forward the question in the work, I don't answer it.' [...]

The very authenticity of the work depends, for Perry, on this refusal to take responsibility: 'In our times, maintaining authenticity for me involves dealing with the changing role of being an artist. I think that's an important question. How do I inhabit this role now, when my work is in demand and it can command quite high prices and I can see in other peoples' eyes that they want me to take command? I want to go. It's not my job really. It might be a job for another artist, but it's not my job.' [...]

Behind Perry's work stands a sort of sadness — the plangency of anticipated disappointment — which clings to the kind of masturbatory fantasies he returns to again and again. Perry draws attention to this expectation of failure, of not achieving the looked-for pleasure, of loss and regret, in several modes as he seeks to specify his role as artist, and this must surely make us pay attention. In the domain of fetish and fantasy, repetition is the endlessly deferred anticipation of a pleasure which is always less than the best that might have been. After the fantasy comes the reality — but the reality will, as every fantasist knows, always fail to live up to the fantasy.

Then too there is Claire. Grayson Perry's artistic agenda is already set out in his self-presentation as 'tranny potter', the disappointingly not quite-perfect-enough illusion of the adorable little girl in the beautifully embroidered dress. Describing the role he sees for himself as an artist, Perry says he wants to have his hand on the shoulder of the viewer as they come to terms with his work, that he is there, quietly and submissively, having embraced his own sense of inferiority, having relinquished his status as powerful male figure in the art world. But it is Claire's hand we find on our shoulder, warning us that after the rapture of anticipation we should be ready to settle for disappointment. That is what gives Grayson Perry's work its extraordinary power and contemporary importance.

Sandra Taylor – *Australia*

Clay seems to suit my restless nature. Straight away my hero was Bob Arneson and later Jun Kaneko whose respect for cause and effect made me acutely aware of my own lacking. Then there was Viola Frey whose giants made me feel as if I was caught up in the ravages of a natural disaster. Generally, I make work about what's close to my own back door.

Wandering around the streets looking out for the odd, the weird and the quirky has always been a bit of a hobby and sometimes an inspiration. Now and again I come across an honest little cottage whose hedges and gnomes just glow with

Sandra Taylor (Australia)

FIGURE **140**
Sculpture, *Final Merger*, 1996.
Hand-modelled earthenware
with layered and multi-fired
underglaze colours, fired in
oxidation, 57 x 37cm
(22½ x 14½in.).
Photograph: Sandra Taylor

Evelyn Grant (Canada)

FIGURE **141**
Teapot, *How and Why* (from
'Woman's Work' series), 1998.
Slipcast and handbuilt earthen-
ware with low-fire glazes and
china paints, fired in
oxidation, 42.5 x 32.5cm
(16¾ x 12¾in.).
Collection of Burlington Art Centre, Canada
Photograph: Evelyn Grant

contentment. Some houses and their people are very symbiotic while others just can't seem to work each other out. Some houses are so embellished with every attention lavished on them while their people remain neglected and unhappy. Then again some houses look quite miserable and their people don't seem to notice.

The creeping 'mansionisation' of Australia is now in epidemic proportion. If you're unhappy with your current situation then true happiness awaits you with a change of lifestyle: a fabulous house and garden of your dreams straight out of the catalogue. But when does a multi-mortgaged and still struggling couple get to play out their dream lifestyle when they now have five bathrooms and five toilets to clean, a perfect lawn with a curved swathe of tamed pencil pines diminishing in size to a small dot (looking remarkably like a question mark) to manicure? What sort of lives are we inventing for ourselves?

This work is from a series called 'Romantic Dividends' [see Figure 140] and is about the often unhappy situations we create for ourselves in our search for what we think will bring us happiness.

Evelyn Grant – *Canada*

During the past 25 years, I have refined my technical narrative and ceramic skills. My work is a collage-like combination of surface treatment, imagery and form, used to develop the content. Upon reviewing my work at this time, I can clearly see my own personal development in the issues I choose to explore: women's issues, family issues and political commentary. I do this work because I am compelled to. The fact that it is accessible and understood by others is a bonus.

The 'Woman's Work' series was created during a period when I was struggling to maintain a clean house, raise children, work at a demanding job, and in my free time produce works in clay. My mother was a traditional stay-at-home 1950s mom, and in the back of my mind, I have always had her as the model for the wife and mother I was supposed to become. Unfortunately, the soul-satisfying part of my existence had to be done on my own time, late at night and on weekends. The form and images on 'Woman's Work' represent the stacking up of the roles I was playing, and the dichotomy of the lovely tea party, followed by the not-so-lovely clean up. *How and Why* [Figure 141] is a large teapot for a large issue. The piece examines the personal dilemma I was wrestling with as to why I should continue to pursue working as an artist, when at times it proved to be so difficult. The answer: Fame and Fortune, of course!

I feel it is important, as is the case with Victorian majolica that my pieces retain their functionality. The object can function on several levels, as a teapot meant for use and handling, and as an image meant to be thought-provoking and controversial.

PATTI WARASHINA (United States)

FIGURE **142** (left)
Sculpture, *Crow Whisper* (from 'Real Politique' series), 2003.
Slipcast, pressmoulded and handbuilt earthenware with multiple-fired underglazes, metal stand, fired in oxidation, 180.3 x 45.7 x 35.6cm (71 x 18 x 14 in.).
Photograph: Rob Vinnedge

FIGURE **143** (right)
Sculpture, *Tule Lake Retreat* (from 'Real Politique' series), 2003.
Slipcast, pressmoulded and handbuilt earthenware with multiple-fired underglazes, metal stand, fired in oxidation, 172.5 x 45.7 x 30.5cm (68 x 18 x 12 in.).
Photograph: Rob Vinnedge

Patti Warashina – United States

The name of this series is 'Real Politique'. The dictionary defines this term as 'an expansionist national policy having as its sole purpose the advancement of national interest'. Along with many others, I am very intrigued and absorbed by current affairs. I read a number of periodicals, and stay abreast of what is happening while captivated by the news on TV. I sometimes think of myself as a voyeur looking from outside into our world, trying to stay abreast of new situations that affect the world. With globalisation, technology, and governmental policies, civilisation is sometimes profoundly changed overnight.

This brings me to my current work in the studio. While working on the 'Mile Post Queen' series, one of my female figures had the gestures and feeling of a masked French circus figure, perhaps in a side-show. Since my work generally is narrative and sometimes autobiographical, I could see my interest in world issues combine with the absurd atmosphere of a festive circus. This is the basis of this series displayed in a circus ring atmosphere, called 'Real Politique'. *Crow Whisper* [Figure 142] — a ballet skirt, on second look, is a red-hot saw blade invading the habitat of the crow looking on. *Tule Lake Retreat* [Figure 143] shows a watch and guard tower at the Japanese relocation centre in Idaho, during World War II, where many were held without effective counsel and without being charged, in conditions likened to a prison camp . . .

Craig Mitchell – *United Kingdom*

My work explores contemporary culture and universal themes but also responds to current events both political and personal. Everything in my life, every chance comment, every potentially insignificant interaction and childhood memory is mixed into the melting pot of my work. Realising slightly surreal ceramic creations is my way of relating to the increasingly bizarre reality which forms the fabric of our daily lives.

The discovery in the late 1980s of the work of Scottish painter Steven Campbell was an important turning point in my creative development; notably the use of bold, cartoon-like figures and a bright colour palette in his narratives. In my own work I try to express ideas using humour to 'sugar the pill', sometimes creating unlikely scenarios or ridiculous juxtapositions that draw the reader in to these tales with a smile before being faced with a mildly chiding finger.

An important strand running through my work is food, and I have explored ideas that include its production, consumption and promotion. Love and relationships form another important theme in my work, in particular looking at the different character traits between men and women. In *Hothouse* [Figure 144], a man crouches on a pier fanning the flames of desire, whilst his sweetheart propagates and nurtures home sweet home. Will the combination of their different priorities achieve the perfect balance? The spindly pier reminds us that maintenance is essential, or fragility and possible collapse will ensue. Further male personality traits are explored in *Miro's Washing Machine* [Figure 145]. A surreal mechanism requires the operator to develop non-existent multitasking and organisational skills. As he smugly performs he awaits approval from an imagined female audience.

CRAIG MITCHELL (United Kingdom)

FIGURE **144** (above)
Sculpture, *Hothouse*, 2003.
Nylon fibre-strengthened
earthenware with underglazes,
glazes, enamels, lustres and metal,
fired in oxidation, 110 x 100 x 20cm
(43⅕ x 39⅓ x 8in.).
Photograph: Shannon Tofts

FIGURE **145** (below)
Sculpture, *Miro's Washing Machine*,
2003.
Nylon fibre-strengthened
earthenware with underglazes,
glazes, enamels, lustres and metal,
fired in oxidation, 40 x 60 x 30cm
(15¾ x 23⅔ x 11¾in.).
Photograph: John K. MacGregor

195

LÁSZLÓ FEKETE (Hungary)

FIGURE 146 (above)
Sculpture, *Self-Liberating Statue*, 1995–96.
Slipcast and assembled coloured clays and porcelain, with glazes, lustres and decals, fired in oxidation, ht: 69cm (27in.).
Photograph: Gyula Tahin

FIGURE 147 (above right)
Sculpture, *The Thief of Baghdad*, 2002–03.
Slipcast and assembled porcelain with glazes, lustres and decals, fired in oxidation, ht: 36cm (14in.).
Photograph: Gyula Tahin

László Fekete – *Hungary*

I live in Budapest, Hungary in Central Europe and my environment has had a major impact on my work. This part of Europe can be regarded as a huge, always busy passageway, where different cultures, ideas, religions, armies, goods, people, empires, etc. have been constantly on the move from the East to the West and vice-versa over the past three to four thousand years.

In my city you can find an especially high number of old monuments from early Roman times, since the Danube River was located on the border of the great Roman Empire. How many peoples and empires have followed after them? Everything was destroyed and rebuilt, pulled down and restored, exterminated, resettled and burned down again, yet from each era something has remained. For example in Hungary, there have been ten to eleven basic political regime changes in the 20th century alone, each affecting our lives and also our way of thinking, our attitudes and our mentality.

The monument-like *Self-Liberating Statue* [Figure 146] shows how we have so often been liberated by some of our 'big brothers.' It is a dark work inspired for the most part by the many public monuments (some excellent, some less so), that can be found throughout Central Europe. Add to them the injuries, the defacing with hammers, the spraying of graffiti, and the stupid commercials, and their true nature is revealed — damaged, broken, shot into, sprayed upon, etc.

The story of *The Thief of Baghdad* [Figure 147] showing a figure carrying a broken vase is quite peculiar. I fired the figure and the vase as early as the fall of 2002 and they stood like that until the spring of 2003. It was at that time that I watched on TV a citizen of Baghdad looting Saddam's palace and hurrying home with a giant vase on his back. I then immediately knew what to do with

WALTER OSTROM (Canada)

FIGURE **148**
Iraqi War Soap Dishes, 2003.
Thrown and pressmoulded
earthenware with maiolica
glaze and painted stains,
fired in oxidation,
15 x 17cm (6 x 6⅔in.).
Photograph: Julian Beveridge

my undecorated pieces. I selected items from my stock of decals to reflect that particular narrative; palaces, triumphant arches, bellowing stags ready for the hunt, lots of gold, etc.

Walter Ostrom — *Canada*

Pottery has always functioned as a container for cultural, economic, spiritual and aesthetic information. My work is utilitarian, but I have always combined and composed historical images, materials and techniques to reflect an informed contemporary view of both utility and ornament. Although keenly interested in current events, this is the first time that I have directly addressed political issues in my work.

These *Iraqi War Soap Dish* souvenirs are literal and traditional [see Figure 148]. There is a long and rich tradition of commemorative ceramics. I am sure that the Franklin Mint is even now working on something brave and patriotic. Utilitarian pottery is unique because it can be subversive. The soap dish format is the beginning of my 'Lady MacBeth' series dealing with all those events that white liberals would like to wash off their hands.

I began these pieces while living in Italy during the period preceding and during the invasion of Iraq. The images I used are very much a bastardisation of Italian *istoriato* imagery, e.g. ribbons, figures, plants and globes. My motivation in making this work was to deal with my own feelings of powerlessness in the face of these events.

The central images shown here are of the world on fire and of the weeping willow (complements of a Halifax tombstone), both obvious symbols of disaster

197

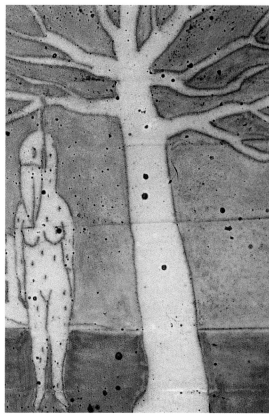

BIRGITTE BÖRJESON (Denmark)

FIGURE **149** (above left)
Bowl, untitled, 2004.
Thrown and altered
stoneware, with slips,
sgraffito and salt glaze,
fired in reduction,
dia: 60cm (23⅔ in.),
ht: 42cm (16½in.).

Photograph: Pernille Klemp

FIGURE **150** (above right)
Detail of untitled vessel
form, 2002.
Thrown and altered
stoneware, with slips,
sgraffito and salt glaze,
fired in reduction,
w: 27cm, ht: 20cm
(w: 10⅔in., ht: 8in.).

Photograph: Pernille Klemp

and death. The ribbon with the words 'Axis of Evil' played against 'Bush' and 'Blair' offer an alternative interpretation of the events. Lastly, a signature 'Woe' on the backs of the dishes is an ordering of my assistant's and my own initials, in a manner that seems appropriate to this particular tragedy.

Birgitte Börjeson – Denmark

I find it difficult to express in words my intentions in presenting some of these 'stories'. The most fundamental theme I feel compelled to explore is that of 'good' and 'evil'. The on-going wars around the world, in particular the most recent, and to me unnecessary war in Iraq, provoke constant feelings of help-lessness and frustration [Figure 149]. At the same time I try to maintain hopes for a better world in the future.

Like the ancient Greek potters who scratched images of their daily lives onto their *amphorae*, I also try to come to terms with life around me, and to 'scratch' my stories into the vessels that are a collaborative work with my husband, Hans Börjeson. We are thus able to exorcise our feelings to some degree, and perhaps present imagery that might strike a chord of empathy in the viewer.

The animal-like representations [Figure 150] are in some cases symbols for eternity, in others for innocence and the plight of the underdog. They are also no doubt influenced by our long sojourn in Africa, a country rich in compelling imagery of animals and stories about animals.

Paul Mathieu — *Canada*

In a culture of consumerism and entertainment, the creative act must remain radical and subversive. The last place where this might be possible is within craft practices. I see ceramics (and pottery) as an independent, autonomous and specific art form. It is that specificity that my work explores, regarding such concepts particular to craft practices as decoration, function and containment, in a unique relation to time, to history and to human experiences.

The current series of salt and pepper shaker 'Disasters' [see Figures 151 and 152] was started in 1999 as a retrospective journey exploring major and minor events of the 20th century: from the Titanic to the Holocaust; from the Hiroshima Bombing to Tienamen Square; from Kennedy's assassination to the AIDS crisis; and to more or less inconsequential events, like the crash death of Princess Diana in Paris; the O.J. Simpson murders; or the Monica Lewinsky-Bill Clinton Affair.

The innocent, familiar, functional, decorative and commemorative format of the salt and pepper shakers reinforces our ambiguous relation to these events and brings them subversively into our homes and daily lives. This reaffirms the need never to forget that remembrance and memory must follow us even in the most ordinary and domestic circumstances. Due to the particular physical nature of ceramics and its specific relation to time, these objects, like all ceramic objects, have the potential to be around for a long, long time and may one day be all that is left of these events — ceramics is the memory of humankind.

PAUL MATHIEU (Canada)

FIGURE **151** (left)
Salt and Pepper Shakers / 'Disasters' series, *Shoah 1933–45*, 1999.
Slipcast porcelain with enamels and lustres, fired in oxidation,
15 x 10 x 10cm (6 x 4 x 4in.).
Photograph: Rory McDonald

FIGURE **152** (right)
Salt and Pepper Shakers / 'Disasters' series, *W.T.C., 09–11–01*, 2002.
Slipcast porcelain with enamels and lustres, fired in oxidation,
25 x 10 x 10cm (10 x 4 x 4in.).
Photograph: Rory McDonald

PAUL SCOTT (United Kingdom)

FIGURE 153 (above)
'Scott's Cumbrian Blue(s)'
series, *Foot and Mouth No.5,
Carving Platter, 10/10*, 2003.
Screen-print on-glaze decals
on Royal Worcester bone china
platter, fired in oxidation,
42 x 32cm (16½ x 12½in.).
Photograph: Paul Scott

FIGURE 154 (below)
'Scott's Cumbrian Blue(s)'
series, *The Nuclear
Vignettes, Seascale Pigeon
Landscape*, 2003.
Ceramic form with porcelain
slip and on-glaze screen-print
collage, fired in oxidation,
40 x 25 x 14cm
(15¾ x 10 x 5½in.).
Photograph: Paul Scott

Paul Scott – *United Kingdom*

I have always been primarily interested in images related to the ceramic surface. In particular I am interested in the depiction of landscape on ceramic surfaces; in the way ceramic engravers plundered fine art landscape paintings reproduced as engravings for book illustrations, and adapted them and other

pictorial sources for decorative purposes on the surface of mass-produced industrial ceramics. Working in a similar way, I deconstruct old engravings (made for ceramic prints, as well as book illustrations) and extract specific elements in order to digitally manipulate and collage them with other images (my own photographs and drawings).

Using the vocabulary of symbolic pattern and the visual language of 'blue and white' (industrially produced ceramic decoration), with the duality of the ceramic medium (form as image, image as form), my work variously examines the effects of industrialisation, pollution and cultivation on differing landscapes. Landscapes can be seen as fantasy or pastoral decoration, as producers of food, as sources of energy and consumer products, and as escapes from urban living. A separate, but related strand of my work sometimes more openly commemorates (or comments on) political events or attitudes.

In early 2001, my own village in rural North Cumbria was in the middle of the largest outbreak of Foot and Mouth disease ever to hit British agriculture. For several months the grisly process of culling and disposing of infected animals (or those suspected of infection) haunted our community, and affected our lives profoundly. The smell of burning pyres was mingled with the rotting stench of decomposing sheep and by night bonfires lit up strangely silent skies. Friends found their jobs suddenly gone or their livelihoods under constant threat. It was hard to believe that life would ever return to normal. I felt it important to mark these dark times with some commemorative pieces [see Figure 153].

The 'Scott Collection: Cumbrian Blue(s) Seascale Pigeon' series commemorates the following event:

In 1998, pigeons roosting at the Sellafield Nuclear Reprocessing plant in Cumbria, England, were found to carry levels of radiation, which were described by a company spokeswoman as 'significant'. The general public was advised not to handle, kill or consume any pigeon found within a ten-mile radius of the Sellafield plant. The advice was given on the basis of preliminary monitoring of the mainly feral pigeons by BNFL and on the supposition that feral pigeons were unlikely to travel more than that distance in their feeding habits.

Greenpeace highlighted the serious health risks posed to the public by these pigeons, and pointed to the requirement for the birds to be classified as Low Level Waste. 'How can BNFL pretend that they have their plutonium factory under control when they have nuclear waste flying over the fence?' said Dr Helen Wallace of Greenpeace. Despite their acceptance of the Greenpeace analysis the pigeons' classification as Low Level Waste and the company's determination to wipe out the entire flock because of the contamination levels, BNFL maintained that there was no risk to the public.

PAUL DAY (United Kingdom, France)

FIGURE **155** (above)
Sculpted relief, *St. Gudule and the Devil*, 1999.
Carved unglazed terracotta, fired in oxidation, 140 x 70 x 40cm (55 x 28 x 15¾in.).
Photograph: Jean–Claude Planchet

FIGURE **156** (right)
Sculpted relief, *Chatelet CCTV*, 2002.
Carved unglazed terracotta, fired in oxidation, 92.7 x 81.3 x 48.3cm (36½ x 32 x 19in.).
Photograph: J.P. Muzard

Paul Day — *United Kingdom, France*

The political content of Paul Day's relief sculptures is revealed in his acute observation of 'human behaviour' situations. The viewer is presented with characters in sometimes 'real', sometimes allegorical situations that move through familiar yet distorted urban landscapes, and make us question our perception and responses to all things familiar and accepted. The artist shares with us the following insights into his work:

> For me, a great work of art happens when brilliant observation and wonderful emotional understanding are coupled to a supremely intelligent use of compositional form. The resultant vision portrays a convincing world, not dissimilar to the one we know, yet fundamentally different from it. This artistic world is governed by a poetic appreciation of form and is full of insight into the human predicament. Figurative art remains a terrific vehicle for thought and can superbly illustrate intellectual concepts, yet what really matters is not how the art speaks to the critical faculty in my brain, but how it resonates within my very emotional, intellectual and spiritual core.
>
> I am a student working under the influence of my masters (Donatello, Breughel, Spencer, etc.), hoping one day to have created to the best of my ability a visual art form that resembles me and speaks to others on my behalf. The challenging and joyful path I travel to get there is ultimately what gives the whole thing meaning, but I am delighted when someone else is genuinely moved by what I make.
>
> Relief sculpture is about a delight in picture making and the use of light and shadow to colour a work. It is the contradiction between drawn perspective and real space, creating visual ambiguities and distortions, that fascinates me. Relief sculpture represents better than anything our experience of architecture and depth. It is when we are on the move that space reveals itself to us. Imagine walking through a city and seeing the buildings move around you. If you stop, then it is the movement of other things that describes the space.
>
> *St. Gudule and the Devil* [see Figure 155]: Gudule is the patron saint of the Cathedral in Brussels. She was followed by the Devil who tried to extinguish the light by which she read her Bible, blowing it out with his foul breath. The foulness of his breath is like the polluting traffic fumes that will one day extinguish life from the city.
>
> *Chatelet CCTV* [Figure 156]: The wide-angle lens of a CCTV camera has recorded a distorted vision of Saturday afternoon in the Métro in Paris — angry youths, snogging couples, happy families and a *sans abri* who sees the world through his own distorted lens — a bottle. It is he who imagines the train driver to be a skeleton and the train a vehicle to take lost souls to the underworld. Perhaps his insight is closest to the truth.

203

Contemporary Narratives:

The Object as Message and Metaphor

12

I n this chapter I present images of works that are less 'human-figure' oriented in painted and sculpted form, such as seen previously. These works might be regarded as more 'allusive' narratives in the form of thought-provoking objects or the juxtaposition of such objects. The presented content (from the artists' point of view) exhibits a full range of ideas, from personal reflections to political statements. It is the objects themselves and their contextual arrangement that convey the given specific message, or become the metaphor or symbol for an idea. These messages are more indirect, and demand of us as viewers the task of identifying and interpreting familiar objects, and their symbolic and associational roles. We are then obliged to re-evaluate these roles along with our own responses to them, in the hopes of expanding or sharpening our own perceptions and creating our own narratives.

Antje Scharfe – Germany

The vessel can be perceived in a variety of ways: rounded, volumetric, and above all, as a functional container. Then there are my 'vessels', generally not round, usually flat and without a container-opening, denying all volume [Figure 157]. Since they have abnegated their function, their meaning must be found elsewhere as ideas. Relevance and volume are established as ideas through a compositional still-life composed of such individual 'vessels'. Space, dimensions and volume need to be interpreted through the interaction and interrelationship between vessel, still-life and observer. That process of observation, and of placing familiar objects into an altered context leads the viewer to a redefinition of what is familiar, and to the creation of a subjective narrative.

OPPOSITE PAGE

ANTJE SCHARFE (Germany)

FIGURE **157**
Wall Installation, *Kitchen 1*, 2002.
Modelled and slipcast stoneware, porcelain and glass, fired in oxidation, 78 x 53cm (30¾ x 21in.).
Photograph: Bernd Kuhnert

Sylvia Hyman – United States

Now that I'm 86, I can see that my work has changed along with my life. During the first 45 years I flexed my wings, working in two and three dimensions with a variety of media as varied as paint and gold. Then I discovered that clay was the medium in which I could best express my ideas, observations and emotions. I wanted to learn everything I could about clay: its origins, its history of use, and the various kinds of clays and their physical properties.

About ten years ago my imagination turned to a more intimate form of sculpture in the genre known as *trompe l'oeil*. As subject matter, I choose familiar objects such as old boxes or baskets and fill them with contents that both convey information and stir the mind: documents, letters, old papers, scrolls of music, architects' blueprints, even crossword puzzles — all made of stoneware and/or porcelain. I try to capture not only the appearance of things but also their essential nature, giving equal weight to meaning and to visual impact.

Storytelling is not what I set out to do when I conceive ideas for my works — and yet, they do seem to ultimately tell a story or to convey a message. These are however not straightforward, and may be interpreted in different ways.

Genesis 7 [Figure 158], the story of Noah and the flood is of course a familiar story from The Old Testament. In my sculpture, the woven ark-shaped basket is quite porous and would hardly survive a flood let alone protect the scrolls contained in it. My screen-printed porcelain scrolls in both print and illuminated calligraphy tell the same story in four languages: Arabic, Akkadian (ancient Babylonian), Hebrew, and English. The ancient story was saved in cuneiform on clay and now my work has preserved various versions of this story in clay as well. It's interesting to note that the cultures of the Middle East that once had so much in common have become so divergent in present-day ideology.

SYLVIA HYMAN (United States)

FIGURE 158
Sculpture, *Genesis 7*, 2003. Slab-built porcelain and stoneware, with screen-printed and stamped underglazes, fired in oxidation, 30.5 x 45.7 x 25.4cm (12 x 18 x 10 in.).

Courtesy of Vanderbilt University Divinity School

Photograph: John Cummings

Karen Dahl – *Canada*

As a child leafing through art books, and later visiting art galleries during my travels, I have always gravitated towards early European still-life depictions — the more realistic, the better. Not surprisingly, the objects surrounding me in everyday life, both natural and man-made, have always inspired me. I am a compulsive collector and I adore the bizarre and unusual.

I use faithfully reproduced, familiar objects as visual tools to seduce viewers into my work. Such objects readily elicit emotional responses, conscious or otherwise. I exploit this by assembling the objects in sometimes unexpected ways, and satisfy my attraction to the bizarre by occasionally including peculiar objects or puzzling circumstances. The narrative is in the individual objects, whereas the combined allusion is broad and amorphous and may vary according to the experiences of the viewer. My work is *trompe l'oeil* with layers of mystery, reflection, humour and occasional menace.

In *Round and Round — Life Goes On* [Figure 159], we all have our own alligators of angst nipping at our heels. Travelling through the dark and mysterious places of life we try to move forward, but sometimes we come back inadvertently to where we started and we repeat our mistakes. Some of us sit above it all, blissfully oblivious to the mayhem. The grocery list reminds us of the grind of daily chores, and yet the book 'Chums' provides a foundation of friendship. We long for more days off… .

In *Race* [Figure 160], life is a struggle to get ahead and we are always trying to surmount one obstacle or another. It's often a messy process, and sometimes confusing, but generally we persevere. Wind us up and we race around. Still, you gotta laugh… .

KAREN DAHL (Canada)

FIGURE 159 (left)
Sculpture, *Round and Round; Life Goes On*, 1998. Handbuilt and slipcast earthenware components, with underglazes, glazes and lustres, multiple-fired in oxidation, 21 x 28 x 24 cm (8¼ x 11 x 9½ in.).
Photograph: Karen Dahl

FIGURE 160 (right)
Sculpture, *Race*, 1999. Handbuilt and slipcast earthenware components, with underglazes, glazes and lustres, multiple-fired in oxidation, 23 x 41 x 21cm (9 x 16 x 8¼in.).
Photograph: Karen Dahl

PAUL A. DRESANG (United States)

FIGURE **161**
Sculpture, *Donny's Bag*, 2001.
Slab-built, thrown and pressmoulded porcelain with slips, underglazes, lustres, enamels, screen-printing and transfers, fired in reduction, 35 x 56 x 50cm
(13¾ x 22 x 19⅝in.).

Photograph: Joseph Gruber

Paul Dresang – *United States*

What draws me to clay is the precise way in which it can record my touch and the extraordinary way it can be made to resemble any other material. These inherent qualities of mutability and sensitivity to touch, whether coarse or refined, begin the process of narration and lead to the communicative function of the object. What is needed is only the desire to communicate, and the requisite making skills.

The versatility of porcelain as a medium has constantly intrigued me, with its ability to 'simulate' the warmth of skin, or the feel of wood, leather or metal. The seduction lies in the creation of a *trompe l'oeil* work that can confound and challenge the viewer and begin a dialogue. Pieces like *Donny's Bag* [Figure 161] reveal familiar objects in quirky and unusual combinations.

These pieces are meant to have the potential of 'layered' associations that might evoke a story in the mind of the viewer, rather than recount a particular established narrative. The 'real' narrative in fact begins to occur with the observer filling in the gaps of a personal story, that might be very different from any which I propose.

JURIS BERGINS (Latvia)

FIGURE 162
Sculpture, *Candlestick*, 2002.
Slipcast bone china com-
ponents, with on-glaze
colours and transfers,
fired in oxidation,
24 x 22 x 18cm
(9½ x 8⅔ x 7in.).
Photograph: Juris Bergins

Juris Bergins – *Latvia*

Porcelain is my 'canvas' for expressing ideas and feelings in three-dimension. I live in a country traditionally torn between the values of Eastern- and Western-European political, social and ideological currents. The post-1989 years, with the decline of communism and the influx of Western European influences have had an important impact on my work.

For example, in *Candlestick* [Figure 162], I allude to the burning out of a candle as a metaphor for the ending of the century 1900–2000. I juxtapose portraits of historic Latvian political figures with imagery of tinned consumer goods, both signifying the fluctuations of power and ideology in a century where independence was gained and lost two times.

209

HOLLY HANESSIAN (United States)

FIGURE **163**
Wall in installation, *Luck*, 2002.
Handbuilt and thrown porcelain components, with terra sigillata, fired in oxidation, 76.2 x 53.4 x 12.7cm (30 x 21 x 5in.).

Photograph: Patrick Young

Holly Hanessian — United States

I have always enjoyed the dichotomy of visual clues inherent in narrative art. For the last 25 years I have woven various stories into my studio art practice. At times I have selectively told parts of them in an effort to give sublime meaning to the narratives. There have been other moments, however, when the narratives have been so blatant that I have had to step back and screen my thought process in order not to give away the entire story to the viewing audience.

I have also struggled with the question of writing directly on the work to make the words apparent. To disguise the literal meanings of these words, I have developed a cursive handwriting style. This writing is further obscured through the ways I begin and end sentences, and how I activate the surface with layers of slip and other materials.

My most recent work involves using ceramic cursive text as a seductive and accessible way to tell stories about how chance, fate and luck play an important role in our lives [see Figure 163].

This work cycle came as a response to a series of difficult life choices related to death, fecundity and progeny. I began creating a series of book-related works with cradles and abstracted female and male body parts, combining them with ideas on luck, chance and fate. The work has handwriting on it, both my own and others', as well as ceramic letterforms that create words which recombine with other ceramic forms, providing a new narrative.

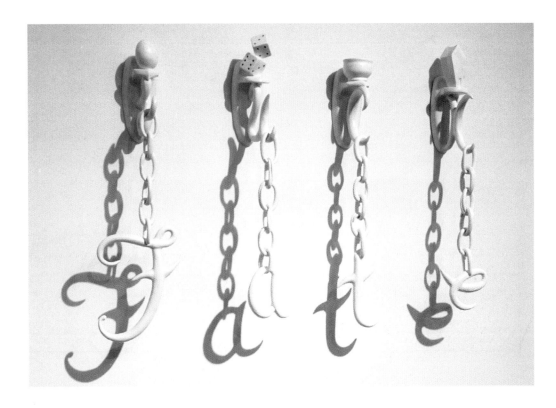

Gudrun Klix – *Australia*

The fact that I can work clay directly with my hands unmediated by tools, allows me to record moments in time and to express moods and feelings that might otherwise be more difficult to express using other media. When working I aim to allow the clay to develop its own rhythms, and not to consciously determine the outcome. I try to watch what evolves, being open to what develops. Ideally the artist and material become partners in a process that arises from some subconscious level. Taken together the work can be seen as a kind of personal narrative that is a record of feelings and responses to places and situations.

To a large extent my work is about travel and personal journeys. My first major journey took place during childhood, when my family fled from the Russians. These journeys tend to have psychological and symbolic significance; they are journeys of self discovery, about who I am in relationship to people and new situations, about capabilities, limitations and challenges, and as well as about discovery of place.

The boat forms, which I've been making since the 1990s are like private diaries [see Figures 164 and 165]. Through their material physicality they are connected to the earth and to our relationship with it. I'm intrigued with how versatile this single form can be, referring at various times to leaves, seed pods, water, waves, mountains, organic life forms, even fire. They are not only about physical journeys and places visited, they are also about the experiential and the emotional, the questioning of self, aloneness, pain, pleasure, and to a large extent the wonder of place.

GUDRUN KLIX (Australia)

FIGURE **164** (below)
Sculpture, *Fissure*, 2004.
Handbuilt and pressmoulded earthenware, with acid-patinated manganese/copper glaze, fired in oxidation, 84 x 18 x 14cm
(33 x 7 x 5½in.).
Photograph: Blue Murder Studios

FIGURE **165** (bottom)
Sculpture, *Night Journey*, 2004.
Handbuilt and pressmoulded earthenware, with acid-patinated manganese/copper glaze, fired in oxidation, 85 x 19 x 30cm
(33½ x 7½ x 11¾in.).
Photograph: Blue Murder Studios

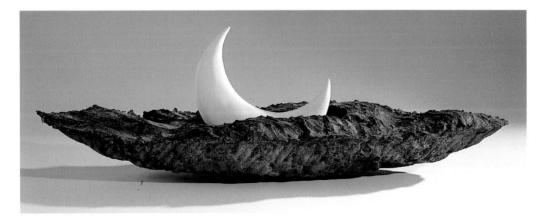

KIMIYO MISHIMA (Japan)

FIGURE 166 (below)
Installation, *Another Rebirth*,
2003.
Waste clay, burnt garbage
slag and glass, volcanic ash
and resin, silk-screen
printing, copper wire,
fired in reduction,
1990 x 1550 x 350cm
(783½ x 610¼ x 137¾in.).
Photograph: Narihumi Kato

OPPOSITE PAGE

FIGURE 167 (above)
Installation, *Copy 82*,
1974–82.
Waste clay with paper, silk-
screen printing, matt glaze,
fired in oxidation,
500 x 1000 x 1000cm
(197 x 393½ x 393½in.).
*Photograph courtesy of Museum of Art,
Yamagushi*

FIGURE 168 (below)
Installation, *Work 2000 —
Record of Twenty*, 2003.
Fire bricks with screen
printing, fired in reduction,
1700 x 650 x 15cm
(669¼ x 256 x 6in.).
Photograph: Narihumi Kato

Kimiyo Mishima – *Japan*

In the 1950s I was interested in creating collage works on canvas of printed matter, using scraps of newspaper, ad posters, magazines, and so on. One day I found that the many lumps of printed paper scraps littering my studio seemed to have a presence of their own. This pushed me into exploring three-dimensional works, and I examined many kinds of materials and eventually found myself working with clay.

Clay was not only malleable and easy to manipulate, but it exhibited the same fragility that I was exploring in the subject matter itself. This inherent material fragility became a constant metaphor for the 'fragility', or tenuous qualities of information as disseminated in contemporary society. It was this uncertainty and fear in our information-filled present-day lives that I wished to convey in a humorous and ironical way.

In my installations [see Figures 167 and 168] information (printed matter) which has been transformed into ceramics, has had the meaning of its existence newly substantiated and solidified. These works have become the record of our daily information-filled lives and the inevitable passage of time.

In the work *Another Rebirth* [Figure 166] I have deliberately used burnt-off fused garbage slag, combined with cast tile factory clay to support the printed matter image. The metaphor again is clear — printed information itself quickly becomes rubbish, no longer valid, informational detritus as meaningless and marginal as the materials on which it is printed, the future clutter of our lives.

Liu Jianhua – *People's Republic of China*

In the catalogue *Regular/Fragile* — *Liu Jianhua* (Translation: Karen Smith), Pi Li describes the recent works of Chinese artist, Liu Jianhua, as follows:

> Liu Jianhua has been concerned with the obsessiveness of culture toward the individual, and has continually created a discord between symbols as a means of revealing the existence of this oppressive power in culture. With the use of feminine symbols like the *cheongsam* [a tight-fitting Chinese dress] in *Obsessive Memories* [see Figure 169], he began to contemplate his work in an internationalised, globalised cultural context. Through the absence of the individual and the presence of eroticism, he fosters a ruminative attitude on the part of the viewer toward the work, which hints at the true relationship between the Western art world and the contemporary art of Third World countries.
>
> Assuming the guise of a cunning court jester, Liu pretends to do his best to conform, but all the while utilises the constant shifts from sculpture to multi-colour glazed ceramic object to make the creator (a Third World artist) disappear from art (Third World art). Ultimately, he serves up the de-personalised outer shell on blue-and-white and *famille rose* porcelain, creating in the name of culture an exotic feast at which there are no individual entities — not even the artist himself as an individual — but only 'culture' and the nominalism of culture. [...]
>
> To Euro-centrists, the interpretation of contemporary Chinese art involves the process of decoding Chinese symbolism, but to contemporary Chinese artists intent on seizing the opportunity, this very Chinese symbolism represents the only means by which they can internationalise their art. [...]
>
> Unlike many contemporary Chinese artists, he no longer directs his questions to party politics or the political system, but extends his sight to the issue of individual existence, and combines it with the Western right of cultural choice and such issues as diversity, pluralism and viewing.

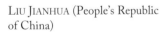

LIU JIANHUA (People's Republic of China)

FIGURE 169
Sculpture, *Obsessive Memories*, 1999.
Slipcast porcelain, with underglaze cobalt, celadon glaze and lustres, fired in oxidation, 58 x 36 x 32cm (23 x 14 x 12½in.).

Photograph: Huang Xi

214

 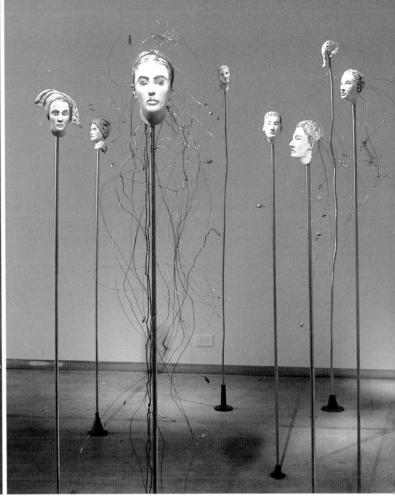

Judy Moonelis — United States

The emotive implications of anatomical study inform much of my sculptural work. Medical illustrations and anatomical models are resources along with the visually seductive scientific methods of collecting, ordering and cross-referencing materials.

Connections between our inner world and our external environment are primary. Porous, elastic boundaries separate these worlds: botanical, vascular, hydraulic, electrical, neural, biological, emotional, molecular and architectural. Our bodies are mirrored in our surroundings. Angles of branching, whether of veins, tree limbs, roots or rivers, rely on similar underlying principals. 'Inversion' [Figure 170] is from a series based on breath. The bronchial tree, a central structure in the human respiratory system, resembles an inverted tree or botanical root — branching forms essential to life.

A strong interest in the human senses led me to an exploration of the sense of touch. In the 'Touch Portraits' series for example [see Figure 171], I considered the primacy of touch as a perceptual tool, the vital meaning of touch, and the profound effect of its absence. The microscopic internal world of touch receptors was integrated with external portraits. The wire forms, like the touch receptors, are highly sensitive to motion and vibration.

JUDY MOONELIS (United States)

FIGURE **170** (left)
Hanging sculpture, *Inversion*, 2002.
Handbuilt white earthenware, fired in oxidation, 109.2 x 78.7 x 30.5cm (43 x 31 x 12in.).
Photograph: Malcolm Varon

FIGURE **171** (right)
Installation, *Touch Portraits*, 2000.
Handbuilt porcelain, oxide washes, wire, fired in oxidation, ht: 152.4 to 213.4cm (60 to 84in.).
Photograph: Cathy Carver

215

RICHARD SLEE (United
Kingdom)

FIGURE **172**
Sculpture Grouping, *Blanket
Bay (Up the Wooden Hill)*,
2000.
Handbuilt earthenware with
coloured transparent glazes,
found objects, fired in oxidation, approx. 1000 x 1000cm
(393½ x 393½in.).
Photograph: Zul Mukhida

Richard Slee – United Kingdom

I grew up in the ceramic landscapes that inhabited the post-Victorian Northern English interiors of grandparents and spinster aunts. These claustrophobic but exotic velvet environments were havens from the sparse and uniform visual realities of post-war Britain. Each ornament in these landscapes had its tale of place or event, imagined or real. Spode willow pattern plates would elicit a tale of an imaginary journey that would change at every telling.

These are the foundations of my belief that the object can hold a narrative that can evoke many layers of meaning. For now I don't wish for my work to be escapist or to be a manifesto, but wish simply to read the contemporary in life as an interpreter.

Blanket Bay (Up The Wooden Hill) [Figure 172]: I wonder if, and hope that every child of this island has played in Bedfordshire, the infantile LSD of Albion. This patchwork landscape of shiny coloured shards is populated by a fanciful tribe which emerged from Far Eastern factories. In their romantic aloofness they are frozen in a dance both between themselves and us. I wrote this statement for a group show with the theme of the landscape entitled 'Get Real' which toured the UK. It's interesting in that the language I'm sure is local and the narrative depends upon a knowledge of English culture. The title comes from a once popular saying 'up the wooden hill' (stairs) to blanket bay (the child's bed) and its variation 'up the wooden hill to Bedfordshire' a pun on the real English county of Bedfordshire. 'The infantile LSD of Albion' contains a double meaning, LSD referring to the pre-decimalization pound sterling of the UK, and to the more universal hallucinogenic drug. Of course the second sentence is meaningless if you live in Asia.

Catapults [Figure 173]: this is part of a series of made ceramics combined with ready-made additions. These are indoor catapults for a conflict that can never happen. Linked and conjoined they embrace or struggle for a futile freedom. The handmade and false wooden look to the ceramic reflects a British obsession with DIY [do-it-yourself?], but on the other hand are they two Y-chromosomes, an example of the 'supermale' syndrome?

Domestic Bedroom Snake [Figure 174]: the albino and iridescent rose-printed, chintz-decorated snake slithers and slides along the floor. This is simply an ironic comment upon the feminisation of styling in the suburban bedroom. The taming of the beast . . . ?

FIGURE **173** (top)
Sculpture, *Catapults*, 2004.
Earthenware, rubber, leather and metal, fired in oxidation, 30 x 40cm (12 x 15¾in.).
Photograph: Phil Sayer

FIGURE **174** (bottom)
Sculpture, *Domestic Bedroom Snake*, 2003.
Handbuilt earthenware, with underglaze printing and lustre, fired in oxidation, l: 71cm (28in.).
Photograph: Zul Mukhida

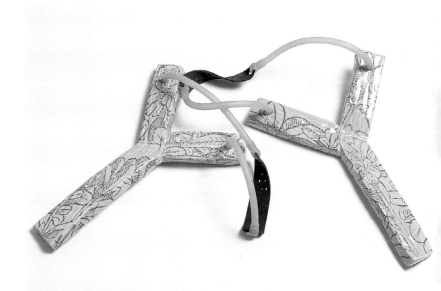

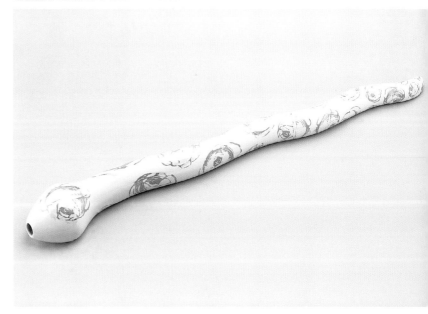

Conclusion

T wo of mankind's most ancient arts have been brought together in this book, and I hope coherently and enjoyably. The art of ceramics and the art of storytelling remain undisputed as relevant art forms by the very nature of their longevity and their continuity to this day. However we may choose to express and renew our narratives, their subject matter still remains central to the important issues we face, both as individuals and as members of a community, regardless of our culture and ethnocentricity.

The myths and fables of the past are renewed as parables of the present: the greed and cupidity found in 'Atalanta and Hippomenes' remain as enduring as the quest for fulfilment in love in the *Romance of the Western Chamber*, or the consequences of dissatisfaction that compromised Adam and Eve and led to their expulsion from Eden.

Our myths are omnipresent and inescapable, and the narrative is with us to stay for as long as potters, painters, writers and filmmakers endure. In closing, I would like to quote Joseph Campbell from his milestone book, *The Hero with a Thousand Faces*:

> Throughout the inhabited world, in all times and under every circumstance, the myths of man have flourished; and they have been the living inspiration of whatever else may have appeared out of the activities of the human body and mind. It would not be too much to say that myth is the secret opening through which the inexhaustible energies of the cosmos pour into human cultural manifestation. Religions, philosophies, arts, the social forms of primitive and historic man, prime discoveries in science and technology, the very dreams that blister sleep, boil up from the basic, magic being of myth.
>
> The wonder is that the characteristic efficacy to touch and inspire deep creative centers dwells in the smallest nursery fairytale — as the flavour of the ocean is contained in a droplet, or the whole mystery of life in the egg of a flea. For the symbols of mythology are not manufactured; they cannot be ordered, invented, or permanently suppressed. They are spontaneous productions of the psyche, and each bears within it, undamaged, the germ power of its source.
>
> [...] In the absence of an effective general mythology, each of us has his private, unrecognised, rudimentary, yet secretly potent pantheon of a dream. The latest incarnation of Oedipus, of Beauty and the Beast, stand this afternoon on the corner of Forty-Second Street and Fifth Avenue, waiting for the traffic light to change.

FIGURE **175**
Plate with 'Atalanta and Hippomenes'. Italy, Venice, The Veneto c.1555–70. Tin-glazed earthenware, dia: 25.5cm (10in.).
Gift of George and Helen Gardiner
Courtesy of The Gardiner Museum of Ceramic Art, Toronto

219

Sources and Recommended Reading

Ancient Greece

Bulfinch, Thomas; *Bulfinch's Mythology*, Thomas Y. Crowell Co., Inc., NY, 1970.

Graves, Roberts; *The Greek Myths*, Penguin Books, London, 1992.

Hamdorf, Friedrich Wilhelm; *Hauch des Prometheus: Meisterwerke in Ton*, Staatliche Antikensammlung und Glyptothek, Munich, 1996.

Lorenz, Susanne; Schmölder-Veit, Andrea (Eds.); *Herakles Hercules*, Staatliche Antikensammlung, Munich, 2003.

Rasmussen, Tom; Spivey, Nigel; *Looking at Greek Vases*, Cambridge University Press, UK, 2003.

The Maya

Goetz, Delia; Morley, Sylvanus Griswold; *Popul Vuh: The Book of the Ancient Maya*, Dover Publications, Inc., NY, 2003.

Reents-Budet, Dorie; *Painting the Maya Universe: Royal Ceramics of the Classic Period*, Duke University Press, Durham & London, 1994.

Taube, Karl; *Aztec and Maya Myths*, The British Museum Press, London, 2002.

China

Beurdely, Cécile and Michel (Transl.: Watson, Katherine); *A Connoisseur's Guide to Chinese Ceramics*, Harper and Row Publishers, NY, London, 1974.

Curtis, Julia B.; *Chinese Porcelains of the Seventeenth Century: Landscapes, Scholars' Motifs and Narratives*, China Institute Gallery, China Institute, NY, 1995.

Kotz, Suzanne (Ed.); *Imperial Taste: Chinese Ceramics from the Percival David Foundation*, Percival David Foundation of Chinese Art, London, 1989.

Medley, Margaret; *The Chinese Potter: A Practical History of Chinese Ceramics*, Phaidon Press Ltd., Oxford, 1976.

Pierson, Stacey; *Designs as Signs: Decoration and Chinese Ceramics*, Percival David Foundation of Chinese Art, London, 2001.

Persia

Atil, Esin; *Ceramics from the World of Islam; Freer Gallery of Art*, Smithsonian Institute, Washington, 1973.

Caiger-Smith, Alan; *Lustre Pottery: Technique, Tradition and Innovation in Islam and the Western World*, Faber and Faber Ltd., London, 1985.

Guest, Grace D.; Ettinghausen, Richard; 'The Iconography of a Kashan Luster Plate', *Ars Orientalis, The Arts of Islam and the East*, Vol. 4, 1961.

Jenkins, Marilyn; *Islamic Pottery, The Metropolitan Museum of Art*, NY, 1983.

Shreve Simpson, Marianna; 'The Narrative Structure of a Medieval Iranian Beaker,' *Ars Orientalis, The Arts of Islam and the East*, Vol. 12, 1981.

Shreve Simpson, Marianna; Kessler, Herbert L. (Eds.); 'Pictorial Narrative in Antiquity and the Middle Ages', *Studies in the History of Art*, Vol. 16, National Gallery of Art, Washington.

Watson, Oliver; *Ceramics from Islamic Lands*, Thames and Hudson, NY, 2004.

Japan

Kakuzo, Okakura; *The Book of Tea*, Charles E. Tuttle Co., Rutland, Vermont and Tokyo, 1956.

Leach, Bernard; *Kenzan and His Tradition*, Faber and Faber, London, 1966.

Mikami, Tsugio, (Transl.: Herring, Ann); *The Art of Japanese Ceramics*, Weatherhill, NY, Heibonsha, Tokyo, 1972.

Sato, Masahiko; *Arts of Japan 2: Kyoto Ceramics*, Weatherhill, NY and Tokyo, 1973.

Wilson, L. Richard; *The Potter's Brush: The Kenzan Style in Japanese Ceramics*, Freer Gallery of Art, Smithsonian Institute, Washington, 2001.

European Tin-glaze Traditions

Alloin, Élise; Borel, Thierry; Bormand, Marc; Bouquillon, Anne; Gaborit, Jean-René; Labbe, Laurence; Lepeltier, Catherine; *Les Della Robbia: Sculptures en terre cuite et émailée de la Renaissance italienne*, Réunion des Musées Nationaux, Paris, 2002.

Caiger-Smith, Alan; *Tin-Glaze Pottery in Europe and the Islamic World*, Faber and Faber, London, 1973.

Carnegy, Daphne; *Tin-Glazed Earthenware from Maiolica, Faience and Delftware to the Contemporary*, A&C Black (Publishers), London, 1993.

Graves, Alun; *Tiles and Tilework of Europe*, V&A Publications, London, 2002.

Hess, Catherine; *Italian Maiolica: Catalogue of the Collections*, The J. Paul Getty Museum, Los Angeles, 1998.

Hess, Catherine; *Maiolica in the Making: The Gentili/Barnabei Archive*, Getty Research Institute for the Study of Art and Humanities, Los Angeles, 1999.

Meco, José; *L'art de l'azulejo au Portugal*, Bertrand Editora, Lda, 1985.

Stephan, Karin (Ed.); *Della Robbia: A Family of Artists*, Scala, Istituto Photographico, Florence, 1992.

Watson, Wendy M; *Italian Renaissance Maiolica from the William A. Clark Collection*, Scala Books Ltd., London, 1986.

Watson, Wendy M.; *Italian Renaissance Ceramics from the Howard I. and Janet H. Stein Collection and the Philadelphia Museum of Art*, Philadelphia Museum of Art, 2001.

European Porcelains

Atterbury, Paul (Ed.); *The History of Porcelain*, Orbis Publishing Limited, London, 1982.

Battie, David (Ed.); *Sotheby's Concise Encyclopaedia of Porcelain*, Conrad Octopus Ltd, London, 1990.

Charleston, Robert J.; *World Ceramics*, Chartwell Books, Inc., New Jersey, 1968.

Chilton, Meredith; *Harlequin Unmasked: The Commedia dell'Arte and Porcelain Sculpture*, The George R. Gardiner Museum of Ceramic Art with Yale University Press, New Haven and London, 2001.

Contemporary Ceramic Narratives

De Barañano, Kosme; Picasso: *A Dialogue with Ceramics: Ceramics from the Marina Picasso Collection*, Fundación Bancaja, Spain and Tacoma Art Museum, Tacoma, Washington, 1998.

Forestier, Sylvie; Meyer, Meret; *Chagall Keramik*, Hirmer Verlag, Munich, 1990.

Girard, Xavier (Ed.); *La Céramique Fauve: André Metthey et les peintres*, Réunion des Musées Nationaux, Paris, 1996.

Jardine, Lisa; *Grayson Perry*, Victoria Miro Gallery, London, 2004.

Koplos, Janet; Borka, Max; Stokvis, Willemijn; Poodt, Jos; *The Unexpected: Artists' Ceramics of the 20th Century*, The Kruithuis Collection, Harry N. Abrams, Inc., Publishers, NY, 1998.

Morgenthal, Deborah; Tourtillott, Suzanne J.E. (Eds.); *The Penland Book of Ceramics*, Lark Books, NY, 2003.

Mathieu, Paul; *Sexpots: Eroticism in Ceramics*, A&C Black (Publishers) Ltd., London and Rutgers University Press, New Jersey, 2004.

McCully, Marilyn (Ed.); *Picasso: Painter and Sculptor in Clay*, Harry N. Abrams, Inc., Publishers, NY, 1998.

McPherson, Anne; 'The Sculpture of Jeanclos', *American Ceramics*, Vol. 10, No. 3, Winter, 1993.

Mulryan, Lenore Hoag; *Ceramic Trees of Life: Popular Art from Mexico*, UCLA. Fowler Museum of Cultural History, Los Angeles, 2003.

Sayer, Chloë; 'A Lover of Clay: Tiburcio Soteno Fernándes', *Artes de Mexico*, Numéro 30, Invierno, 1995–96.

Scott, Paul; *Painted Clay: Graphic Arts and the Ceramic Surface*, A&C Black (Publishers) Ltd., London, 2001.

Stevenson, Michael; *Hylton Nel*, The Fine Art Society, London and Michael Stevenson Contemporary, Cape Town, 2003.

Waller, Jane; *The Human Form in Clay*, The Crowood Press Ltd., UK, 2001.

Narrative and Philosophical

Campbell, Joseph; *The Hero with a Thousand Faces*, Princeton University Press, New Jersey, 1973.

Carrol, Lewis; *The Annotated Alice, Alice's Adventures in Wonderland & Through the Looking Glass*, Bramhall House, NY, 1960.

Carter, Angela (Ed.); *The Virago Book of Fairy Tales*, Virago Press, Ltd., London, 1991.

Homer; (Transl.: Voss, Johann Heinrich; Rupé, Hans; Bertheau, Martin); *Iliad*, Tempel Verlag GmbH, Darmstadt, 1956.

Homer; (Transl.: Voss, Johann Heinrich; Weiss, E.R.; Bertheau, Martin); *Odyssee*, Tempel Verlag GmbH., Darmstadt, 1956.

Jones, V.S. Vernon; *Aesop's Fables*, Avenel Books, Crown Publishers, Inc., NY, 1985.

Shah, Idries; *Tales of the Dervishes: Teaching Stories of the Sufi Masters over the Past Thousand Years*, Panther Books, Ltd., UK, 1973.

Simon, Henry W. (Ed.); *The Complete Sonnets, Songs and Poems of William Shakespeare*, Pocket Books, Inc., NY, 1951.

Index

Acknowledgements

It is said that one picture is worth a thousand words, but in the case of a book of this nature, we are dealing with both. Since the pictures are not my own, and the words have come from many sources, I would gratefully like to acknowledge all the help that I have received.

I would first like to thank Linda Lambert and Alison Stace at A&C Black Publishers in London for all their help and forbearance in nursing me through problems and delays. My thanks also to Penny and Tony Mills for the book's design, which has made it a visual delight. Thanks to Alan Smith in Montreal for word processing and corrections, and also for attempting to keep me computer literate.

My very special thanks to David Whiting for his major contribution to this book's Chapter Six.

The following people affiliated to museums have provided me with the image and text sources that have so enriched my historical chapters: first and foremost at the Gardiner Museum of Ceramic Art in Toronto, Christina Green, Sue Jefferies and Diana Wolfe; at the Freer Gallery of Art, Smithsonian Institution in Washington, my thanks to Rebecca Barker, Louise Allison Cort, Dr. Massumeh Farhad and Angela Gerardi; at the Walters Art Museum in Baltimore, thanks to Elizabeth Flood and Christianne Henry; at the Wallace Collection in London, thanks to Melanie Oelgeschlaeger and Rosalind Saville; at the Percival David Foundation of Chinese Art in London, thanks to Elizabeth Jackson and Stacey Pierson; at the Chinese Institute in New York, thanks to Pao Yu Cheng; at the J. Paul Getty Museum in Los Angeles, thanks to Jacklyn Burns and Catherine Hess; at the Metropolitan Museum of Art in New York, thanks to Ian Wardropper; at the Museum voor Hedendaagse Kunst, 's-Hertogenbosch, thanks to Wil van Gils and Yvonne Joris; at the British Museum in London, thanks to Colin McEwen; at the Staatliche Antikensammlung in Munich, thanks to Irene Boesel and Dr. Vinzenz Brinkmann; at the Graphische Sammlung Albertina in Vienna, thanks to Dr. Ingrid Kastell; at the Museu di Ceràmica in Barcelona, thanks to Maria Antonia Casanovas; at the Victoria and Albert Museum in London, thanks to Terry Bloxham, Judith Crouch, Catherine Davis, Alun Graves, Rachel Lloyd, Luisa Elena Mengoni and Jennifer Opie; and at Scala/Art Resource in New York, my thanks to Ryan Jensen.

For specific text sources, I am extremely grateful to: Esin Atil, Mary Beard, Dory Reents-Budet, Alan Caiger-Smith, Joseph Campbell, Angela Carter, Meredith Chilton, Garth Clark, Richard Ettinghausen, Léopold L. Foulem, Pascale Galipeau, Tamar Garb, Alun Graves, Grace Guest, Robert Hillenbrand, Lisa Jardine, Gloria Lesser, Pi Li, Tony Marsh, Anne McPherson, Stacey Pierson, Chloë Sayer, Marianna Shreve Simpson, Paterson Sims, Karl Taube, Patsy Vanags, Sigrid Weigel, Richard L. Wilson, and this book's many contributing artists.

The following people, galleries and organisations have been helpful in providing imagery and information in those chapters dealing with contemporary ceramic narratives: Roussina Valkova at *American Ceramics* in New York; Marta Donaghey at Contemporary Ceramics in London, Michael Mohammed at the Fine Arts Society, also in London; Renate Wunderle at Galerie B-15 in Munich; Bianca Landgraaft and Hans Kaufman at Galerie Bianca Landgraaft in Belgium; Garth Clark Gallery in New York; Helen Drutt in Philadelphia; Leslie Ferrin Gallery in Lenox, Massachusetts; Frank Paluch at Perimeter Gallery in Chicago; Suzann Greenaway at Prime Gallery in Toronto; Calvert Barron at Rena Bransten Gallery in San Francisco; and finally Kathy Stephenson at Victoria Miro Gallery in London.

For special photo permissions I am grateful to Mme Mathilde Jeanclos in Paris, to Barbara and Justin Kerr in New York, to David Lavender in London and to Jan Thijs in Montreal.

For proofreading, thanks to John Blazina, Alan Caiger-Smith, Meredith Chilton, Charlotte Davies, Gabriele Schnitzenbaumer and Sean McCutcheon.

Finally, I am grateful to the following people for their help and support: Heide Granger in Florence; Jean-Paul van Lith in France; Janet Mansfield in Sydney, Australia; Paul Mathieu in Vancouver; Paul Scott in the United Kingdom; Judith Schwartz in New York, and Eric Wong and Ann Roberts in Ontario.

Last, but not least, my heartfelt thanks go to all the ceramic artists who have participated in this project. This book should be a celebration of their work.